CH00762006

BEHEADED

The killing of a journalist

by JV Koshiw

Artemia Press Ltd

www.artemiapress.biz

Published by Artemia Press Ltd
2003

ISBN 0-9543764-0-4

Printed by Bookcraft, CPI Group,
Midsomer Norton, UK

Artemia Press Ltd
84 Crescent Road
Reading RG1 5SP
England

Dedicated to Lucy

Author's note on the spelling of names and places

Traditionally, Ukrainian names and places have been transliterated into English from the Russian. When Ukraine became independent in 1991, Ukrainian became the official state language. Therefore, all Ukrainian names and places have been transliterated from Ukrainian. Hence, the capital of Ukraine is Kyiv and not the Russian equivalent, Kiev. The same goes for Chornobyl (Chernobyl), Dnipro (Dnieper), Lviv (Lvov), Kharkiv (Kharkov), Odesa (Odessa), etc.

The rule is followed also for names, for example Mykola rather than Nikolai; Borys (Boris), Dmytro (Dmitry), Mykhaylo (Mikhail), Oleksandr (Aleksandr), Petro (Pyotr), Serhiy (Sergei), Volodymyr (Vladimir), etc.

Author's publications

J.V. Koshiw has published more than 70 articles on current affairs in Ukraine during 1998-9, while deputy editor of Kyiv Post, Ukraine's only English newspaper. Under the pseudonym of Viktor Haynes, he jointly authored with Olga Semyonova, *Workers against the Gulag*, published in 1979 in UK by Pluto Press, in France by Maspero, and in Sweden by Barrikaden. With Marko Bojcun, he co-authored *The Chernobyl Disaster*, London, Hogarth Press, 1988.

In 1997, the Canadian Institute of Ukrainian Studies at the University of Alberta published his research paper, *British Foreign Office Files on Ukraine and Ukrainians, 1917-48*.

During 1990-95, he worked as a TV journalist with HTV-Wales on documentary films on Chornobyl and with BBC Inside Story on the Sellafield nuclear reprocessing plant.

CONTENTS

Contents

Preface

On the eve of the year 2000, pundits predicted doomsday scenarios for much of the world, especially Ukraine. Millions of old computer chips that could not read 2000 would cause planes to fall from the sky and nuclear power stations to shut down, or even worse. Nothing like that happened anywhere, including Ukraine.

But something awful did happen in Ukraine in the year 2000 to a bright, young, energetic and relatively prominent broadcasting journalist. Georgi Gongadze disappeared on September 16 and was found beheaded on November 2.

Soon afterwards recordings appeared implicating the president of Ukraine in ordering Gongadze's kidnapping. One of his guards had secretly recorded the president saying this, before fleeing the country on November 25, first to Europe and then to America.

Since his departure, the whistle blower Mykola Melnychenko has drip-fed excerpts from his vast collection of recordings to the internet. They show the president, Leonid Kuchma, issuing orders to punish his critics – journalists, politicians, and businessmen – with imprisonments, beatings and kidnappings. They reveal the spying by his security service on everyone of interest to him – from political allies to opponents. His international reputation slid even further when a recording showed him approving the sale of military radar to Iraq in violation of UN embargoes.

Despite this mountain of evidence, no legal measures have been taken against Kuchma. He simply denies the crimes and claims the recordings have been fabricated. Furthermore, he doesn't allow a credible investigation to take place and instead has created a cover-up where every tiny event has multiple explanations, like a gigantic hall of mirrors. The only institution empowered by Ukraine's constitution to investigate him – parliament – is under his control. Demonstrations, some violent, have failed to dislodge him.

The purpose of this book is to present the evidence in the disappearance and murder of Gongadze in order that justice may be done. I have chosen first to introduce the three key individuals involved – Gongadze, Kuchma and Melnychenko – and then to present in chronological order the evidence and analysis.

Gongadze's was not the first politically motivated disappearance. In my many trips to Ukraine, I met two people who also disappeared for similar reasons.

Mykhaylo Boychyshyn, I first met in August 1989. He was a leading activist of Rukh (Movement for the reconstruction of Ukraine), then involved in transforming Ukraine from a Soviet republic to an independent state. I saw him again in 1991, when he was managing the presidential campaign for the former Soviet political prisoner Vyacheslav Chornovil, and I joined them in a mini-van on their campaign trail across Ukraine. On a shoestring budget, Boychyshyn took on the might of the former Soviet state machine, which was batting for the former communist party ideologue, Leonid Kravchuk. The ex-communist boss won, but Chornovil came second with 26 per cent of the vote.

In 1994 Boychyshyn disappeared from the center of Kyiv. Despite what the government claimed was its biggest ever man hunt, he was never found. In 1999, Chornovil died in an accident that his supporters alleged was organized by a government death squad.

In February 1998, Ihor Svoboda – whom Boychyshyn had introduced me to – was seized by armed men and never seen again. He was an assistant to Odesa's mayor, Edward Hurvits, whom Kuchma ousted from office later that year.

After Gongadze disappeared, I decided to write a book, as this time there was evidence of who was behind this ghastly crime. I did not know Gongadze personally, but I knew about him, as did most people who followed closely the 1999 presidential elections. Readers will have to decide for themselves whether the book does justice to Gongadze as well as to Kuchma.

1

Fighter to journalist

For Ruslan and Lesya Gongadze, May 21, 1969 should have been a day to celebrate the birth of identical twins. Instead, tragedy struck. Someone stole one of the boys from a maternity hospital in the Georgian capital Tbilisi. He was never found. They named the remaining baby Georgi, or Giya for short.

Thirty-one years later, on September 16, 2000, Giya would suffer his brother's fate. He too would disappear, but in another capital city, Kyiv. But unlike his twin, Giya was found – beheaded.

The boys' father was Ruslan Gongadze, an architect – their mother, Lesya Korchak, a dentist. They had met and married in the western Ukrainian city of Lviv, where both attended the university, and moved to Tbilisi in November 1967.

When Giya was six years old, his parents divorced. Ruslan remarried and had another son. Lesya stayed single and continued to live and work in Tbilisi until she returned for good to her hometown Lviv in 1994.

Giya was brought up by his mother in Tbilisi, where in school he excelled in athletics and, in the mid-1980s, qualified for the Soviet Olympic reserve squad in the 100 and 200

Giya and Ruslan

meters sprint. From an early age he was multilingual – learning Georgian, Russian and English in school and Ukrainian at home. In 1986, he enrolled at the Institute of Foreign Languages in Tbilisi to specialize in English. After a year, he was called up into the army and served in Ashkhabad, Turkmenistan, on the border with Iran. "I paid so he wouldn't go to Afghanistan," said his mother, explaining how she kept him out of the Soviet-Afghan war.

He came back from the army in May 1989 and joined his father, who was a leading political activist in the movement to separate Georgia from the USSR. The Secretary General of the Communist Party, Mikhail Gorbachev, had ignited the break-up of the superpower unwittingly by proclaiming glasnost – understood by the public as free speech. Nationalists across the USSR rushed to take their republic out of the "prison of nations". Georgia headed the stampede to leave Russia's embrace.

Gorbachev attempted to halt the process by force. This only exacerbated the break-up of the USSR. On April 9,1989, Soviet troops, attempting to disperse nationalist demonstrators on the streets of Tbilisi with shovels, killed twenty people, mostly women and children.

The massacre radicalized Georgians like Ruslan and Giya Gongadze. They threw themselves into the task of creating an independent Georgian state. Ruslan headed the National Front for a Free Georgia. Giya, then 20 years old, became the Front's information spokesman. In 1989-90, he traveled to the Soviet Baltic republics and Ukraine to seek allies for the organization and its quest for Georgian independence.

In Ukraine's capital Kyiv, in September 1989, Giya on behalf of the front attended the first congress of Rukh (the Popular Movement for the Reconstruction of Ukraine) – then a loose coalition of political groups and individuals that had as their goal the democratization of the Soviet republic of Ukraine. But the congress didn't go according to plan and instead it began Ukraine's road to independence. Leading members of the communist party in Ukraine participated in the event with the hope of controlling the nationalists' clamor for independence. The future first president of Ukraine, Leonid Kravchuk, then the republic's communist party ideologue, took an active part in the five-day conference. His people in Rukh – notably the conference's chairman, Dmytro Pavlychko – ensured that the congress did not pass any critical resolutions against the communist party. Even those calling for the closure of the Chornobyl nuclear power plant – where the world's worst nuclear accident had occurred in 1986 – were banned from the microphone. However, the activists at the conference could not be halted by podium manipulations and Rukh fell into the hands of the dynamic and articulate former political prisoner, Vyacheslav Chornovil.

In an attempt to gain popularity, Ukraine's communist elite, with the Kremlin's approval, removed the first secretary of Soviet Ukraine's communist party, Volodymyr Shcherbytsky – who for twenty years had ruled this Soviet republic with an iron fist. Shcherbytsky reacted by committing suicide. The shocked communist elite and its successors have never revealed the truth about his suicide.

In 1989, Giya also attended the first non-communist music youth festival in Ukraine – Chervona Ruta (Red Rue) – held in Chernivtsi. There he fell in love with Marianna Stetsenko. In August 1990, he and Marianna married and settled in Lviv. He got a job teaching English and sports, and studied at Lviv University's department of Romance-Germanic languages.

It seemed that Giya's short political career was over and he was settling down to start a family. But he found himself in the midst of Ukraine's own national revolution, and nowhere more so than in Lviv, where Rukh supporters fought pitched battles with the police for the control of the streets. The deciding moment for Ukraine came in August 1991. In reaction to the attempted coup in Moscow against Gorbachev, on August 24, 1991, Ukraine's Soviet parliament voted almost unanimously to declare Ukraine independent and ban the communist party.

This unexpected development delighted Rukh supporters – but it also deprived Rukh of its monopoly of the independence banner. It meant that the former Soviet elite would continue to hold political and economic power in independent Ukraine.

Ukraine's parliament announced that all registered residents in Ukraine on August 24, 1991 were citizens of Ukraine. This included Giya, but not his mother Lesya who at the time lived in Georgia.

On Dec 1, 1991, while voters in Ukraine voted in a referendum to approve the parliament's vote of independence and to elect its first president, Georgia was in a state of civil war. Giya decided to return after hearing that his father was being hunted down as a traitor.

3

Jan.14, 1992 – Giya and his step-brother
in front of the Georgian parliament building in Tbilisi

The Georgians, who had formed an independent state in April 1991, had turned on each other. After becoming president in May, the former Soviet political prisoner Zviad Gamsakhurdia became ruthless, paranoid and corrupt. His political conflict with his former allies in parliament turned increasingly violent. The president declared 32 political opponents "enemies of the state" and ordered their arrest. Twenty-eighth on the list was Ruslan Gongadze, a leading member of the Georgian parliament and head of the Radical Union of Georgia. Ruslan evaded his captors by hiding in a basement near the parliament building before making his escape from Tbilisi.

On December 22, 1991, in Tbilisi, anti-Gamsakhurdia demonstrators were killed by government troops. Militias controlled by various parliamentary parties counter-attacked and civil war flared.

In the last days of 1991, in the midst of the fighting, Giya returned to Tbilisi. He turned up at his mother's apartment holding a Kalashnikov. "Mother, I have come to defend my father's honor and his name" – she recalled him saying. He and his mother fought on the

4

rebel side. "My son never fired a shot. He took part in the fighting as a medic, bringing the wounded to the hospital." As Giya drove an ambulance picking up the dead and wounded, his mother nursed the wounded in a makeshift hospital located in the basement of the parliament. However, after snipers killed a number of medical personnel, Giya didn't hesitate to shoot back with his Kalashnikov.

On January 14, 1992, President Gamsakhurdia fled Tbilisi and the fighting stopped. The opposition took power, and soon afterwards appointed Edward Shevardnadze – the former Soviet foreign minister under Gorbachev – as president.

Next day, January 15, Giya returned to Lviv. He found that his wife had left him. Her mother had convinced her that a man who could leave her for Georgia was not fit to be her husband.

Unmoved by his wife's departure, Giya decided to continue to promote the Georgian cause in Ukraine. He created a Georgian cultural center in Lviv – naming it after the Georgian prince Bagrationi – which doubled as the Georgian Information Agency. While registering the center with the authorities, he met Myroslava Petryshyn, his future second wife. Together they wrote an article about the Georgian civil war – "The tragedy of the leaders" – published by the Lviv newspaper *Post-Postup* in 1992.

Giya soon returned to Tbilisi with the intention of giving up politics and starting a business. He changed his mind after interviewing the wounded from the civil war at the military hospital where his mother worked. "I took him by the hand and told him that instead of getting involved in business he should write about these victims. He decided to make a documentary film on the Georgian civil war. I got him a camera and he made a film called 'The pain of my land'." In February 1993, Ukraine's third national channel, UT-3, broadcast Giya's documentary on the Georgian civil war.

Georgia's independence had unleashed demands for the same from its two major ethnic groups. In 1992, Ossetians in eastern Georgia and Abkhazians in northwest Georgia declared independence. Georgia blamed Russia for provoking them. Armed conflicts flared in Abkhazia and Ossetia as Georgia attempted to contain its rebellious minorities.

Giya volunteered for the war in Abkhazia. The authorities rejected him for military duty on the grounds that, as the son of Ruslan Gongadze and a Ukrainian citizen, he was more useful for propaganda work in Ukraine. He returned to Lviv to take up his "diplomatic" assignment and threw himself into a frenzy of activity to get Ukraine to back Georgia in the inter-ethnic conflict.

In Ukraine, he found only the fringe paramilitary organization UNA-UNSD (Ukrainian National Assembly-Ukrainian National Self-Defense Organization) ready to commit itself wholeheartedly to the Georgian cause. Gongadze appeared at their public meetings in Lviv to raise recruits to fight for Georgia. The aims of UNA-UNSD – "to get rid of communists and criminals from Ukraine and to fight Russian expansionism" – coincided with the interests of Georgian nationalists. In July 1993, UNA-UNSD's Argo battalion led by the loquacious Dmytro Korchynsky arrived in Tbilisi to fight in Abkhazia.

Giya stayed in Ukraine for the first half of 1993 because of his father's illness. In March 1993, the Georgian government had sent Ruslan to a hospital in Kyiv for an operation to halt the spread of cancer. Giya came to Kyiv to be with his father. On August 5, 1993, Ruslan died at the age of 49. Giya returned to Tbilisi with the body.

Following the funeral, Giya began filming a documentary on the Ukrainian nationalist volunteers fighting in Abkhazia. He had raised the money for the film by selling his Kalashnikov.

The war in Abkhazia had already been raging for almost a year. The fighting had begun in August 1992, when the Georgian government sent its National Guards to Abkhazia's capital, Sukhumi, to put an end to the rebellion. The Abkhazian rebels led by Vladyslav Ardzinbai, reinforced by other Caucasians, including Chechens, and backed by Russian military aid, responded by seizing most of Abkhazia and surrounding its capital, Sukhumi – trapping over 100,000 Georgians. In September 1993, the Georgian government, in return for a ceasefire, removed its soldiers and heavy guns from Sukhumi.

But as soon as the Georgian troops left, the Abkhazians advanced on Sukhumi. A rag-tag army of irregulars defended the city. President Edward Shevardnadze – trapped inside the city – appealed to Russian

President Boris Yeltsin to stop the attack. "In the war, 2,031 civilians killed and 5,802 wounded … 1,500 residential buildings destroyed. No water, bread, light and hope is fading", he wrote to Yeltsin, who ignored his pleas.

On September 17, Giya left Tbilisi for Sukhumi with his camera to film the fighting. He arrived in style. Dressed in a First World War British style officer's uniform with high leather boots, he attracted sniggering remarks from the volunteers. After only a few hours in Sukhumi, the news came that the Abkhazians were preparing to attack the city. That night Giya was mobilized. In the early morning, he found himself on the front-line along the Gumista River. It was here that the enemy made its major assault. As Giya stood in a trench, an artillery shell exploded over his head. Shrapnel peppered him in twenty-six places across his body, including his right hand. The steel helmet he was wearing saved him from certain death. Two others standing near him were killed by the explosion. The embedded shrapnel was to stay with him for the rest of his life; it was used to identify his body.

Giya's wounding was mentioned in a dispatch from Sukhumi published in the Tbilisi newspaper, *Svobodnaya Gruziya (Free Georgia)*, September 21, 1993. He was rushed to a field hospital where he called attention to himself by demanding that his bag with videocassettes be retrieved from the front line, recalled a local fighter, Konstantyn Alaniya, or Koba, who was to become his friend for life. Giya's persistent requests for his film bag paid off, as volunteers retrieved it under fire.

That Saturday night medics placed Giya and other seriously wounded on a plane for Tbilisi. This proved to be the last Georgian plane, after President Shevardnadze's, to leave Sukhumi before the Abkhazians occupied the city.

Koba stayed on in Sukhumi with the irregulars, fighting from an ever-decreasing area of the city. He escaped with other Georgian fighters along a mountain corridor. To this day, Koba, along with 200,000 Georgians who fled, has not returned to Abkhazia. In 1995, he left Georgia and settled as a refugee in Lviv, where by chance he met Giya.

At a Tbilisi military hospital, Giya's mother tended his wounds, but her fear was that he might die of malnutrition. "Times were awful. There was no food, electricity or heating, nothing to cook on" – Lesya recalled – "and no bread either". She wanted to get him out of Georgia, but had no money. The government had not paid her and the hospital staff since the start of the civil war in December 1991. She collected money from friends and relations to get him out of Georgia. After two weeks in the hospital, he flew to Lviv in October 1993. There was not enough money for her to leave, and besides, "I couldn't leave the wounded", she said.

Despite his life-threatening ordeal, Giya had his films about the Abkhazian conflict, which he edited into the documentary – "The shadows of war" and which was shown on Ukrainian TV.

His return marked the end of his fighting for Georgia. He married Myroslava and in 1997 had twins. But his struggle to be a journalist in Ukraine proved to be deadlier than his fighting for Georgia.

1998 – Myroslava and Georgi with twins Nana and Solomiya

2

Peasant to president

The man many hold responsible for Georgi Gongadze's disappearance had a Soviet style rags to riches story. Born into a poor family on an impoverished Soviet collective farm, Leonid Kuchma became the director of one of the most important Soviet enterprises – a factory making intercontinental missiles. After the collapse of the USSR in 1991, he continued his meteoric rise in the newly independent Ukraine. He became its second prime minister in 1992 and its second president in 1994; re-elected in 1999. At the time of Gongadze's disappearance in September 2000, Kuchma had reached the apex of his career. Following the revelation on November 28 that he was behind the disappearance, his political career began a downward spiral.

The peasant

Leonid, or by his diminutive Lyonya, was born on the Chaykino (meaning seagull) collective farm on August 9, 1938. Chaykino is located in a very isolated area of Ukraine – tucked in near the border with Russia and Belarus. No one seems to know why the place was named after a sea bird never seen in the area.

Lyonya's formative years of poverty were made worse by the absence and then death of his father. When Hitler's armed forces attacked the USSR in June 1941, Lyonya was less than three years old. His father, Danylo, mobilized into the Red Army, retreated with it as the Nazis occupied the whole of Ukraine. He perished fighting the now diminishing German Army in 1944 near Kursk, not far from Chaykino.

Lyonya, his sister, brother and mother survived the Nazi occupation, the 1947 famine in Ukraine, and Chaykino's poverty. Hunger was a perennial problem. Everyone in the village had one goal – "to survive", recalled Lyonya's classmate, Oleksandr Dubyna.

The Chaykino collective farm was miserably poor. For all the time Kuchma lived there, it had no electricity, telephone, main drainage or running water. People lived in earth houses – dwellings with walls made of dried mud mixed with straw and thatched roofs – and had outdoor wells and outside toilets.

Lyonya liked reading and mathematics, but the local school offered only the barest necessities for a rudimentary education. Chaykino's school building of seven classes was just another earth house. Kuchma's classmate, Nataliya Kysla, remembered that the class had only one mathematics book and no exercise books. Children used scraps of paper to write on. "Often there was no ink, and the teachers prepared it from elder, ash, or something else. We used quill pens just like in Pushkin's time."

The school had a simple library, and the future president spent much of his free time there. He recalled in a newspaper interview that most of the books were in Ukrainian (though his future Soviet career would be mostly in Russian). For his secondary education, from 14 years of age, Lyonya attended a school in the nearby collective farm of Kostobobriv, also not very well endowed.

The director

At the age of 17, Lyonya went to continue his studies in Ukraine's industrial city of Dnipropetrovsk. His excellent memory and math skills earned him a place to study engineering. Dnipropetrovsk – with apartment blocks, electricity, drainage, public transport, shops and all the other attributes that came with Soviet modernization – must have been a gigantic leap into the future for the teenager from Chaykino.

In Dnipropetrovsk, Lyonya studied, worked and made a career in rocket engineering and the communist party. In 1960, he got a job at Yuzhnomash (Pivdenmash in Ukrainian) missile design plant. It served the nearby Yuzhnomash missile manufacturing plant – which built the intercontinental missiles that, when tipped with nuclear warheads, made the USSR a world super power.

Kuchma used the communist party to rise to the top of the Soviet "classless" society. At this time, Dnipropetrovsk was the ideal place to to reach the higher ranks of the elite. In 1966, Leonid Brezhnev, a native son of the Dnipropetrovsk region, had become General Secretary of the Soviet Communist Party – the top post in the USSR. He not only brought members of the Dnipropetrovsk elite to the center of power in Moscow, but installed them in the republican capital – Kyiv. The Dnipropetrovsk communists, led by Volodymyr Shcherbytsky, ran Ukraine as their fiefdom until the collapse of the USSR. (Kuchma continued the tradition. On being president, he placed over 200 of his friends, referred to by some as "the Dnipropetrovsk mafia", in leading positions in the government.)

Another reason for Kuchma's rapid rise in Dnipropetrovsk was his marriage in 1962 to Lyudmyla Tumanov, whose family were important members of the local communist elite. As the missile design bureau and the production plant were top secret, anyone working there – and more importantly anyone who wanted to hold top posts – had to be not only vetted but also to have the right connections. Lyonya from Chaykino did not have the connections, but his wife did. Her father Henadiy was a leading rocket engineer and local communist stalwart, and her brother Yuriy would become a KGB officer.

At the missile design bureau, Kuchma headed the Komsomol – the young people's branch of the communist party. Then in 1975, at the age of 38, he became the head of the design bureau's communist party. In 1981, he became the design bureau's chief engineer – the second senior post after the general-director.

In 1982, he moved to the missile manufacturing plant as the head of its communist party. At the same time, he improved his professional position at the plant as the first deputy to the general builder. In 1986, at the age of 48, he reached the top – general director of Pivdenmash manufacturing plant. He now joined the top ranks of the Soviet "Red Directors" and received all the corresponding privileges, including his own Tupolev airliner and a country house with servants.

The prime minister

As the Soviet state began to implode because of its unresolved political and economic problems, Kuchma vacillated between saving the USSR and creating an independent Ukraine. On January 9, 1990, the Dnipropetrovsk newspaper, Prapor Yunosti, quoted him as being against independence. One month later, at the February 1990 plenum of the communist chiefs of Ukraine, Kuchma supported the minority position in the party calling for "full economic and political sovereignty of Ukraine as a state".

In the March 1990 Soviet Ukrainian parliamentary elections, which for the first time in Soviet history allowed non-communist candidates to take part, Kuchma was elected as a communist from the Dnipropetrovsk Oblast (region). In parliament, he belonged to the 239-strong communist majority that kept the lid on the 111 pro-independence minority.

The attempted coup in Moscow, August 19-21, 1991, by advocates of a strong centralized USSR, made Ukraine's elite fear for their survival. On August 24, 1991, Ukraine's parliament led by its speaker and communist leader, Leonid Kravchuk, voted overwhelmingly for independence. Only four deputies voted against, and Kuchma was not among them.

Three of the four MPs who voted against independence were "nationalists" – Serhiy Holovaty, Valeriy Ivasyuk and Laryssa Skoryk. (Ironically, ten years later all three would play a major role in accusing the now President Kuchma of being responsible for the murder of Georgi Gongadze.) They had voted against independence because they had felt the communist elite's sudden turn to nation building was a ploy to take power for itself.

It became clear after some time that Ukraine's party elite wanted their own state so that they could become rich. Like Kuchma, they were communists not for the ideology but the economic privileges. Along with their vote for independence, they banned the Soviet communist party. They allowed the creation of a reformed communist party led by Oleksandr Moroz, called the Socialist Party.

Parliament's declaration of independence was overwhelmingly approved in a referendum on December 1, 1991, when 90 percent of the population voted for it. A fantastic result considering that only two years earlier, advocating independence meant a long prison sentence or early death from confinement in a labor camp. Each of the 27 regions of Ukraine voted for independence, even the overwhelmingly Russian populated Crimea, where the vote was just over 50 percent.

On the same day, the voters elected the first president of Ukraine, Leonid Kravchuk, who won with 20 million votes out of the 30 million votes cast. He saw off his nearest challenger, the former dissident and now leader of the nationalist Rukh party, Vyacheslav Chornovil, who got only six million votes or 26 percent of the vote.

Kuchma took part in the presidential election as the campaign manager for the "New Ukraine" candidate, Ihor Yukhanovsky, who received less than a million votes. The New Ukraine group were radical advocates of reforming the state owned economy. Kuchma, along with other "Red Directors", like Volodymyr Shcherban, had joined the group in parliament after independence. (By the time of the Gongadze affair, many of these radicals had became Kuchma's fiercest political opponents – among them Viktor Pynzenyk, Taras Stetskiv, Volodymyr Filenko, and Ihor Yukhanovsky.)

Independence provoked a mad scramble by the elite to grab state property – preferably to sell it for dollars on the world market and put the proceeds into their own foreign bank accounts. Every official, from the first president, Leonid Kravchuk, down to the local ranks seemed to be stealing from the state.

The uncontrolled rush for state assets created a new elite, popularly called oligarchs – defined as those who enriched themselves on state funds and property. It happened not only in Ukraine, but across the former Soviet Union. The previously totally state-owned economy was being privatized without the rule of law. The cunning and above all the well politically-positioned were taking what they could for themselves. One method of becoming rich quickly was to sell off Soviet military equipment to warring sides in conflict areas around the world. Another was to sell abroad precious metals like titanium, and steel products. Internally, the main game was to acquire properties, from apartments to hotels to factories. This primitive accumulation was often accompanied by gangster style violence.

This free-for-all plunged Ukraine even further into the economic abyss then it had been as part of the USSR. In the first year of independence, Ukraine's gross national product (GNP) declined faster than even Russia's, though the latter was less politically stable. Only the former Soviet republics in Trans-Caucasia and Central Asia had a worse economic decline, but many of them were involved in civil or inter-republic wars. Ukraine's decline was worse than Yugoslavia's, surprisingly, as that country was embroiled in a full-scale civil war. All Ukraine had was tension with Russia over the Crimea, but no fighting ever took place.

As the economic decline accelerated, Ukraine's parliament looked for a savior. A consensus developed that Leonid Kuchma, the director of one of the Soviet Union's most important missile plants, would make the ideal prime minister to reverse the economic collapse. Kuchma appealed not only to the former members of the Soviet elite but also to the radical reformers, as he was a member of the pro-reform New Ukraine group. On October 13, 1992, parliament approved Kuchma as Ukraine's second prime minister by an overwhelming vote – 316 to 23, with 14 abstentions.

Kuchma as prime minister began by asking for and receiving emergency powers for six months. However, his dictatorial decisions only made the economy worse. His first major economic decree abolished the Soviet ruble, the currency still shared with Russia. He replaced the ruble with the karbovanets – a Soviet Ukrainian word for ruble – which against the dollar soon proved to be worthless. In 1993, inflation was 10,000 percent. This was one of the highest inflation rates ever recorded in peacetime Europe. The new currency failed because Ukraine had nothing of value to replace the ruble with. In East Germany, for example, the local currency was replaced with the West German deutschemark. Ukraine inherited almost no foreign reserves from the USSR. The new Russian government had seized for itself all the foreign Soviet assets – currencies, investments and properties.

In response to the public outcry about the uncontrolled plunder by officials, Prime Minister Kuchma declared war on corruption. On November 18, 1992, he recommended the creation of a cabinet commission to combat "Mafia like activities" which would have strong investigative and punitive powers, including removing the immunity which members of parliament (MPs) had from prosecution.

While the prime minister preached against corruption in public, he engaged in it in private. The MP Hryhoriy Omelchenko – a former police and state security service investigator specializing in economic crimes – had documented allegations of corruption against Kuchma while he was prime minister. They show that in the spring of 1993, Kuchma and his deputy prime minister Yukhym Zvyahilsky had transferred 12 million DM from state reserves into their private accounts as well as those of other highly placed individuals and their children, including a Swiss account of Oleksandr Kravchuk, the son of President Kravchuk. Sharing ill-gotten money with the president was a way of protecting oneself from prosecution. Omelchenko further alleged that three people involved in this money-laundering affair had been murdered in order to keep Kuchma's money laundering a secret.

The former economic crime investigator has made additional detailed charges of corruption against Kuchma. He claims that prime minister Kuchma had dealings with a shady company headed by Oleksandr Volkov, who subsequently became one of Ukraine's most powerful oligarchs.

According to Omelchenko, Kuchma supplied Volkov with dollars from the state treasury to buy and sell valuable commodities for private gain. In return, Kuchma supposedly received a share of the profits made from the sales. In 1993, on at least two occasions, Kuchma allegedly transferred $6 million from the state treasury to Volkov's company. The first $6 million was to buy fuel in Russia to sell in Ukraine. The second was to buy coal in Ukraine and sell it in Moldova.

Volkov apparently deposited millions of dollars made on such deals on his and Kuchma's foreign bank accounts. In 1997, the Belgian authorities accused Volkov of money laundering and froze his accounts with more than $3 million. Ukraine's legal authorities have refused to investigate any of these allegations.

The president

Prime Minister Kuchma and his Minister of Economy, Viktor Pynzenyk, took Ukraine's economy into the abyss. Surprisingly, the population did not turn violent against the state. People simply became depressed and disillusioned, and turned to strikes and crime to outlive the economic crisis. Many began to idealize the former communist state as a heaven and to support the newly-legalized "back to the USSR" communist party led by Petro Symonenko. On August 24, 1993, on the first anniversary of Ukraine's independence, parliament, under pressure from large-scale strikes, voted to hold unscheduled presidential elections in the summer of 1994.

Kuchma resigned as prime minister in September 1993 and retreated into heading the Ukrainian Union of Industrialists and Entrepreneurs. There he plotted with his former Red Directors and his business partner Volkov, to launch himself as a presidential candidate. His main opponent would be the incumbent president, Kravchuk, who as president would have to take responsibility for the economic collapse, regardless of the fact that it was his prime minister who had created an economic crisis.

Kuchma successfully posed as the person better able to rescue the economy from the abyss and, surprisingly, even received support from the resurrected and growing communist party. Its leader, Petro Symonenko, campaigned for Kuchma not only on the poor state of the economy but also on the national question. He saw Kuchma, who campaigned in Russian, as being more pro-Russian than Kravchuk, who campaigned in Ukrainian. Fearing that Kuchma's victory would bring the communists to power, nationalists led by Vyacheslav Chornovil flocked to the side of their old communist enemy Kravchuk. The socialists, led by the parliamentary speaker Oleksandr Moroz, also came out against Kravchuk, but only for his economic policies.

In the July 10, 1994 presidential elections, Kuchma beat Kravchuk by 52 percent to 45 percent, to become the second president of Ukraine. As future events would show, both the communists and nationalists perceived Kuchma incorrectly. He was not about to unite Ukraine with Russia. The single most significant process during Kuchma's first presidential term on office from 1994-99 was the consolidation of the oligarchs over the state and private property. The public was not aware of this process as the mass media was censored by the state, with the oligarchs increasingly taking it over.

The March 29, 1998 parliamentary elections marked the oligarchs debut onto the political stage. The oligarchs for the first time came out of the shadow economy and appeared at the head of new political groups and parties. Elected to parliament were names that the public had hardly ever heard before, like Oleksandr Volkov, Viktor Pinchuk, Andriy Derkach, Hryhoriy Surkis, Viktor Medvedchuk, and Yuliya Tymoshenko, and familiar names too, like Pavlo Lazarenko and Yevhen Marchuk. A parliament which until then had been a forum for ideological battles between the communists and nationalists now had new players whose interests focused almost exclusively on making more money out of the state.

There were many other powerful oligarchs who didn't' make it to parliament. The powerful oligarchs from Ukraine's heavy industrial heartland – the Donbas – were not represented. Their debut would come after the March 2002 parliamentary elections.

In the 1998 elections, the oligarchs and their parties won around 80 of the 450 seats. But within two years, the oligarch parties would double the number of seats in parliament by buying off members from other parties. In the March 2002 parliamentary elections, they won the majority, and selected the parliament's speaker and his two deputies.

The oligarchs formed their factions in parliament with populist-sounding names. For example, oligarchs Viktor Pinchuk and Andriy Derkach, called their faction Working Ukraine. The president's favorite oligarch, Oleksandr Volkov, named his group in parliament Rebirth of Regions, while outside of parliament, he created the

Democratic Party. The oligarchs Hryhoriy Surkis (owner of the Dynamo Kyiv football club and a lot more) and Viktor Medvedchuk appeared as leaders of the Social-Democratic United party (SDP(U). A group of gas and oil traders had the nerve to appear in parliament as a Green Party, thanks to advertisements aimed at gullible young voters paid for by the oligarch Vadim Rabinovich, who couldn't enter parliament on account of taking Israeli citizenship. Another oligarch party was the National Democrats, led by then prime minister, Valeriy Pustovoytenko (1997-1999).

The Working Ukraine oligarchs were especially close to the president. Pinchuk had created an industrial conglomerate through family ties, first through his first wife in Dnipropetrovsk and then through his marriage to the president's daughter. His huge financial empire includes some of the most profitable factories in Ukraine. He entered parliament in 1998 with a strong influence on the mass media through his ownership of Ukraine's biggest newspaper, *Fakty*. Since then he has added the TV station ICTV.

The other Working Ukraine leader, Andriy Derkach, had also used his family connections to become very rich and powerful. His father, Leonid, has had a close relationship with Kuchma from the time they both worked together at the rocket factory in Dnipropetrovsk. While Kuchma rose to become the plant's director, Leonid Derkach became its KGB head. After Kuchma became president in 1994, he appointed Derkach to head Ukraine's customs service, and his son a presidential adviser. Soon after the 1998 parliamentary elections, Leonid Derkach became the chief of the state security service.

The young Derkach, born in 1967, like Pinchuk, made huge profits by avoiding customs duties on importing gasoline and other products. Also like Pinchuk, he has invested his surplus wealth in the mass media, most notably the Kyiv newspaper *Telegraf* and ERA TV on Ukraine's first state channel.

Oleksandr Volkov has been by far the most important oligarch for Kuchma. Their relationship goes back at least until 1993, when he and prime minister Kuchma used state funds to conduct private business deals. During the 1994 and 1999 presidential elections, Volkov managed Kuchma's campaign funds. Until 1998 when he entered parliament, he along with the young Derkach served as advisers to the president. Volkov entered parliament in a by-election in September 1998, probably to gain immunity from prosecution following charges of money-laundering by the Belgian authorities.

Hryhoriy Surkis and Viktor Medvedchuk have been, compared to the other oligarchs, more successful in forming a real political party, the SDP(U). It even belongs to the Socialist International, which unites European social democratic parties like the British Labour Party. It has created a popular base in a number of cities and even regions, like the Transcarpathian Oblast. Surkis and Medvedchuk have a large slice of the mass media, as they control Ukraine's most watched TV channel, Inter, and the capital's largest newspaper, Kievskiye Vedomosti.

The oligarch Vadim Rabinovich exercised a great influence in the 1998 parliamentary elections. He splashed money across the political spectrum, which even included the nationalist Rukh party. The source of his wealth has made him very controversial. The US government has refused him entry because it claims he has been involved in international criminal activities. His media interest in Ukraine has been extensive, as co-owner of the TV company Era along with Andriy Derkach. He had strong interests in Ukraine's second TV channel, Studio 1+1, until he lost it in 1998 after an acrimonious row with the other owners. He also owns a few newspapers in Ukraine.

Following the parliamentary elections, the president's power over parliament gradually increased along with the growing influence of the oligarchs. The populist right – Rukh and Reform-and-Order – helped by aligning themselves with the oligarchs against the left who controlled parliament. However, as will be shown, the Gongadze affair would gradually unite the populist left and right parties against the president and the oligarchs.

The challenger

It has not been smooth sailing for Kuchma with the oligarchs. In August 1997, one of Ukraine's major oligarchs, Pavlo Lazarenko, rebelled against Kuchma, declared his intention to challenge him for the presidency. Kuchma had dismissed Lazarenko as prime minister on July 2, 1997, ostensibly because Lazarenko had retired at his own request for health reasons, but in fact probably because of his overzealous acquisitiveness at the expense of other oligarchs, who complained to the president. He might have accused him of using too much violence against other oligarchs to achieve his aims.

Kuchma had brought Lazarenko from Dnipropetrovsk where he was governor of the oblast (region) to the center of power by making him first deputy prime minister (August 5, 1995 – May 28, 1996) in charge of the energy sector. Lazarenko used his position to give the private company United Energy Systems of Ukraine (UESU), headed by the able Yuliya Tymoshenko, the monopoly over natural gas in

May 1997 – President Leonid Kuchma with Prime Minister Pavlo Lazarenko on his right and parliament head Oleksandr Moroz on his left
(Photo UNIAN)

20

Ukraine. As UESU trading increased, so did the kickbacks to Lazarenko which were sent to Swiss banks – estimated by the Swiss authorities to be about a billion dollars. Despite this large-scale corruption, Kuchma rewarded Lazarenko with the post of prime minister on May 28, 1996.

Not all oligarchs found it agreeable that Lazarenko should be the exclusive beneficiary of this multi-billion dollar industry. He was opposed by a powerful group from the Donetsk, who as the "Donetsk mafia" – as opposed to Kuchma-Lazarenko's "Dnipropetrovsk mafia" – were excluded from the halls of power in Kyiv.

In 1996, a series of assassinations of Donetsk oligarchs rocked the country. At the end of March 1996, a burst of automatic gunfire in Kyiv's city center killed the director of the Russian natural gas supplier Itera-Ukraine, Oleksandr Shvedchenko, a former governor of Donetsk Oblast. On May 16, 1996, in the courtyard of his apartment building in Donetsk, assailants pumped six bullets into Oleksandr Momot, the head of the Donetsk Industrial Union – the club for the Donbas oligarchs. In November 1996, on the tarmac of Donetsk airport, machine gun fire mowed down the godfather of the Donetsk oligarchs, the MP Yevhen Shcherban, along with his wife and a host of bodyguards.

The Donetsk oligarchs apparently retaliated. In June 1997, on the road to Kyiv's Boryspil Airport, a remote-controlled bomb blew up a car carrying Lazarenko. These violent incidents were probably behind Lazarenko's "retirement" on July 2, 1997.

Lazarenko could have retired to a life of luxury with his billion dollars stashed in foreign accounts. Instead, he responded with fury and declared his intention to replace Kuchma. He poured money into the mass media and took over a political party called Hromada (Community) to prepare it for the parliamentary elections in March 1998.

Kuchma reacted by using the courts to close down Lazarenko's newspapers. Despite the silencing of Lazarenko's media outlets, Hromada got over 35 seats in the elections, including one for Lazarenko and the UESU director Yuliya Tymoshenko.

In parliament, Lazarenko created an alliance with the communist, socialist and peasant parties, who together had about 200 of the 450 seats. Now he was in a position to pose a political threat to the president. Using his charisma, Lazarenko galvanized the fragmented left to take control of parliament. After an unprecedented two-month long marathon to elect the parliamentary speaker and his two deputies, when at least two dozen candidates for speaker failed to obtain at least a simple majority, Lazarenko's candidate, the peasant leader Oleksandr Tkachenko, won. It looked as if Lazarenko was set to take on Kuchma in the October 1999 presidential elections.

But in early December 1998, disaster struck. The Swiss police arrested Lazarenko on a charge of money laundering as he attempted to enter the country on his Panamanian passport.

Back in Ukraine, Lazarenko's arrest equally shocked and embarrassed the country. The pro-presidential mass media made sure the incident was fully reported, as no quarter was given to an enemy of Kuchma.

Though the event ended Lazarenko's chances of becoming president, he did not give up the battle. After the Swiss freed him on bail of $2 million, he returned to Ukraine. On January 22, 1999, Hromada nominated him as their candidate in the coming presidential elections.

President Kuchma demanded that parliament remove Lazarenko's immunity from prosecution so he could be tried for corruption. If not, he said, he would call for a referendum to dissolve parliament. When it became clear that his left-wing allies would desert him, Lazarenko fled Ukraine for Greece on February 15, 1999.

On February 17, Prosecutor General Mykhaylo Potebenko presented the accusations against Lazarenko to parliament. It voted 310 to 39 to lift his immunity from prosecution. Though his former comrades – the communists, socialists and peasants – embarrassed by the much-publicized arrest, voted to remove his immunity, the communist and socialist leaders, Symonenko and Moroz, out of respect for their fallen comrade, abstained.

Meanwhile, Lazarenko left Greece for the USA, where he owned a $17 million mansion, formerly occupied by Hollywood film star Eddy

Undated – Pavlo Lazarenko and his business partner Petro Kurychenko
somewhere in north-west America on holiday (Photo UNIAN)

Murphy. The "pile" has 41 rooms and five swimming pools, all on 18
acres of land in Novato, about 30 km north of San Francisco.

On arrival, he claimed political asylum. The American authorities
instead decided to arrest him, and charge him with laundering $114
million in the States. Again, the pro-presidential mass media had a
field day. As of October 2002, Lazarenko was still awaiting trial in a
prison in California.

This was a spectacular fall for the super-rich and powerful
Ukrainian politician. His goal of becoming Ukraine's president was in
tatters. In contrast, President Kuchma's chances of re-election received

23

a tremendous boost from Lazarenko's arrest. In the coming presidential elections, he could present himself as a fighter against corruption.

An oligarch

On his official salary as president – about six thousand dollars a year – Kuchma could not be rich. However, a former guard, Mykola Melnychenko – who secretly recorded the president – has said in a sworn statement that the president had over $2 billion in private accounts. So how has Kuchma become a billionaire? Melnychenko explained in his affidavit:

> An analysis of the recordings of the conversations in the president's office of L.D. Kuchma gives me the basis to conclude: President L.D. Kuchma robbed over $2 billion from the state, a large part deposited on his foreign accounts or accounts he controls, including those through his trusted individual Oleksandr Volkov.
>
> (Source: Statement sworn in New York by Mykola Melnychenko to the Prosecutor General S.M. Piskun, Sept. 27, 2002.)

Furthermore, Melnychenko accused Kuchma of acting like a Mafia chief extorting money from his subordinates. He swore that Kuchma compelled oligarchs to pay regular dues:

> Kuchma has created a state racket – an extortion system – in which all businessmen, who he calls oligarchs, are obligated to pay him large sums in foreign currency. This money L.D. Kuchma obtains in cash, which is then deposited on his overseas accounts or accounts controlled by O.M. Volkov and other individuals.
>
> (Source: Ibid.)

These accusations showed how far Kuchma had travelled from poverty stricken Chaykino. As president and apparently the top oligarch, the peasant boy had reached the apex of political and economic power in Ukraine.

3

Guard to whistleblower

Sept. 1999 – Guard Mykola Melnychenko behind President Leonid
Kuchma in Sevastopol (UNIAN)

President Kuchma's image took a radical turn for the worse with the
appearance of recordings made secretly in his office by his guard,
Mykola Melnychenko. They revealed a petty, spiteful, foul-mouthed,
xenophobic, anti-Semitic, and a criminal personality that surprised
even his strongest critics.

Melnychenko was born on October 18, 1966, in the village of
Zapadynka, near the town of Vasylkiv, south-west of Kyiv. He joined

the KGB during his military service, and when the USSR was on the verge of collapse found himself at the Kremlin, as a guard for the first secretary of the Soviet Communist Party, Mikhail Gorbachev. In 1993 he returned to Ukraine and in 1994 got a job as a guard at the president's office. He was employed there until he made his escape with his wife and child to the Czech Republic in November 2000. Reporters accompanying President Kuchma often saw Melnychenko in his presence, and many photographs show this to be the case.

His role in the presidential guard service was safeguarding the president's communications and conducting counter-electronic surveillance – an ideal position to record the president. He explained why he recorded the president in an interview by a parliamentary committee.

> I started making the recording or, to be precise, documenting the Ukrainian president, after I witnessed – when carrying out my professional duties – President Kuchma giving a criminal order; having found out that the order was fulfilled I continued to document further events.
>
> (Source: Melnychenko's interview on video by parliament's Gongadze committee presented to parliament on Dec. 12, 2000)

In a statement on video, Melnychenko explained what that criminal order was:

> I learned by accident about the order by Ukrainian President Leonid Danylovych Kuchma to organize a terrorist attack on the presidential candidate Nataliya Vitrenko with the purpose of politically destroying [the presidential candidate] Oleksandr Oleksandrovych Moroz.
>
> (Source: Melnychenko statement presented on video to parliament on Dec. 14, 2000)

Melnychenko has been vague on when he heard this order, when he began recording and how many hours he recorded. It can be assumed from his statements that he recorded for a year, from the grenade attack on Vitrenko on October 2, 1999, to October 2000, when he left his job at the president's office.

But how did he record without being caught, as guards work in pairs and often rotate? "The digital recorder was [placed] precisely in the presidential office under the sofa. There is a sofa in the presidential office to the left [of the president's desk] and the recorder was under it," he told parliament's Gongadze committee. The recorder he used was a Toshiba SX-1, which could record "four hours and 25 minutes", he told Tom Warner, the *Financial Times* correspondent in Kyiv.

> *FT*: Right. That's not enough to record an entire day. So someone was turning the machine on and off throughout the day, to record the important meetings?
>
> M: Yes.
>
> *FT*: How was that possible, if the recorder as you've said was hidden under the president's sofa?
>
> M: I made a remotely controlled switch and attached it to the back of the recorder.
>
> (Source: Tom Warner, www.ft.com/Ukraine, Sept. 15, 2002.)

But was Melnychenko working alone? How could he without anyone else's help exchange the memory card and the batteries, and remove and replace the recorder without ever being noticed, for a period of a year? He has repeatedly said that he was the only person who placed the recorder under the sofa and retrieved it.

Skeptics find this unbelievable. If its true that he worked alone, he was either lucky or the president's guard service was incompetent. It has been suggested that the recordings were copied from recordings made by the state security service – with or without Kuchma's permission. Melnychenko has denied this.

Are the recordings genuine?

At least five electronic laboratories or experts have carried out authenticity tests on Melnychenko's recordings. They include the American BEK-TEK Corporation, the Dutch Institute of Applied Scientific Research (TNO), Ukraine's National Institute of Court Experts (NICE), an unidentified British expert employed by Kroll Associates of New York, and an unidentified laboratory working on the behalf of the International Press Institute (IPI) in Vienna.

Only the American BEK-TEK Corporation expressed a strong view on why the recordings were genuine. Both the Dutch Institute of Applied Scientific Research (TNO), and the laboratory working on the behalf of the International Press Institute (IPI) in Vienna, didn't find any alterations or editing in the recordings, but they both concluded that because the recordings were digital, it was impossible to say whether they had been manipulated. IPI suggested that the best way to decide authenticity was to compare the discussions on the recording with corresponding events taking place outside the president's office. (This book will show that events taking place outside the president's office did coincide with the president's discussions.)

Ukraine's National Institute of Court Experts (NICE) and the unidentified British expert employed by Kroll Associates, found the recordings to have been falsified. Ukraine's NICE test will be discussed in chapter 22, and the Kroll test in chapter 27. Though both of these tests come to the same conclusion, they do so for different reasons. The Ukrainian test will be shown to be politically motivated, while the Kroll tests will be shown to be fundamentally flawed.

The BEK-TEK tests were the most rigorous. Only BEK-TEK received from Melnychenko his full cooperation. He made available some of the "master copies" of the recordings – the memory cards, and his "tools" to make the recordings: a Toshiba digital recorder, an Olympus voice recorder, two cellular telephones, two remote switching devices and several other pieces of equipment.

On Feb. 7, 2002, Bruce Koenig of BEK-TEK, a former FBI agent and an internationally recognized expert in audio and video recordings, tested five excerpts from the president's July 3, 2000 discussions on Gongadze. The BEK-TEK conclusions and the contents of these five excerpts recorded on July 3, 2000 can be found in Appendix 1. In brief, in these discussions, Kuchma ordered that Gongadze should be seized and dumped in Chechnya as a punishment for publishing critical articles on his internet site.

Koenig's tests concluded that there were "no indications of alterations or edits to the audio data in the five designated areas" on the two files tested. "No phraseology or sentence structure was pieced

28

together by using individual phonemes, words or abort phrases". In other words, the recordings were authentic.

Melnychenko personally delivered Koenig's test results to Ukraine's embassy in Washington D.C.. The government responded immediately, not with an interest in the tests but with revenge. In Kyiv, Ukraine's foreign ministry summoned the US Ambassador Carlos Pascual to demand Melnychenko's extradition.

BEK-TEK carried out a second test at the request of Ukraine's parliamentary committee on Gongadze. It was on a minute excerpt of an original "master" recording with the president saying on July 7, 2000 that the MP Oleksandr Yelyashkevych should be hit so hard so that he would "never get up again".

In a sworn affidavit, dated February 16, 2002, Koenig said he tested this excerpt, given to him in a file on a 16 MB SmartMedia card. His conclusions were identical to those he reached on the Gongadze excerpts.

Recordings available to the public

A few months after Melnychenko fled Ukraine in November 2000, about 45 hours of his recordings (30 hours of actual recordings and 15 hours of excerpts) were made available to the public by the Vienna based International Press Institute (IPI), which received a copy for testing from a member of the parliamentary committee to investigate the disappearance of Gongadze.

Since the release of the IPI collection, Melnychenko has released a steady flow of transcripts – not all dated or accompanied by sound recordings. They contain the intricate details of how the president of Ukraine governs, most of them mundane, but also include numerous criminal acts, some with international ramifications.

The quality of many transcriptions is in doubt. If Ukraine was a normal country, a special government commission would be created to have the recordings professionally transcribed and annotated. This is especially important because the recordings vary enormously in their sound quality. As there is no such commission, Melnychenko and others have taken upon themselfs to select recordings and release them to the public. Often it is not clear on the internet who released the transcripts, and without annotation it is not clear what the discussions were about. This method of transcribing is wholly unsatisfactory from understanding what the conversations were about. A reputable commission has to be formed which would take responsibility for the transcription and prepare them for prosecution. But this will not happen until Kuchma's dominance of the state ceases, as he will not allow a genuine investigation to take place.

The future of the recordings, said to be over 1,000 hours, in Melnychenko's possession is not clear. He has come under very strong pressure to hand over his whole collection to the US government. From the day he arrived in the US to take up the political asylum granted in April 2001, the US justice department and a grand jury in San Francisco have demanded he hand over his complete collection. He has refused – despite threats of imprisonment – because he says the recordings contain Ukrainian state secrets.

FT: How much of your recordings did you bring with you to the US?

M: I don't have anything in America. All my recordings are in a safe location in Europe. I can't bring them into the US because then I would be obliged to turn them over to the justice department.

The main thing now is to get moving on making transcriptions, and then to investigate the crimes discussed. We need to find some kind of consensus. I have the impression that US agencies have intelligence information, and no small amount. They simply need confirmation. They also need to confirm who is working as spies for other countries in Ukraine, or for Ukraine. But that is secret information and that I will not turn over.

(Warner, Ibid.)

Melnychenko feels personally threatened. In "Killing the Story", the BBC TV documentary on Gongadze, he told the reporter Tom Mangold that he was in hiding in the United States from Kuchma's assassins – "Sooner or later they will get me, I know how they work".

4

Crushing STB

President's Leonid Kuchma's first term in office (1994-9) earned him international notoriety as a repressor of the mass media. On May 3, 1999, marking the international day for press freedom, the New York based Committee for the Protection of Journalists (CPJ) included Kuchma among the world's six worst abusers of the mass media. He was included with an unenviable company of dictators: Slobodan Milosevic of Yugoslavia, Jiang Zemin of China, Fidel Castro of Cuba, Alberto Fujimori of Peru, and Laurent Kabila of the Democratic Republic of Congo.

What did President Kuchma do to deserve this dishonor? In announcing its awards of shame, CPJ stated: "Using tax and libel laws as instruments of his hostility to journalists, Kuchma runs roughshod over any expression of opposition. His tacit acceptance of violence against the press has encouraged bombings of newspaper offices, assaults on reporters and editors, and a general climate of fear and self-censorship. His tax policies force print and broadcast outlets without foreign support to seek financial aid from businesses and politicians who then extort favorable publicity." President Kuchma threatened to sue CPJ, but nothing came of it.

In May 2000, CPJ again awarded the Ukrainian president this title, this time for repressing the mass media which did not support his re-election in 1999. The subjection of the TV station STB during the elections stood out as the most glaring example of Kuchma's abuse of power. Thanks to the secret recordings of the president's guard, CPJ's charges against President Kuchma have been confirmed.

STB, a small private national TV broadcaster, found itself under siege after announcing in early 1999 that it would provide airtime to all candidates taking part in the presidential elections scheduled for

31

October. It also challenged the president by announcing it would broadcast the daily parliamentary proceedings, which the president had banned from state TV and radio, because he saw parliament as a forum to criticize him. In addition, STB started a series of documentaries on sleazy operations by Kuchma's oligarchs, focusing on how they milked the state energy sector for private gain.

The reaction to STB's announcements was lethal. Unidentified hit squads carried out a serious of ruthless measures against its personnel. On February 23, 1999, an assassin shot dead STB's investigator and security official, retired Lt. Col. of the interior ministry, Oleksandr Deneiko, on the staircase of his apartment building in central Kyiv. On February 26, STB cameraman Serhiy Korenev was attacked and robbed of his camcorder and tapes. On the night of March 1, arsonists set fire to the cellar under the apartment of STB President Mykola Knyazhytsky. On March 3, at six in the morning, two masked men broke into the apartment of STB's commercial director, Dmytro Dahno, and threatened to kill him and his pregnant wife if the TV station did not halt its anti-presidential activities. In June, the head of the STB's managing board, Volodymyr Syvkovych (a former advisor to President Kuchma), fled the country after receiving death threats. Syvkovych, who represented the air carrier Vita, which held a 32-percent stake in STB, was seen as the villain by the president.

The terror against STB employees was accompanied by official attempts to close down the station. In early May 1999, the State Inspectorate for Electrocommunications – responsible for the safety of TV frequencies – threatened to withdraw STB's license supposedly for emitting harmful radiation. On June 8, the government halted STB's satellite broadcasts to its affiliates around the country, while other government departments repeatedly charged STB with health-and-safety violations.

After repeated tax inspections, on August 26, 1999, tax officials froze STB's bank accounts. To appease the presidential administration, beginning from September, STB became noticeably pro-Kuchma. This was not enough for the president, as STB had crossed the political Rubicon by not supporting him initially.

A secret recordings by Melnychenko provided the hard evidence that the president was behind the campaign to destroy STB and the threat to the life of its top executive, Syvkovych. In an undated recording released by Melnychenko – probably from early October 1999 – Kuchma discussed STB with the head of the tax office, Mykola Azarov:

[Kuchma] Now, we should decide about STB.

[Azarov] How?

[Kuchma] How? Take everything away from them, disconnect them, they are illegal – Though they have, how to put it.

[Azarov] Yes. Giving up.

[Kuchma] Giving up. What they, the motherfuckers, so much filth – Syvkovych – Syvkovych must be exterminated by all means.

[Azarov] I told you about – about STB, he has asked …

[Kuchma] Syvkovych saw [US Ambassador to Ukraine Stephen] Pifer and complained to him. Then they wrote a letter to the state [indistinct, maybe US State Department] that we are persecuting the press here.

(Source: Radio Liberty Episode 15, pravda.com.ua, March 13, 2001.)

By mid-October Syvkovych had surrendered to the presidential administration. He sold his company's stake to a off-shore company called Norcross Corporation, which was controlled by managers of the Russian oil giant "LUKoil", and which already had a share in STB. On October 13, Syvkovych quit to prevent the station from being closed down and 1,000 employees becoming redundant. Afterwards, Norcross' person at STB, Oleksiy Fedun, the channel's first vice-president and financial manager as well as the cousin of a Lukoil top executive, took control of the station from Syvkovych.

Serhiy Kutsy, a presidential adviser and former head of the President Press Office, was appointed the new managing director. He took the position without resigning his post of presidential adviser, as the law requires; instead he took leave from the job in the president's office.

On October 20, with less than two weeks to the October 31 presidential elections, Kutsy implemented a strictly pro-presidential regime. A number of STB journalists left or were pushed out, but most accepted reality and stayed. It was not surprising that with Kutsy's appointment, the threats against STB came to an end.

American officials used the example of STB to criticize Ukraine's government. On October 14, the US secretary of state, Madeleine Albright, mentioned that during Ukraine's election campaign there were problems relating to freedom of speech and cited STB as an example. Her deputy, Strobe Talbott, in an interview published on Oct. 23, in *Zerkalo Nedeli*, also gave STB as an example of a freedom of speech problem in Ukraine.

The STB incident is evidence that the Melnychenko recordings are genuine, what was being said in the president's office coincided with what was taking place outside.

Gongadze's baptism of fire

Kuchma's conflict with Lazarenko and the repression of the mass media had a great effect on Georgi Gongadze who was working in the broadcasting media. In a newspaper interview in 1998, Gongadze expressed the view that the Lazarenko-Kuchma conflict deprived the public of the chance to learn what was really happening in society. He said that it covered up the state of oligarchs headed by the president and predicted that many "Watergates" awaited Ukraine. This was the case, he said, "because simply there is not a single publication that the oligarch clans do not control and censor", he told the *Den* newspaper on Nov. 11, 1998. This was rather a prophetic statement, considering that his disappearance would trigger the biggest "Watergate" type scandal a head of state has yet to experience.

Gongadze's first encounter with the president's wrath occurred in early 1997. He was presenting from Kyiv the TV analytical news program called Windows-Plus (Vikna-Plus) along with Artem Petrenko and Andriy Tychyna. He first came across President Kuchma's sensitivity to reporting when he presented the fact that president had stacked his government with acquaintances from his hometown of

Dnipropetrovsk. The program was "sharp and uncompromising and had no equal on Ukrainian TV", wrote the *Den* newspaper media correspondent Nataliya Ligachova on May 8, 1997.

All Gongadze said was that President Kuchma had appointed over 200 of his associates from Dnipropetrovsk to top political posts in the government. They included Prime Minister Pavlo Lazarenko, the former governor of Dnipropetrovsk Oblast, and the head of the National Security and Defense Council, Volodymyr Horbulin, who had worked at Pivdenmash missile factory with Kuchma.

In western democratic countries, the news that a president had given his friends positions of power would be met with the response "what's new". This takes place after every American presidential election. But Kuchma reacted angrily. He ordered his state security agents to threaten Gongadze and the other journalists at Windows-Plus.

The president saw this program on TV while on holiday at the Truskavets health spa in the Carpathians. "They [the staff] said he shouted profanities when he saw it. For almost two weeks after the broadcast, all kinds of state security services 'shook' us and the Lviv people [the local broadcasters]", recalled Gongadze.

This was the first time, Gongadze said, he had felt the psychological terror of the president's bullying and it scared him. "I am afraid", he told the *Den* interviewer Ligachova. Kuchma had even expressed his anger at Gongadze personally to Georgia's president during a state visit. "Even during [President Edward] Shevardnadze's visit, Kuchma complained that there is a Georgian here who accuses me of procreating my own clan," the interviewer reported Gongadze as saying.

On the eve of the March 1998 parliamentary elections, Gongadze found himself in the political spotlight, as a victim of the president's refusal to allow his opponents in parliament air-time on TV and radio. In the autumn of 1997, parliament led by the speaker Oleksandr Moroz had challenged the president for influence over the mass media. It voted to sponsor a TV and radio program to provide a national forum for all political parties to publicize their views before the elections. In January 1998, the president responded by banning this program from being broadcast on state TV and radio.

Gongadze's name figured prominently in this president-parliament confrontation. Parliament had appointment Gongadze and Serhiy Naboka – a highly regarded journalist and former Soviet political prisoner – to present the program, "Your Choice", weekly on state TV and daily on state radio.

On January 16, 1998, the information minister, Zenon Kulyk, announced that state broadcasters would not air these two programs. He claimed that parliament's decision was "unconstitutional", as state TV and radio came only under the jurisdiction of the president.

The fact that Gongadze had been appointed to present "Your Choice" was given by the *Den* newspaper as one of the reasons why the presidential administration had rejected it for broadcasting. Its article, dated January 17, 1998, described Gongadze as "a very strong and independent journalist", and said that if Gongadze had not been appointed, then the president's office would not have reacted so negatively to the program.

Gongadze was bitter. "I finally understand that no-one needs objective information in Ukraine – not the executive government, and not the majority of those who take part. For the elections, there is not a single independent news program on Ukrainian TV", he told *Den*.

President Kuchma took additional vindictive measures to limit parliament's influence in the media. He stopped the broadcasts of parliamentary proceedings on state TV and radio. Also, he removed parliament's influence over private broadcasters by paralyzing the operation of the eight-member National Council of TV and Radio, whose job it was to license broadcasters. He did this by not reappointing his four appointees, leaving the four parliament appointees without a quorum and unable to take any decisions.

The national council's paralysis continued well beyond elections. Kuchma replaced his four appointees only after the October 1999 presidential elections, when his supporters had the majority in parliament. With all his measures to control the mass media, the president ensured that during the run-up to October 1999 his opponents would not have influence over state or private broadcasters.

5

Re-election fraud

At a press conference in the summer of 1999, Kuchma announced that he would run for a second term in office. With his main political rival Pavlo Lazarenko in an American jail and the mass media under his control, it seemed he had a good chance to be re-elected.

However, what was against him was the poor performance of the economy during his first term in office. Given that in 1994 he had been elected on the promise to turn the economy around, re-election should have been out of the question. In the fifth year of his presidency, the vast majority of the population was still miserably poor, earning around $100 a month. During his first term in office, not a single year had registered economic growth – a significant failure considering that from 1995 almost all the former communist states in eastern Europe and the former Soviet republics saw their economies grow.

His only achievement was to have vanquished hyperinflation, but not inflation. Inflation fell from the fantastic 891 percent in 1994 to the still serious 16 percent in 1997. There was hope in the first eight months of 1998, as it fell to single figures. But this was dashed by the Russian financial crisis in August 1998. Ukraine's inflation again increased to double figures in 1999.

One important reason why the economy was performing poorly during Kuchma's first term was because corruption undermined its growth and foreign investment. A company's fortune depended on political connections – foremost with the president – and only then on the market place. International investors who did not have these connections found Ukraine one of the world's least desirable places to invest and conduct business.

In 1998, Transparency International, the US organization monitoring corruption around the world, placed Ukraine as the 21st worst corrupt society, tied with Bolivia. In its 2000 survey, Ukraine fell to the third most corrupt state in the world, just better than Nigeria and the former Yugoslavia. Transparency International also identified Ukraine, along with Russia, as a leading world center for money laundering.

Ukraine's image was further tarnished by another survey. London's Economist Intelligence Unit, in its May 2000 review of 60 countries judged by the quality of their business environment, put Ukraine fourth from the bottom. Only Iraq, Iran and Nigeria came lower.

So how would a president – presiding over a shrinking economy, intolerant of media criticism, and with a negative world image – set out to contest his re-election? The strategy devised by the Kuchma camp was for him to stand against someone who was even less electable, like the leader of the communist party, Petro Symonenko. But first he had to get make sure he would not run against the more electable candidate, the socialist leader, Oleksandr Moroz.

Eliminating a candidate with grenades

What could Kuchma do to disgrace the socialist leader? He would find it difficult to accuse him of corruption, as Moroz prided himself on not having enriched himself at the expense of the state. At best one could accuse him of having had corrupt political allies, like Lazarenko and Tkachenko, but this would not be good enough to disgrace him.

Moroz's presidential campaign had started promisingly. On August 24, 1999, he and three other candidates – the former state security service chief, Yevhen Marchuk, the Cherkasy mayor, Volodymyr Oliynyk, and the parliamentary speaker, Oleksandr Tkachenko – met in Kaniv at the burial mound of Ukraine's bard – Taras Shevchenko – and made a dramatic announcement. Using Shevchenko's grave as a patriotic backdrop, the four candidates – dubbed by the media the Kaniv-4 – proclaimed their intention to choose a single candidate to stand against Kuchma. The reporters present at this event said that Moroz was expected to be the Kaniv-4's chosen candidate.

On Sept. 29, Marchuk announced that he would withdraw his candidacy in favor of Moroz. Oliynyk and Tkachenko were expected to do the same. Kuchma's worst scenario looked like coming true – he might have to stand against Moroz, and not the communist leader Symonenko. Then occurred a violent incident that destroyed Moroz's chances of becoming president.

At 8 pm, on Saturday, October 2, two grenades were thrown at the presidential candidate Nataliya Vitrenko and her supporters as they left an election rally in the small factory town of Inhulets near the city of Kryvyi-Rih. The grenade explosions injured 45 people, including Vitrenko, and two of her party's MPs – Volodymyr Marchenko and Nataliya Lymar. "I got shrapnel wounds to my legs and stomach" Vitrenko told Ukraine's first state TV channel (UT1) on October 3.

This event shocked the nation. It also shattered Moroz's presidential hopes, as within an hour of the explosions, Ukrainian state media bombarded the public with the news that the attackers were linked to Moroz.

The relentless media attacks on Moroz continued into the next days and weeks. On Sunday, October 3, 1999, the day after the attack, UT1 in special news bulletins unreservedly placed the responsibility for the attack on Moroz. The well-groomed TV newsreader Oksana Marchenko (soon to be wife of the oligarch Viktor Medvedchuk) linked Moroz to the terrorist attack in no uncertain terms. "It has become known to Ukrainian Television News [UTN] that Serhiy Ivanchenko, an election agent of Oleksandr Moroz in electoral constituency No 33, was the organizer of the attempt on the life of presidential candidate Nataliya Vitrenko".

UT-1, controlled by the president, had within hours of the event decided who was guilty. It accused Ivanchenko of driving the "terrorists" (his brother and his friend) to the venue by car, giving them the grenades, and then disappearing from the scene. In this vein, the state and the private mass media owned by the president's friends tarnished Moroz's image. In all the news broadcasts Moroz was linked to Ivanchenko. There was no proof that Ivanchenko or the "terrorists" were to blame for the incident.

Attempts by Moroz to counter this propaganda failed. The state TV and radio president, Vadim Dolhanov, ignored a resolution by Ukraine's parliament to give Moroz the right to rebut the charges. On October 12, Moroz, accompanied by members of parliament and journalists walked into the national broadcasting house in Kyiv to confront Dolhanov (whose wife, Susanna Stanik, was the justice minister). After a heated discussion, Dolhanov promised Moroz the right to reply on the channel's flagship news program, 7-Days, shown on Sunday evenings. But the next day, Dolhanov reneged on his promise, and accused Moroz and his supporters of attempting to commit a terrorist act – the seizure of the broadcasting center.

Vitrenko, who recovered soon after the incident, supported the government accusations against Moroz, creating more problems for him. Her accusations were based on her political animosity to Moroz. She had been a close associate of his but split from the socialist party in 1996 to form the progressive socialist party. Many of her critics claim that she was created and groomed by the president's office to weaken Moroz.

After the grenade throwing incident, pre-election surveys showed that Moroz would be out of the running, receiving even fewer votes than the injured Vitrenko. But they also predicted that Kuchma would not win outright, as this required him to get more than fifty percent of the vote, but would come first in the field of 13 candidates. The prediction was that he and the communist party candidate, Petro Symonenko, would contest the elections in a second round, with the possibility that Vitrenko might come second instead of Symonenko.

Adding to Moroz's difficulty was the collapse of the Kaniv-4 on October 14. The former state security service chief, Marchuk, decided not to stand down in favor of Moroz, and the others did the same. Their decisions further undermined Moroz's public standing.

The predictions also said that in the second round, Kuchma would win by a few million votes, regardless of whether he stood against Symonenko or Vitrenko. This was exactly what happened.

In the first round of the elections, on October 31, 1999, Kuchma came first with 36 percent of the vote (9.6 million), smack in the middle of what the voter surveys predicted. Symonenko was second with 22 percent (5.9 million), which was much more than the surveys had predicted. Moroz did much better than the predictions with 11 percent (or 3 million). Support for him had improved after its collapse following the grenade-throwing act. Vitrenko was just behind Moroz with just under 11 percent. But three left-wing candidates – Symonenko, Moroz and Vitrenko – amassed an impressive 44 percent of the vote. Marchuk received more votes than the surveys had suggested – seven percent or 2.1 million votes. The remaining eight candidates received well below five percent of the vote each. A respectable 70 percent or 26.3 million voters took part in the first election round.

But who ordered the grenade attack against Vitrenko? A year later, President Kuchma was accused of this act by his guard Melnychenko. "When carrying out my work responsibilities, I learned by accident about the order by Ukrainian President Leonid Danylovych Kuchma to organize a terrorist attack on the presidential candidate Nataliya Vitrenko with the purpose of the political destruction of Oleksandr Oleksandrovych Moroz" (statement made on video and shown in parliament on Dec. 14, 2000). Melnychenko has yet to explain how he heard about the grenade-throwing incident.

The incident cries out for a full investigation, as June 15, 2001, three people, Serhiy Ivanchenko, his brother Volodymyr, and Andriy Smoilov, were each sentenced for this incident to 15 years of imprisonment. All claimed they had been framed by the authorities.

Melnychenko has provided only a short excerpt on this incident. The excerpt was undated. In it Kuchma was assured by the state security chief Derkach, the interior minister Kravchenko and an unidentified person that Ivanchenko's brother would confess to the accusations made against him. Derkach guaranteed that it would be forced out of him by putting him in a cell with 30-40 prisoners. "On the Ivanchenko affair, everything is going according to plan. There are no hitches." – he told the president. Kuchma stated that all the blame for the incident had to be directed towards Moroz. (This excerpt was released by Oleksandr Moroz on June 21, 2001. He said the conversation took place sometime in the middle of the summer in 2000.)

Election cheating

President Kuchma helped to fix his re-election, according to undated transcripts released by Melnychenko. But from the context of the discussions, these excerpts contained discussion that took place between the first and second rounds of the election – October 31 and November 14, 1999. They show Kuchma instructing his subordinates to threaten local officials with tax irregularities, unemployment and even imprisonment, if their district or farm didn't vote for him. In the election fixing discussions with the head of the tax office, Mykola Azarov, Kuchma ordered him to sack tax inspectors if they did not apply sufficient pressure on officials in rural areas of the central oblasts (regions) of Ukraine, where support for Moroz was the strongest.

[Azarov] Good day.

[Kuchma] Hello. Sit down, We'll have some tea. So, I have some [tasks] for you. You should get together all of your fucking tax inspectors – from the districts, or, I don't know, if only from the oblasts regions. And warn them: those who lose the elections in the district will not work after the elections.

[Azarov] ?

[Kuchma] We won't even let a single [loser] remain. Well, you understand, to every last rural district. You should sit down with every head and fucking tell them: either you sit in the fucking jail – as I have more on you than on anyone else, or you produce votes. Right or wrong?

[Azarov] I understand – everything will be done.

[Kuchma] Now I'm gonna tell this to [interior minister] Kravchenko. And then you will tell the same that they should talk with each collective farm head.

[Azarov] OK. Starting from the district department heads, right?

[Kuchma] [Speaking by phone to Kravchenko] I have Azarov here. Well, there is this scheme. They pretty well have a case on every collective farm head. They should be gathered together in every district so that the police and tax service chiefs can tell them: guys, if you don't fucking give as much as is necessary, then tomorrow you will be where you should be – yes. Well, we should gather all the guys, so to say – well, except for the western oblasts [Western Ukraine], not necessary. But those fucking central oblasts – Kherson, Kirovograd, Chernihiv, fucking Cherkasy – all these oblasts. Yes, we should ... they should be clear, we are not gonna play fucking games with them anymore. I said that yesterday at a meeting. I said – though you are elected by the people, but ... And that is it, I said. Let him think about it (laughing). OK. Those fucking bitches, bloody collective farm heads. All of them. I said yesterday: they all act like landlords, barons. Immediately after the elections, the toughest order should be introduced.

[Azarov] Of course.

[Kuchma] We must not relax. Second, we must win with a formidable margin. This is important as well. You understand. When they say – two or three per cent, it is not a victory. That is why we should do it so that none of the villages, not a fucking place can say that it protesting – it is a total protesting electorate, ... – that is why they didn't vote for you.

[Azarov] Well, right. Although, not all of them are for Moroz.

(Source: Episode 2, pravda.com.ua, Feb. 11, 2001)

In another, conversation with Azarov, President Kuchma again ordered him again to apply pressure on officials in those districts where he didn't do well in the first election round:

[Kuchma] You have the [first round] election results, in the districts, all of them.

[Azarov] Right.

[Kuchma] Tell them – guys, this is your fucking work – forcing collective farm heads to fucking dance to our tune.

[Azarov] I will talk to Kravchenko now. Vitaliy has done it for the western oblasts.

(Source: Episode 4, pravda.com.ua, Feb. 11, 2001.)

Siphoning state funds

Melnychenko has also produced evidence that the president funded his re-election campaign with millions of dollars from state funds. In the recordings, the president asked Ihor Bakay, the head of the state oil and gas company Naftohaz to provide $250 million for his re-election fund, controlled by the MP Oleksandr Volkov.

President Kuchma had formed Naftohaz – a state gas and oil conglomerate – in February 1998 and appointed Bakay to head it. Naftohaz essentially took over the role played by Lazarenko's UESU, and, like it, had the monopoly over natural gas and oil production and distribution in Ukraine. And like for Lazarenko, this company became a source of funds for officials to enrich themselves. However, Melnychenko's recordings show that Naftohaz's head failed to provide $250 million as instructed, and kept as much as half of it for himself.

During the election campaign, Kuchma's fundraiser, Oleksandr Volkov, complained that Bakay had not come up with the promised funds for the campaign:

[Kuchma] Listen, how's Bakay?

[Volkov] Nothing new since then. I told you yesterday we need 900,000 [dollars]. Today I called him and said: do you have conscience? You are an animal, if you think that Volkov goes first and you stay aside, with what? You will follow me. Now [MP and gas trader Oleksandr] Abdullin visited me, now he's gone. He says, give me the payment order, I gave him one payment order [indistinct] – This was to Yura.

[Kuchma] And where is Bakay?

[Volkov] I was told [he is] at the Cabinet of Ministers, there, there.

[Kuchma] I need to discuss something with him. He has transferred 10m. But what is 10m if 20m dollars is needed till the end of the month. Well, give the account number where to transfer [the money], I will think it over whom to give it to.

[Volkov] I think to [MP, and leading oligarch in Crimea and the president's former son-in-law, Anatoliy] Franchuk.

[Kuchma] No, I need one more [indistinct] to Franchuk.

[Volkov] Really?

[Kuchma] Yes.

[Volkov] OK.

(Source: Episode 1, pravda.com.ua, April 23, 2001.)

In another excerpt the Kuchma can be heard in a telephone conversation telling Bakay off for not providing enough funds. "[Kuchma] I was looking in your eyes and you told me, 'I will provide 250m dollars for your election campaign'" (Source: Episode 2, Ibid.).

After the election, on February 10, 2000, the head of tax office, Azarov, told Kuchma that Bakay had pocketed some of the money promised for his re-election:

> [Azarov] … when Oleksandr Mykhaylovych [Volkov] and I sat down [we found that] what Bakay had in real terms given over to the election campaign was roughly half of it, and it was not accounted for. Volkov did not even get 184m.
>
> (Source: IPI, ZL1002, Feb. 10, 2000.)

Azarov also expressed his concern that he covered it up so poorly that "any stupid" tax inspector could discover it:

> [Azarov] Well, about this Naftohaz. I invited Bakay, as we have agreed, and showed him everything. My people worked on that, I trust them. I spoke to Oleksandr Mykhaylovych [Volkov], and found out, how much came in total. And I literally told him [Bakay]: "Well, Ihor, you have put at least 100m [dollars] in you pocket, at least. I understand that, of course, I will not set you up. I give you two weeks, a month at the most. (Then I showed him all the schemes). Destroy them, these, so to say, your papers, which prove directly or indirectly all of your – you did it foolishly and stupidly." And I showed him that he did everything foolishly and stupidly.
>
> [Kuchma] Good.
>
> [Azarov] Well, things have got moving now.

[Kuchma] Well – Mykola Yanovych – I told him: "Listen, honey, we all are not going to cover your ass".

[Azarov] He should have some brains.

[Kuchma] I agree with you. I agree with you.

[Azarov] Well, he could have done it in a smart way. But no, he did it so that any stupid inspector could see his false schemes. Even a stupid one.

[Kuchma] Well, listen, everywhere he did it, there is complete impunity.

[Azarov] Absolutely. Well, we have agreed with this Bakay, he should go to a hospital for some time. Well, roughly, a week, two weeks, a month. Well, maybe six weeks, it does not make any difference, but he has understood what he should do. The only thing I want, I want your support, if this moron does not do it, then I will, so to say.

[Kuchma] Well, I will tell him tomorrow.

(Source: Ibid.)

Kuchma was re-elected in the second round on November 15 with 56 percent (15.9 million) of the vote. Symonenko received 38 percent (11 million) of the vote. Another six percent (1.7 million) had spointed their ballots. The unpopular president had won as his advisers had suggested he would, by standing against an even less popular candidate.

Oct. 31, 1999 – President Kuchma, wife Lyudmyla and grandson at a polling station in Kyiv (Photo by Vasyl Artyushenko / Irex-ProMedia)

6

Gongadze goes to America

Following President Kuchma's re-election on November 14, 1999, many journalists felt angry and cynical about the methods he used to get re-elected. Few journalists seemed angrier than Gongadze, who had personally felt the president's threats.

It was in the 1999 elections that Gongadze rose to prominence as a journalist, thanks to his controversial radio broadcasts and appearances on a weekly national TV news program. He had his own program on Kyiv's Radio Continent, 100.9 FM. The station – owned and managed by the maverick Serhiy Sholokh – was an oasis of free speech in Ukraine's capital. For two months, September 1 to October 31, Gongadze presented a daily two-hour news and discussion program called "The First Round". It did what most of the media would not do; it not only gave a platform to all the candidates, but it came out against Kuchma for president.

Many journalists saw Giya's public calls not to vote for Kuchma as suicidal. "When Gongadze and I used to walk into the cafe at the Central Election Commission headquarters, our fellow journalists would greet us with shouts of 'Here come the kamikazes!'", recalled Sholokh, the radio's director. Gongadze called on people to vote either for the former State Security Service head Yevhen Marchuk or the socialist leader Oleksandr Moroz, both of whom accused Kuchma of corruption and being unfit for another term in office.

What gave Gongadze national prominence were his weekly appearances, from June until October, on Epicenter, the TV news discussion program presented by Vyacheslav Pikhovshek, which was broadcast on the national private TV channel Studio 1+1. Each of the thirteen presidential candidates appeared in turn on Epicenter. Its format consisted of the presenter, Pikhovshek, introducing the candidate and then allowing journalists to throw questions at him or her. The program gave Gongadze the opportunity to grill all thirteen candidates, and he earned a reputation for asking tough questions.

"Pikhovshek chose Giya because he was a bright man, asked good questions, had a lot of experience in television, and could perform well in front of a camera", recalled the Kyiv Post reporter Katya Gorchinskaya, who also appeared on Epicenter. "He appeared regularly because Pikhovshek wanted him to ask awkward questions to give the program balance" said the journalist Olena Prytula.

Giya once said he viewed the Epicenter format as revolutionary for Ukrainian TV because journalists could ask politicians awkward questions. "I am anxiously awaiting Kuchma's appearance (on Epicenter). I have a number of questions to ask him, if they invite me to appear", Giya told *Den*, Oct. 1, 1999.

On October 17, Kuchma appeared on Epicenter. Gongadze asked an awkward question, about why he didn't fire the Interior Minister (equivalent to the chief of the national police) Yuriy Kravchenko as he had failed to solve major crimes:

> [Giya] Today, despite the fact that weapons are being found and explosions take place, Kravchenko is riding high. Do you not think that this is incompetence? People who cannot find the guilty criminals, should not be in their jobs. First of all, they are compromising you. No one cares whether Kravchenko knew or did not know about something that is his responsibility.
>
> [Kuchma] Excuse me sir; I do not know your name.
>
> [Giya] Georgi Gongadze.
>
> [Kuchma] So, Georgi, this is a question to the Security Service of Ukraine and not to the Interior Ministry. Serious changes have taken place at the Security Service since that time. It is the Security Service that is responsible for economic security.
>
> (Source: Epicenter, 1+1, Oct. 17, 1999)

Gongadze's awkward question elicited a confusing answer. Kuchma, rattled by the tone and substance of the question, answered incoherently that the question had to do with economic security and should be referred to State security service. The question, an oblique reference to the throwing of the grenades at Vitrenko and her supporters, and the discovery of firearms in the suspect's house, was the responsibility of the interior minister.

Following the appearance of all thirteen presidential candidates, Pikhovshek announced that Epicenter would start a new format. All the presidential candidates would be invited over five days to debate specific topics in the week before the polling day.

In the first debate, Kuchma came out poorly in contrast to other candidates. Immediately afterwards, the remaining debates were cancelled and Epicenter did not appear until well after the election. Pikhovshek claimed that he had had a heart attack and the program could not continue without him, as he was its presenter and author.

The journalist Gorchinskaya said she witnessed Pikhovshek's heart attack. "I was there when they called the ambulance. He walked out of a studio during a live TV broadcast because he thought he was having a heart attack. I was there when the doctors were giving him drugs."

However, skeptics claimed that if Pikhovshek was ill someone else could have continued the program in his place. They charged Pikhovshek with pulling the plug on further debates because the president's office wanted to spare Kuchma any more embarrassments.

For other presidential candidates, like Moroz, Epicenter on 1+1 channel was their only chance to publicize themselves nationally. It was impossible to get on the other two key national channels, Inter and especially the state national TV station, UT1. The latter barred Moroz completely except for the few minutes provided officially for each candidate. UT1 had totally dedicated itself to promoting Kuchma. In the last week before the vote, it provided seven hours of positive coverage on Kuchma, as opposed to minutes to the other candidates, reported the European Institute for the Media.

On the eve of the presidential poll, Georgi made an emotional pitch to his radio listeners not to vote for Kuchma.

> I am appealing to all those who are planning to vote for the sitting President. I say this with complete consciousness. Today's regime does not have any right to stay in power. They have had every chance to

improve the situation. They did not do it; in five years they made all of us beggars, moral beggars. And this is their worst sin ... We live today in a Belarus with a yellow-blue flag and trident [Ukraine's national emblem], we are not a state, [we] are only left with trappings.

A telephone caller asked, if you call for a vote against Kuchma, whom should we vote for? "I would be pleased if in the second round the contest was between Marchuk and Moroz. We would be voting not against, but for," replied Georgi." In an answer to another caller, Georgi gave his view on the president:

I somehow managed to appear on Epicenter with the president. You probably saw this program. Everyone sat there upright and quietly. I will tell you my own feelings. In the first half [of the program] I was ashamed of this president and of living in a country headed by this man. I prepared questions that would be sharper, but I understood that there was no sense [in asking them]. ... In the second half I was somewhat scared by what would I do if he stays. When you are ashamed of your government this is catastrophic. ...

(Source: "I am a Georgian, but ready to die for Ukraine", pravda.com.ua, March 3, 2001.)

Georgi was depressed with the results of the first round of the presidential elections on October 31, with Kuchma coming first, Symonenko second, and Moroz and Marchuk out of the race. What angered him was Marchuk's "betrayal". Having made Kuchma's corruption a major plank of his campaign, Marchuk after the first round called upon his supporters to vote for Kuchma in the second. Gongadze, like many other Marchuk supporters, who had worked on his behalf, felt personally betrayed. The question that Marchuk has to answer was why he didn't support Moroz as he had initially promised? As the former head of state security service he must had some information on who threw the grenades at Vitrenko and her entourage?

In the week before the final vote on November 15, Georgi resumed his broadcasts – now named the Second Round – with a vengeance, calling upon the electorate not to vote for either of the two candidates. A futile jesture that didn't stop from Kuchma winning.

Attempts to silence Radio Continent

As the presidential election period began, the authorities reacted to Gongadze's broadcasts by harassing the station's director Serhiy Sholokh. The tax office froze Radio Continent's bank account. From September to October 1999, Radio Continent went to court five times to have its accounts reopened. Even after the courts ruled in the radio's favor, the tax office and its police continued the harassment by demanding more financial documents. "The aim was to force the radio station to be more reserved and obedient", said Georgi.

Like in the case of STB, the director received a death threat, but also it was followed by an attempt on his life. In October 1999, an anonymous telephone caller told Sholokh – "Shut up or we will shut you up". A few days later, a car attempted to force Sholokh off the road, causing him to crash but not get hurt. Immediately afterwards, he returned to his office, when an anonymous caller rang to say, "If you think you are a good driver, you're mistaken. We have warned you." (Fourteen months later, in January 2001, another attempt will be made to hurt or kill Sholokh in a traffic accident, but this time he would discover who was behind it; see Chapter 23 – The provocations). Presidential staff members even telephoned Sholokh directly to demand he stop Georgi broadcasting. Sholokh responded to the attempt on his life with a complaint to the chief of the State Security Service, Leonid Derkach, which went unanswered.

Following Kuchma's victory, Sholokh obtained information that the president's administration was planning to shut down his radio station. In reaction, he and Gongadze resolved to spoil President Kuchma's state visit to Washington DC, which was to begin on December 8, 1999. This audacious move to lobby against him in the American capital would not go unnoticed by the president's men.

Sholokh and Gongadze received a sympathetic ear from the US embassy in Kyiv. During the presidential elections, the intervention by the Ambassador, Steven Pifer, with President Kuchma's office probably prevented the shutting down of Radio Continent. Though the Americans were pleased that the communist candidate didn't win, they were not happy with the way Kuchma had won. They issued visas to Gongadze, Sholokh and a third person, along with a letter of introduction to politicians in Washington. On December 4, Sholokh, Gongadze and the third person flew to Washington DC.

The third person

The "president's favorite reporter" had also joined the lobbying campaign. Olena Prytula, the reporter to the president's office from the Interfax-Ukraine news agency came along with Gongadze and Sholokh. Prytula had worked for one of Ukraine's top news agencies as chief reporter to the president's office from 1995 until the end of the 1999 presidential elections.

She was appointed to Ukraine's "White House" by the then director of Interfax-Ukraine, Oleksandr Martynenko. In November 1998, Martynenko became President's Kuchma's press secretary. While reporting on the president, Prytula continued to have a good personal relationship with her former boss.

Like Georgi, Olena was born outside Ukraine, in Zavolzhe, Gorky Oblast, Russia. She and her future husband, Volodymyr Prytula, studied engineering at Odesa Polytechnic. After graduation, they both received jobs at a top secret Soviet naval electronics plant in Sevastopol, then a city closed to foreigners and the headquarters of the Black Sea Fleet.

Following the collapse of the USSR and the closure of their military plant, they both decided to become journalists. "When the [Soviet] Black Sea Fleet split [into Ukrainian and Russian navies], we wanted to report the events from the Ukrainian view", explained Olena.

In 1993, she got a job with Interfax-Ukraine, an agency based in Moscow, and in 1995 landed its most important reporting job – reporter to the president's office. "I dedicated my life to the job and was available to report what the president said day and night," Olena said. She became such a fixture at the president's office that Kuchma knew her by sight. He had a habit of always saying hello with the same question: "Olena, what are you up to?"

"As I worked a long time with the president, I saw from the inside everything that was happening there, and the Kuchma I got to know was not completely to my liking – I was disillusioned with Kuchma", she said. What did she find unacceptable about Kuchma? "I cannot say because I consider it would be unethical", she replied. What was unethical she would not say.

In 1997, she met the married Georgi and they started a relationship. It became public in 1999, when Georgi took Olena and not his wife, Myroslava, to a reception for journalists at the American Embassy. Olena also introduced him to her friend Martynenko, the president's press secretary. Gongadze and Martynenko saw each other socially on only a few occasions, like when Martynenko came to Georgi's birthday party on May 21, 1999.

The Olena and Georgi relationship would turn out to be a dangerous symbiosis for the president. While Georgi was a fiery journalist, Olena was a cool-headed, disciplined reporter. Georgi was a journalist viewing the ruling elite from the outside; she saw them close up.

Lobbying in Washington DC

For the American trip, Olena helped Georgi write a petition accusing the Kuchma government of muzzling the mass media during the presidential elections and killing democracy in Ukraine. On December 2, 1999, Georgi read the petition at a round-table discussion in Kyiv on "Libel in Ukraine", organized by OSCE, the Council of Europe and Irex-Promedia (an American government sponsored center for journalism in Ukraine). Altogether, sixty-four journalists in Kyiv signed the petition.

The petition spoke plainly:

During the past few years Ukraine has seen the formation of clan-like, oligarchic political groupings that have instituted antiquated methods of state control, and have led to the practical liquidation of independent television and print media … Such a situation was obviously present during the recent presidential elections, when the press and TV played a 'killer' role, morally destroying the opponents of incumbent

53

President Leonid Kuchma. Millions of dollars were spent on persecuting and discrediting the president's rival. Pressure on national and
local mass media reached unprecedented levels. … If Western political
circles ignore these problems, the present situation will lead to the
establishment of an authoritarian regime, which under the slogans of
democracy will destroy civil society, creating the foundation for
unpredictable developments in Central Europe.

"On December 4, Gongadze, Prytula and I flew to the States with
various documents showing that freedom of speech was being violated
in Ukraine. [The MP Oleksandr] Moroz gave me a sealed folder of
presidential election violations to give to the State Department.
Gongadze had a petition signed by 64 journalists protesting the lack of
press and broadcasting freedom", recalled Sholokh.

At the State Department, they met Ukraine desk officer Mary
Worlick, and Carlos E. Pascual, the former US ambassador to Ukraine
(and from October 2000 again ambassador to Ukraine). At the House
of Representatives, they met aides of congressmen who belonged to
the Ukrainian caucus. They spoke mainly to the aides as most of the
congressmen had already left the capital for their districts on the eve of
the Christmas holidays.

The trio was disappointed with the reaction to their lobbying – "we
know all about the situation in Ukraine and believe that after his re-
election Kuchma will make Ukraine more democratic and free". The
truth was that American politicians welcomed Kuchma's victory
because he kept out the communist Symonenko, and weren't interested in other matters.

Meanwhile, Kuchma's state visit began badly. For a start, the US
Embassy in Ukraine refused to issue visas to the MP Oleksandr Volkov
and the head of state oil and gas company, Ihor Bakay. The State
Department had barred them on suspicion of money laundering activities in America, just like the disgraced former prime minister
Lazarenko. For Kuchma this was highly embarrassing and put him in
bad mood. Volkov was his most faithful political ally who had organized the funding of his presidential elections. Bakay he cared less for,

but it was the principle that offended him.

President Kuchma and his entourage arrived in Washington on December 8, for the Kuchma-Gore Summit and a photo opportunity with President Bill Clinton at the White House. The Ukrainian delegation included the government's major figures, including Vice Prime Minister Serhiy Tyhypko, Finance Minister Ihor Mityukov, National Bank director Viktor Yushchenko, and the newly appointed secretary of the National Security and Defense Council, Yevhen Marchuk.

Word got to the presidential party that three journalists from Kyiv were lobbying against President Kuchma. The Epicenter presenter, Vyacheslav Pikhovshek, who accompanied the presidential party, met the trio to warn them that their lives were in danger: "Do you know what dangers await you for what you are doing here", Prytula recalled Pikhovshek telling them. "Friends, I completely understand your position, but you are affecting such interests that you are threatened with physical harm," was what Sholokh recalled. "You don't realize that you could be killed for what you're doing here" was how Reporters San Frontiers (RSF) reported Pikhovshek's message. Whatever the precise words, they all came down to the fact that the president's men were angry over Gongadze's and Sholokh's lobbying.

Sholokh returned to Kyiv on December 12, while Gongadze and Prytula stayed on to continue their political efforts in New York City. His visit was reported by an Ukrainian-American newspaper under the headline – "Young Ukrainian journalists warn of danger of continued deterioration of press freedom".

> The message brought here by Serhiy Sholokh, general manager of Radio Continent, Olena Prytula of Interfax-Ukraine and Georgi Gongadze, also of Radio Continent, is that the psychological and physical intimidation of the press by the government in Ukraine was not simply a short-term phenomenon related to the re-election of President Leonid Kuchma, but rather, has become a consistent element in the practice of journalism in Ukraine.
>
> This phenomenon of control by intimidation has a dual nature, according to Mr. Gongadze. The first is external, such as the use of

administrative means, for example tax audits, and physical means, such as threats of bodily harm, to keep editors and journalists in line; the second is internal, ever-increasing self-censorship – as editors and journalists refrain from reporting negative information about elected officials, as well as about the so-called financial 'oligarchs,' in order to not suffer consequences later.

(Source: *Ukrainian Weekly*, Jan. 16, 2000)

On December 17, 1999, in New York City, Georgi gave a lecture at the office of the lobbying group, the American-Ukrainian Congressional Committee. He posed the question – "Whither the Titanic of Ukrainian Journalism?" His answer was that Ukraine was on its way to becoming a Belarus or Kazakhstan but not a European type of state. He accused President Kuchma and his supporters of using the mass media to destroy their opponents. He gave the example of Lazarenko, who as the president's prime minister manipulated the press against his critics, and now discovered the same methods being used against him to devastating effect. He described the editorial pressures that journalists in Ukraine had to work under and how they had to write articles dictated by their paymasters.

Gongadze named President Kuchma, the secret police chief Derkach, and the head of the president's office, Lytvyn, as the culprits behind the punishment and destruction of journalists and media outlets that opposed the president's re-election. "He gave examples how the tax police and physical threats had been used against television and radio stations, including Radio Continent," reported *The Ukrainian Weekly*.

Georgi's fund-raising campaign in America was even less successful than his political lobbying. He visited foundations and diaspora organizations in a vain hope of raising funds for the new series of "Free Wave" news programs on Radio Continent he planned to launch after his return to Kyiv. At the conservative foundation, Freedom House, he spoke to its president, Adrian Karatnycky, who recalled that Gongadze struck him as more of a revolutionary than a journalist.

7

Hitting an MP

The year 2000 began with a confrontation between the right and left leading to the creation of two parliaments. The oligarch factions had increased in size by buying off MPs from the other parties. The rightists – the oligarch parties, along with the two Rukh parties and Reform-and-Order, now had the majority and demanded a vote for a new parliamentary speaker. The left-wing speaker Oleksandr Tkachenko refused to allow a vote to take place. On January 21, 2000, the right-wingers walked out and convened a new parliament in Ukraine House, the former Lenin museum in Kyiv. Ukraine now had two parliaments, each declaring the other illegitimate.

On February 7, 2000, an extraordinary meeting took place between representatives of the two parliaments behind closed doors. The outcome was that the communists and socialists gave in to the rightist majority and agreed to the oligarchs taking control of parliament.

Nataliya Vitrenko and her progressive socialist MPs refused to accept the decision and staged a hunger strike in the parliament's assembly hall. At 7:30 am on February 8, about 70 right-wing MPs – led by the oligarchs Surkis, Volkov and Brodsky – evicted the hunger strikers from the session hall. Vitrenko hurriedly called a press conference, charging the oligarchs with beating up three of her MPs.

She and her comrades spent the rest of the day heckling the parliamentary session from the gallery of the hall. (Soon afterwards her progressive socialist parliamentary faction dissolved, having fallen below the statutory minimum of 14 members, as many had left for the oligarch parties. The peasant party, led by the former speaker Tkachenko, also met the same fate.)

The oligarch groups appointed their members to position of power. Ivan Plyushch, a former Soviet bureaucrat and close collaborator of

President Kuchma, became speaker. Viktor Medvedchuk of the Social Democratic United Party got the first deputy speaker post. The second deputy speaker post went to Stepan Havrysh, a member of Regional Rebirth, the party of Kuchma's closest political ally, Oleksandr Volkov. The oligarch factions took over the majority of the parliamentary committees. (On June 1, 2000, parliament dissolved all the investigating committees – many of them focusing on the oligarchs' money laundering and other criminal activities. Later investigating committees were allowed – like the Gongadze committee – but without the legal powers to investigate.)

Watching the February 8th parliament proceedings on closed circuit TV was President Kuchma along with the state security chief Derkach. In a recording by Melnychenko, Kuchma could be heard getting very agitated with the speeches by the MP Oleksandr Yelyashkevych. This former leading member of Lazarenko's Hromada party was asking for a delay in the voting of new procedural rules because it would again tear apart the two warring sides. He complained that the two sides couldn't reach an agreement on the rules because the president wanted only his MPs to control parliament.

This snide remark by Yelyashkevych prompted an outburst of profanities from Kuchma.

[Kuchma] Here is a fucking Yiddish sprout!

[Yelyashkevych can be heard addressing the session, while Kuchma and Derkach speak.]

[Kuchma] He will get [what's coming to him].

[Derkach] Fucking him!

[Kuchma] Fuck him up! Let's [do it]! Let the little Jew be handled by yids!

[Derkach] Be handled and done for. What does he fucking think [he is], the limit? [Let them] beat him a little and say prick!

[Kuchma] Let the yids [handle] the yid! Well, I agree.

[Kuchma names the person that should organize the beating]

[At this moment, parliamentary speaker Ivan Plyushch begins to comment on one of Yelyashkevych's proposals that a recess take place to hold consultations among the leaders of all parliamentary groups. Kuchma, agitated by this, says loudly in his characteristic style that the speaker has to continue the session before the time stipulated by parliamentary regulations expires.]

[Kuchma] Drag it out until 12:00, you motherfucker!

The conversation between Kuchma and Derkach, interrupted for a moment, resumes.

[Derkach] He'll meet his end!

[Kuchma] You arrange everything.

[Derkach] By what date?

[Kuchma] Tomorrow.

[Derkach] Good. He'll be at home!

[Kuchma] Finish [him] off! The fucker will get his. Jew.

Kuchma tried to reach first deputy speaker [Viktor] Medvedchuk by telephone to instruct him to continue the session, but it proved difficult. He told Medvedchuk's secretary that he would get the sack if he didn't connect with him immediately. A minute or two past, and Medvedchuk came to the telephone. The incident showed how Kuchma controlled parliament's proceedings, the kind of interference Yelyashkevych was complaining about:

[Kuchma] Hello! [unintelligible] Listen! There is no need to take an early break. It is necessary to continue until 12. Otherwise, they will celebrate a victory. They will mess up everything. Under no circumstances. Drag it out. Any issues [you like]. Good.

[Kuchma and Derkach again listen to deputy Yelyashkevych's speech.]

[Kuchma] Let them beat him! He's become impudent, that son of a bitch!

(Source: Sworn statement on the Yelyashkevych incident by Mykola Melnychenko to the Prosecutor General S.M. Piskun, Aug. 27, 2002.)

There are two important things about this excerpt. The first is Kuchma's vicious and unbalanced response to Yelyashkevych's suggestion to delay a vote on parliament's procedural rules. The second is that Melnychenko and Yelyashkevych, in their sworn affidavits, didn't name "the Jew" who Kuchma assigned to organize the attack on Yelyashkevych? (His name will not be mentioned here either, except to say that he is a well known oligarch.)

Prior to the attack on February 9, the oligarch Hryhoriy Surkis approached Yelyashkevych in parliament and told him he would be hit over the head with a pipe if he didn't stop criticizing Kuchma. Later that evening, as Yelyashkevych was returning to his room at the Hotel Moskva, located in the center of the city, a few hundred meters from the president's office, a man approached him and hit him with a professional karate like-blow to the face, causing severe injury and pain.

Yelyashkevych survived the attack only to find that the police investigators ignored his charge that he was threatened by Surkis before it took place, and that the threat came from Kuchma. The police registered the attack as hooliganism.

Subsequently the police arrested a former convict Vitaliy Vorobei for the attack. On April 26, 2002, without even informing Yelyashkevych, a court sentenced Vorobei to prison. Yelyashkevych claimed that an innocent person had been imprisoned to cover up a crime by Kuchma, Derkach and the "Jew".

On July 7, 2000, Kuchma again threatened Yelyashkevych. This time he threatened to have him killed if he presented an impeachment resolution in parliament. In a Melnychenko recording, Kuchma told an unidentified MP that if Yelyashkevych presented an impeachment motion he will be hit so hard that he will "never get up again".

In March 2002, Yelyashkevych took refuge in the United States, and was granted political asylum in October 2002.

This incident was very strong evidence – much more powerful than on the STB affair – that the Melnychenko recordings were authentic. It showed a very close correlation between the recorded discussions and events taking place outside the president's office.

8

pravda.com.ua

On January 3, 2000, after a month in the States, Georgi Gongadze and Olena Prytula returned to Kyiv. Prytula went back to Interfax-Ukraine, but not to her old job as the reporter on the president. Georgi restarted his broadcasting on Radio Continent with an hourly "Free Wave" daily news and two weekly discussion programs. "Journalist in the bunker" appeared every Tuesday evening with a guest journalist to discuss news stories; and "Political Ukraine" appeared every Friday evening with a politician to discuss the news.

There was lots of news to report and discuss. In January the parliament had split with each side holding its sessions in separate buildings, but in February it came came back together. But by far the most important issue, at least it seemed so at the time, was the referendum to strengthen Kuchma's powers. On January 15, 2000, Kuchma issued the decree "On the Declaration of the All-Ukrainian Referendum on the People's Initiative" setting April 16, 2000 as the date for the vote on six questions.

On March 29, Ukraine's Constitutional Court ruled that two questions proposed by the president were unconstitutional. Voters could not be asked if they had confidence in parliament; nor could they be asked to hold a referendum on a new constitution, as this was a choice only for parliament, the court said.

The constitutional court did approve the following four questions:

1. Do you agree with the proposal that the president should have the right to disband parliament if it fails either to form a permanent majority within one month, or to approve within three months the national state budget drafted and submitted by the government?

2. Do you agree that there is a need to abolish deputies' immunity from prosecution?

3. Do you agree that the total number of parliamentary deputies should be cut from the current 450 to 300 and appropriate amendments made to the election laws?

4. Do you agree that there is a need to form a two-chamber parliament in Ukraine, one of which will represent and uphold the interests of individual oblasts?

The referendum had been called on the initiative of over 300 groups organized by the Democratic Party, a party sponsored by the MP Oleksandr Volkov. These groups claimed to have collected over 3.3 million signatures from all regions of Ukraine, thus meeting the constitutional requirement to hold a referendum – a minimum of three million signatures from not less than two-thirds of the oblasts.

Gongadze used his radio programs to attack the referendum as a device for the president to gain even more power over parliament and the state. The MP Serhiy Holovaty recalled that he was "one of the rare journalists to allow time on the air to people opposed to the referendum".

The body that unites European MPs – the Parliamentary Assembly of the Council of Europe (PACE) – expressed its concern about the coming referendum which might give the president control over parliament. PACE voted on April 4 to suspend Ukraine's membership should the results of the referendum be implemented.

The referendum on April 16, 2000 went well for Kuchma. Supposedly 29 million people came out to vote, a half-million more than in the second round of the 1999 presidential elections. Each of the four proposals – questions which were difficult to understand – received well over 80 percent approval: 86, 89, 90, and 82 percent in that order. Kuchma was beside himself at the results.

In contrast, his opponents denounced the whole referendum process, from the collection of signatures to the voting, as manipulation and falsification. Ironically, the referendum results were never implemented as the constitutional court ruled they needed a two-thirds approval by parliament, such a majority parliament for Kuchma didn't exist.

The virtual newspaper

On April 16, 2000, the day the referendum took place, Gongadze's internet newspaper, *Ukrayinska Pravda (Ukrainian truth)*, or pravda.com.ua, came on line. Gongadze had left Radio Continent partially because he found it difficult to raise money to pay for broadcasting his programs. His financial agreement with Radio Continent was that his "Free Wave" programs had to be self-financed.

Gongadze had canvassed a wide circle of possible benefactors to continue the Free Wave broadcasts and met with only temporary success. Following the presidential elections, he found raising money increasingly difficult. Some money did come from Kuchma's opponents, like the right-wing MP Anatoliy Matviyenko and the left-winger Oleksandr Moroz. To keep the broadcasts afloat, Gongadze took a loan of $1,000 from the Turbota Credit Union, headed by Halyna Zhulynsky, the wife of the Deputy Prime Minister of Ukraine, Mykola Zhulynsky. This must have been a disguised donation, as he had no means to pay back any loans. The promised money from Ukrainian-Americans never arrived.

Gongadze decided to leave Radio Continent when a benefactor agreed to sponsor an internet newspaper. "In March [2000] a sponsor appeared who provided us with an apartment near Tolstova Ploshcha [Tolstoy Square], computers, and two thousand dollars a month for expenses. I don't know either the name or the details of these people. But I guess that they were connected to Marchuk," said Lyudmyla Frolova, who Gongadze hired as finance manager for the internet newspaper – *Ukrayinska Pravda*. In the economic situation of Ukraine, $2,000 a month, plus an office and computers, was more than enough to have a financially viable internet publication. Journalists in Kyiv could easily be hired for about $250 a month.

Besides hiring a finance manager, Gongadze selected an editor – Olena Prytula. He also brought in his friend from the Abkhazian-Georgian war, Konstantyn Alaniya.

But who was this benefactor? "Petro Poroshenko came up with the money", asserted Radio Continent director Sholokh, who should know. Poroshenko was a well-off businessman (Vinnytsya Sweets Factory, Ukrainian Industrial-Investment Concern and Mriya Bank). At this time he was an MP in SDP(U) led by Medvedchuk and Surkis. In the summer of 2000, Poroshenko broke with SDP(U) to form his own parliamentary faction called Solidarity. It was a collection of businessmen and had nothing to do with the Polish organization of a similar name.

Attempts to verify whether Poroshenko was the sponsor came to nothing. The editor Olena Prytula said she didn't know who the benefactor was, and couldn't even remember the address of the office he had provided.

Gongadze's finance manager, Frolova, believed that the sponsor of pravda.com.ua was the former state security chief, Yevhen Marchuk. This was hard to believe. Kuchma, after his re-election appointed Marchuk to the powerful post of secretary of the National Security and Defense Council. Why would Marchuk feed money to a journalist who specialized in attacking the president he now was serving?

"It's very unlikely Marchuk gave any money" was Sholokh's view. He added, "after Marchuk changed sides and accepted the post of secretary of National Security and Defense Council, Gongadze fiercely attacked him for taking the post and felt personally betrayed by him".

The only thing that Gongadze supposedly told his staff about the sponsor was that his name was "Petrovych". Following Gongadze's disappearance, Marchuk stated that he knew "Petrovych", whom he described as a businessman. He said he couldn't divulge his name because the matter was under investigation.

Gongadze left the day to day management of pravda.com to the editor Olena Prytula. In the first weeks after the launch of his internet newspaper, he took an active part in a journalists' protest action against the attempt to shut down the Lviv newspaper *Express*. A court had ruled that *Express* had to pay Hr 150,000 (about $40,000) in damages – a huge amount for a Ukrainian paper – for a 12-line critical article about an obscure composer. The journalists perceived the ruling as an attempt by the authorities to use libel laws to punish newspapers they didn't like.

The Lviv action soon turned into a national campaign for press freedom in Ukraine. It was dubbed the Freedom Wave and rolled into
Kyiv on May 3, 2000. To mark the occasion, artists and journalists
built a symbolic Freedom Barricade in front of the UNIAN news
agency office building located in the heart of Kyiv on European
Square. On the same day, as a draft law on the mass media was presented in parliament, around 50 journalists, among them Gongadze,
marched along Kyiv's central street, Khreshchatyk, with their mouths
taped in protest against the gagging of the press. They held up placards
with slogans such as "Don't be quiet!" and "Long live freedom of
speech"!

For the last three weeks of May, 2000, Gongadze was absent again
from the office. He and Alaniya went to the town of Vinnytsya to do
promotional work for a mayoral candidate. They created TV, radio
and general publicity items for Volodymyr Vahovsky, a member of the
pro-presidential National Democratic Party (NDP) and Deputy
Governor of Vinnytsya Oblast, in his bid to become mayor. On June
11, 2000, Vahovsky won the election.

Pravda.com.ua was suddenly shut down in the middle of May, while
Gongadze was in Vinnytsya. Heavy-set men walked into the office,
took the computer equipment and told the staff to vacate the prem-
ises. What had caused the benefactor "Petrovych" to change his mind?

The sudden withdrawal of sponsorship followed a scurrilous article
on Marchuk a few days earlier. Pravda published on May 15, "The
Presidential Pretenders – Keep Cool" by Tatyana Korobova. It was
reprinted from the newspaper *Grani* published on that day. The article
lampooned Marchuk, accusing him of wanting to be president at any
price. It also attacked him for being unfaithful to his wife of 34 years
and exchanging her for a young opportunist who wanted to be the
country's first lady. The "opportunist" in question was Laryssa
Ivashyna, the editor of Marchuk's newspaper *Den (The Day)*.
Korobova had been *Den's* leading columnist until Marchuk's
"betrayal" – when he called for his supporters to vote for Kuchma in
the second round of the presidential elections.

Korobova's article also included disparaging remarks about how the head of the president's office, Volodymyr Lytvyn, was grooming himself to become Kuchma's successor. It was possible that following Marchuk's as well as Lytvyn's protests, "Petrovych" withdrew his sponsorship.

It was Prytula and not Gongadze who selected Korobova's article for publication. There was no indication that he was displeased with her work.

Following their eviction, *Pravda* ceased publication for about two weeks. Gongadze returned from Vinnytsya and got it running again in the first week of June 2000. It had another apartment for an office, fitted with computers and an internet connection. This new office at 83 Volodymyrska street in central Kyiv was not far from the previous one on Lev Tolstoy.

May 4, 2000 – Georgi Gongadze at the Freedom Wave rally in Kyiv
(Photo Dmytro Havrysh / UNIAN)

There was a new sponsor, according to the June 12, 2000 secret recording made by Melnychenko. Derkach told Kuchma that the sponsor was the MP Mykhaylo Brodsky – a charismatic and fiercely anti-Kuchma oligarch tied with the Surkis-Medvedchuk oligarch clan. If indeed Brodsky was Pravda's new sponsor, this was a double-edged sword for Gongadze. On the one hand, he had someone who would back him over critical articles about the president, but on the other hand, associating with Brodsky would ensure a place on the president's hit list.

9

The Podolsky kidnapping

This crime incident strongly correlates with a discussion recorded in the president's office. Even if Gongadze had not been murdered, this kidnapping, the crushing of the STB TV, and the hitting of the MP would have been enough to imprison Kuchma and his associates.

On June 9, 2000, Oles Podolsky was attacked after distributing copies of the political bulletin, "We", in front of the interior ministry in Kyiv. One of the key members of "We" was the MP Serhiy Holovaty. The bulletin contained an article – "From the 'referendum' to a society of free citizens" – charging Kuchma with fixing the April 19 referendum in order to acquire dictatorial powers over parliament. The retribution for distributing the publication was terrifying, as a statement issued by "We" showed:

> At 22:30 on Lviv Square three 'unidentified' men hit Podolsky from behind on the head, threw him on the floor of a car and drove 130 km from Kyiv. During the ride, they hit him with a rubber baton and fists, and took his money, passport and personal things. In the area of the village of Petrivka, Pryluky District, Chernihiv Oblast, near a tract of forest, Podolsky was pulled out of the car, violently beaten and forced to dig his own grave. At the end 'the unidentified' warned Podolsky that if he did not stop his political activities, and if he continued to write critical articles against the president and leaders of the interior ministry, and attempted again to distribute "We" publications near the ministry, they would kill him.

> On the morning of June 10, Podolsky, finding himself in the town of Pryluky, gave a statement to the local police. A medical examination confirmed that he had received bodily injuries. As of July [2000] the police had not begun a criminal investigation. In his police statement, Podolsky said that he suspected that the person who ordered the crime

was the Interior Minister Yuriy Kravchenko and that his subordinates carried it out.

During the night of June 10, 2000, a few minutes after the attack on Podolsky, 'persons unknown' set fire to the door of the apartment of "We" member Serhiy Kudryashov, which Podolsky had left five minutes before he was attacked. Only thanks to neighbors, who managed to put out the fire, was a tragedy averted.

(Source: "The July 2000 'We' statement", *Grani*, Dec. 4-10, 2000.)

A Melnychenko recording confirmed that the attacks on Podolsky and Kudryashov were sanctioned by the Interior Minister Yuri Kravchenko. On June 12, 2000, only three days after the kidnapping of Podolsky, the interior minister boasted to the president that he had a special unit to punish his critics:

[Kravchenko] Now about that gang, you remember, that distributed leaflets from Holovaty?

[Kuchma] Yes.

[Kravchenko] I mean the day before yesterday he was located as far as Sumy Oblast, the one who was distributing them. They beat the hell out of him [laughter]. And he's yelling, "It is Holovaty" [laughter]. When he gets home, and the dacha, the door burned out.

[Kuchma] Whose?

[Kravchenko] His [both laughing]. …

[Kuchma] Was he only the only one distributing or.

[Kravchenko] … he, the bastard, came out again with a new pile. That same day, 15 cops – and he was with three bodyguards. Then he came out alone and they shoved him into the car. And he started – "I won't do it again, it is Holovaty. Who is your boss? Who is your boss? I will give evidence". To be brief – I have such a unit, their methods; they have no morals, no nothing. So God forbid that something happens. Simply, I have a group and they have begun to silence things. Now with your permission I will call [the head of the tax office, Mykola] Azarov. I want them also to take part.

(Source: IPI, G1206p2.dmr, 1:35:30-1:39:10, June 12, 2000)

10

The order to kidnap Gongadze

On Monday, June 12, 2000, Leonid Derkach, the chief of Ukraine's state security service (Sluzhba Bespeky Ukrayiny or SBU) appeared in the president's office with a complaint. A "Georgadze" – Derkach mispronounced Gongadze's name – had offended the president with articles calling for him to be replaced with Derkach's son, Andriy.

The state security chief claimed that Gongadze had written the article "Our Ukrainian Putin", under the pseudonym of Sergei Karkov and had it published on June 7, 2000 in one of the leading Russian newspaper, *Nezavisimaya Gazeta*. A summary of the article appeared in pravda.com.ua under the title of "Andriy Derkach – 'the Ukrainian Putin'?"

> [Derkach] Read this, takes exactly three minutes. Read this here. This is about the one responsible for this article that the Ukrainian Putin will be Andriy Derkach [Derkach's son]. This is, all this is by this Georgadze.
>
> [Kuchma] This Georgadze, yes?
>
> [Derkach] Yes, yes.
>
> [Kuchma] You can take care of him?
>
> [Derkach] The time for him to mouth-off will come to an end. I'll crush this fucker. [MP Mykhaylo] Brodsky gave him money, fuck.
>
> [Kuchma] What?
>
> [Derkach] Brodsky gave him money.
>
> (Source: IPI, G1206p2.dmr, 2:23:45-2:30:15, June 12, 2000.)

Kuchma changed the subject from Brodsky to a controversy surrounding the oligarch Hryhoriy Surkis. Derkach said that Surkis was being attacked in the Russian media for publishing articles in his newspapers alleging that Russian oligarchs – Boris Berezovsky, Roman Abramovich, Oleg Deripaska and Misha Chornyi – had bought one of the Ukrainian state's most profitable plants, Mykolaiv Alumina, for next to nothing.

The bad press, Derkach told Kuchma, had angered the Russian oligarchs. Berezovsky's TV station ORT had retaliated with a documentary saying that Surkis had organized a convention of mobsters to support Kuchma in the 1999 presidential elections. The spy chief said he had a video copy of this program and that a person in Kharkiv making copies for distribution had been arrested. He told Kuchma he was awaiting the visit of his Russian Federation counterpart Nikolai Patrushev, director of the Federal Security Bureau (FSB) – the former KGB, who would bring the full and unedited copy of the program.

But Derkach had "Georgadze" on his mind and steered the conversation back to him:

> [Derkach] … I want to let you know why 'Georgadze' is an animal. I simply wanted you to know. The article he wrote is all nonsense; it isn't necessary to anyone. And, this is what he is doing, he wrote such terrible stuff that you shouldn't bother to read …
>
> [Kuchma] Is Hrisha [Hryhoriy Surkis] financing this?
>
> [Derkach] … Leonid Danylovych, you must understand, they do not give directly. They always play a game.
>
> [Kuchma] Gongadze [pronounces his name correctly], yes I will read him. But will you take care of him?
>
> [Derkach] I'll sort this out. I'll put 'Georgadze' in his place. And I'll do the same to those who finance him.
>
> (Source: Ibid.)

Once again an article in pravda.com would cause problems for Gongadze. In May 2000, it was Tatyana Korobova's article saying that Yevhen Marchuk wanted to be president, which caused the loss of a sponsor and the shutting down of its first office. This time it was an article saying that the son of the spy chief should become the next president. But this time it would not lead to the closure of an office but to Gongadze's murder.

The pravda.com article on Andriy Derkach was only a summary of a much longer piece by Karkov. It was simply a promotional piece for Derkach junior. The Karkov article probably wasn't written by Gongadze. The article that appeared in *Pravda* lampooned the Russian article. Neither article could have caused offense to his son. The Russian article flattered young Derkach as the ideal person to become Ukraine's next president. It said he had the experience to bridge the gap between the old communist elite and the new moneyed elite because he was a former KGB officer and an oligarch. It heaped praise on him – calling him an oligarch without scandal, a political centrist, a pragmatist, a progressive, constructive, well educated and forward-looking. Apparently, he not only understood Ukraine's place and role in the world, and had good working relations and contacts both with Russians and Americans. In short, he was the perfect man for Kuchma to hand over the reins of power, just like Putin had been the correct choice for Boris Yeltsin. All pravda.com did was to summarize this Russian article and make fun of it.

Why did Derkach senior bother the head of state with a seemingly trivial article? The security chief knew how sensitive, if not paranoid, Kuchma was about someone replacing him as president. He probably feared that if the president had heard about these articles from someone else, he might have concluded that he was plotting to replace him with his son. Kuchma might even blame him for the rumors circulating in Kyiv that he was terminally ill with cancer and that his days in office were numbered.

Derkach's mention of Brodsky's sponsoring "Georgadze" caused Kuchma to call for action to be taken against the journalist. At first Kuchma repeated "Georgadze" after Derkach, but then he corrected himself and said Gongadze. In contrast, Derkach continued to mispronounce the name.

The question has to be asked, why did the chief of the security service provoke the president against Gongadze? Derkach must have known how Kuchma would respond to him. Either Derkach was just a blundering fool or he was up to something no good.

On June 12, 2000, after Derkach left Kuchma's office, the TV Epicenter presenter, Vyacheslav Pikhovshek, a close professional colleague of Gongadze, came to see the president. They spoke on a number of topics, including the Russian ORT TV program alleging that Kuchma was re-elected with the help of criminal elements. This was the same program that Kuchma and Derkach had discussed earlier in the day. Pikhovshek wanted to know who Kuchma suspected was behind this documentary. The president replied that it was being investigated, and then suddenly without prompting Kuchma launched into a tirade against Gongadze:

[Kuchma] … Behind all the articles which – the article in *Nezavisimaya Gazeta* stands Gongadze. Yes?

[Pikhovshek] What, has he gone completely mad?

[Kuchma] Yes, but he is being financed – I don't want to talk about this now – we are checking this out.

[Pikhovshek] Yuliya [Tymoshenko, the deputy prime minister]?

[Kuchma] No! Our friends, you might say. Well, we have to look into this …

(Source: IPI, G1206p2.dmr, 3:24:31 – 3:27:23, June 12, 2000)

On June 22, Kuchma brought up Gongadze in a meeting with Derkach. After Derkach presented him with more spy reports on his opponents, the president asked him if there was any more information on Brodsky's funding of Gongadze.

[Kuchma] OK. You're also looking into that Georgian Gongadze bastard who is being financed by Brodsky, yes?

[Derkach] We have information. I … we're now watching him closely. Soon we'll completely [banging on the table].

[Kuchma] Should I ask [Surkis' political partner and deputy parliament speaker Viktor] Medvedchuk why does he finance the bastard Brodsky? I, I will do what you say.

[Derkach] Wait awhile. Let them come out more into the open.

(Source: IPI, G2206p1.dmr, 3:32:00 – 3:33:15, June 22, 2000)

On July 3, 2000, after more critical articles in pravda.com, President Kuchma made up his mind to have the "Georgian" [actually a citizen of Ukraine] punished by being dumped in Chechnya:

[Kuchma] Hello [Kuchma speaking through an intercom to the head of the president's office, Volodymyr Lytvyn].

[Lytvyn] Hello.

[Kuchma] Give me the same about *Ukrayinska Pravda* and … And we will decide what to do with him. He has gone too far.

[Lytvyn] I need to begin a [court] case

[Kuchma] What?

[Lytvyn] Start a case? [undecipherable]

[Kuchma] Good

[Lytvyn] The case – we will make in duplicates

[Kuchma] No, I don't need a case.

[Kuchma] *Ukrayinska Pravda* well is simply too much – the scum, fucker, Georgian, Georgian

[Lytvyn] Gongadze?

[Kuchma] Gongadze. Well, who is financing him?

[Lytvyn] Well, he actively works with [socialist MP Oleksandr Moroz], with *Grani* [a newspaper sponsored by Moroz's Socialist Party]. On Saturday I saw …. with [socialist MP Volodymyr] Makeyenko.

[Kuchma] Maybe take MP to court, let the lawyers take it to court. This goes to the prosecutor, right?

[Lytvyn] No, let loose [the interior minister] Kravchenko, in my opinion, decide how, and also [Horbanyeyev? or Komanyeyev?] and Kholondovych [Kholondovych, chief of the main directorate for logistic control – a cover for an interior ministry department specializing in special operations]

[Kuchma] Simply shit – is there any limit, after all, son-of-a-bitch – he needs to be deported – the scum – to Georgia and thrown there on his ass!

[Lytvyn] Take him to Georgia and drop him there.

[Kuchma] The Chechens should kidnap him and ask for a ransom!

(Source: IPI, GO3007p2.dmr, 0:07:38-0:10:45, July 3, 2000)

Thus Kuchma had made his mind up on how he was to punish Gongadze. At first he wanted him to be deported him Georgia, but then decided on the ultimate punishment, Chechnya, where the probability of him being killed was high on account of the bloody war being fought between the Russian armed forces and the Chechens.

Soon after Kuchma's conversation with Lytvyn, the Interior Minister Yuriy Kravchenko entered the president's office. He had come to present his bi-annual report on the state of crime in Ukraine.

He began with small talk about how he had gone to his hometown of Oleksandriya in Kirovohrad Oblast to lay flowers on his mother's grave and to attend the graduation ceremony of the local technical high-school he graduated from in 1970. Kuchma patiently listened out Kravchenko's monologue and then raised the subject of Gongadze:

[Kuchma] So that I don't forget, there's a Gongadze

[Kravchenko] I have heard such a name.

[Kuchma] Well, the scum is the limit

[Kravchenko] Gongadze, he has run through us before – [we have] run into him before

[Kuchma] What?

[Kravchenko] He has gone through us before. We will find him.

[Kuchma] Understand, he writes all the time in some *Ukrayinska Pravda*, he pushes it in the internet, understand. Find out who is financing him?

[Kravchenko] – … I have people …

[Kuchma] But the main thing, I say, ... , as Volodya [Lytvyn] says, the Chechens must kidnap and take him to Chechnya on his ass ... and demand a ransom.

[Kravchenko] – Yes, we will somewhere ... I tell you ... They are such people [laughing] terrific ... [undecipherable], never failing, and don't tell anyone.

[Kuchma] Just drive him to Georgia, that's all.

(Source: IPI, GO0307p2.dmr, starting at 0:49:00, July 3, 2000, and Moroz Tape 2)

Kuchma may have purposely said that Volodya [Lytvyn] suggested that Gongadze be kidnapped and deported. Kravchenko responded to Kuchma's kidnapping order by assuring him that he had the people "the never failing" unit (on a previous occasion he described as having "no morals") to silence his critics.

After receiving his order to commit a crime, Kravchenko launched into his review of the state of crime across Ukraine. After a long report, Kravchenko mentioned that the Kyiv crime boss Kisil (or Mykhaylo Kyselev) had immunity from prosecution because of his political and business status in society. Kisil was a local councilor in Kyiv and had business partnerships with many prominent people, including as it will be shown, even with Kravchenko (they co-sponsored an Olympic champion).

The mention of Kisil provoked the president to ask if the MP Mykhaylo Brodsky was a friend of Kisil's. "Yes" replied Kravchenko. The mention of Brodsky's name triggered Kuchma to return to the question of Gongadze:

[Kuchma] As for Gongadze, apart from working together with Moroz, he writes for Moroz, for his *Grani*, that since the summer has been financed by Brodsky.

[Kravchenko] Well, he is an animal if there ever was one. I wouldn't be surprised if he [Brodsky] didn't have ties with the socialists here. ... Well, we will discover everything about him. ...

[Kuchma] But Brodsky means [parliament deputy speaker Viktor] Medvedchuk and [parliament deputy and oligarch Hryhoriy] Surkis? Through Surkis.

[Kravchenko] That is, there is a tie between them.

[Kuchma] No, they are friends.

[Kravchenko] 100 percent friends!

[Kuchma] I remember that game around (the newspaper) *Kievskiye Vedomosti*. [Surkis bought the newspaper off Brodsky after the government made it impossible to publish it.]. Surkis, yes, I did good for him – fuck, Jew, fuck. And now I'm reading a few of his conversations.

(Source: IPI, GO0307p2.dmr, 1:04:30-1:05:53, July 3, 2000)

Very soon after the meeting with Kravchenko on July 3, Derkach entered Kuchma's office and immediately launched into an attack about an article in pravda.com.ua:

[Derkach] Did you read the [the article]? What a bitch, huh?

[Kuchma] [In] *Ukrayinska Pravda* ? Yes, I did, the whole thing. What are we doing about it?

[Derkach] We're all over him, monitoring all [Gongadze's] communications, checking out all [his] Kyiv contacts. ... He's already slunk over to Moroz.

[Kuchma] Aha! So he's cooperating with Moroz now, is he!

(Source: IPI, G0307p3.dmr, 0:23:44-0:24:12, July 3, 2000)

What was interesting about this conversation was that Kuchma didn't tell Derkach that he had ordered Kravchenko to kidnap Gongadze. The president was not sharing his kidnapping order with Derkach.

On July 3rd, Gongadze wasn't in Kyiv. He had left on June 28 for a ten-day holiday in Turkey with wife and the four-year-old twins. He returned on July 8. While he was away, men claiming to be police press officers had approached several of his friends and employees asking whether he had any connections to criminal gangs. Olena Prytula, the pravda.com.ua editor, said she had investigated these press officers and discovered that they were probably from Derkach's state security service. Kravchenko's people could have only began their operation after July 3, when Kuchma ordered his interior minister to organize Gongadze's kidnapping and deportation to Chechnya.

At the July 3rd meeting, Derkach had showed Kuchma critical articles by the *Grani* journalists Olha Ansimova, Tatyana Korobova and Iryna Pohoryelova as well as by Gongadze. The president reminded his spy chief to make sure that *Grani's* printers in Zhytomyr stopped publishing it.

Derkach also presented the president with reports and telephone intercepts on the MPs Surkis and Medvedchuk. Kuchma seemed to take a special interest in their extra-marital affairs (Radio Liberty transcript no. 9, April 3, 2000). After a discussion about a number of spying reports, including about a military intelligence officer who had spread rumors that Kuchma was terminally ill, the discussion returned to the question of Gongadze:

[Kuchma] Who gives the Georgian the money? This is the question.

[Derkach] I have already told you, this time Brodsky gave the money.

(Source: Ibid.)

A week later, on July 10, Kravchenko came to see the president and found him in a paranoid state about Gongadze:

[Kuchma] So that I don't forget – did you find this Georgian?

[Kravchenko] I'm, we're working on him. That is …

[Kuchma] I'm telling you, drive him out, throw out, give him to the Chechens, let (undecipherable) and then a ransom.

[Kravchenko] We, we think it over. We'll do it in such a way that …

[Kuchma] Take him there, undress him, the fucker, leave him without his trousers, and let him sit there.

[Unknown] The shit [I would …]

[Kuchma] He's simply a fucker.

[Kravchenko] I – today I was informed. We're learning the situations, where he goes, where he walks.

[Unknown] Well, yes, he is somewhere on holiday [Gongadze had returned from Turkey on July 8].

[Kravchenko] We are doing a bit, a little more has to be learned, we'll do it. The team – such eagles – that will do whatever you want. Hence, this is the situation.

(Source: IPI, Gong01.wav.p4, 04:55-5:46, and Moroz 4a)

Once again Kravchenko assured Kuchma he had the unit to carry out Kuchma's order. His "eagles" would do "whatever you want".

Kuchma's punishment for Gongadze was a death warrant, as the chances of him coming back alive from Chechnya were nil. In the summer of 2000, a cruel war was being fought in Chechnya between the Russian armed forces and the rebels. A captive could be killed by either side or by criminal gangs, like the one that in 1998 severed the heads of four employees from a British telephone company.

June 24, 2001 – President Leonid Kuchma and Pope Paul II during his visit to Kyiv (Photo by Valeriy Solovyov/UNIAN)

11

The eagles

How would the interior minister Kravchenko carry out the president's order to hand over Gongadze to Chechen gangsters? He decided to prepare the ground for such a scenario by linking Gongadze and Alaniya to a gangster style killing involving Chechens in Ukraine's port city of Odesa. It proved to be a clumsy attempt to associate them with Chechens.

On July 10, 2000 a person identifying himself as deputy police colonel Oleksiy Bahrov or Bagrov of the Odesa police, called at Radio Continent, according to its director Serhiy Sholokh. The officer said he was investigating the possibility that Georgi Gongadze and a person called Kostya had been involved in the shooting of Chechens at an Odesa cafe two weeks earlier. He claimed that two people with these names were at the cafe just before the shooting saying they were journalists from "Radio Continent in Kyiv". They had shown their identity cards in a red folder, said the deputy-colonel. He wanted to know from Sholokh if Georgi Gongadze and Kostya worked for him. Sholokh presumed that "Kostya" was Konstantyn Alaniya, who was better known by his Georgian diminutive Koba than the more common Kostya.

Sensing a provocation, Sholokh explained to the officer that the press cards shown in the cafe must have been faked. Radio Continent identification cards were not in the standard red folders carried by Ukraine's journalists, but were sealed in plastic and didn't even have Radio Continent on them, but Media-Center, its registered company name.

The visibly embarrassed officer then asked Sholokh to find Gongadze so he could interview him. An interview was arranged for later in the day, but the colonel did not show up – as his provocation was poorly prepared and became too transparent.

There was a shooting in Odesa at the cafe alluded to by the police officer. It occurred on Friday, June 23rd. That evening, a party of Chechens were barbecuing lamb at the Black Sea beach bar called "Zhemchuzhyna", located just below the site of the Odesa cable car. Out of the darkness a gunman fired a number of rounds with an automatic weapon. Five people were wounded and later one of them died – Archek Beslan, a businessman who was prominent in the Odesa Chechen community. The gunman got away but the weapon used in the shooting was found, as well as a car with two grenades inside.

A week after the killing at the cafe, Chechens held a rally in Odesa to protest against this shooting as well as other similar incidents. They claimed that in the previous seven years, 15 prominent Chechens had been murdered in Odesa and the police had failed to bring any of the killers to justice. They also complained about police harassment of refugees from the war in Chechnya.

The stalkers

Following the police officer's visit to Radio Continent, Gongadze became aware that unidentified men were following him. Olena Prytula had noticed from her 7th floor balcony on Lesya Ukrayinka Boulevard that three men were watching Georgi after he left her apartment. Georgi had told her that men were following him wherever he went.

On July 12, it looked to Gongadze as if he was about to be seized. Three cars appeared in front of the apartment building on Volodymyrska Street where the *Ukrayinska Pravda* office was located. They disappeared after Georgi had contacted the office of the MP Anatoliy Matviyenko, which sent an aide to take Gongadze away.

The MP and socialist leader Moroz recalled that Gongadze came to see him after this incident: "Since I left the post of parliament speaker, I have retained good contacts with high-ranking employees from the Interior Ministry, the SBU and other structures. From those sources, I learned that Gongadze had been shadowed. I told Gongadze that something serious was being prepared. However, he could not believe it. He told me later that he went towards a car which was following him and asked –'What are you looking for, why are you shadowing me?' I advised him to write to the Prosecutor General's Office. We hoped that the shadowing would stop, as the security services do not like publicity for their activities" (*Vecherniye Vesti*, Kyiv, Feb. 2, 2001).

On July 14, Gongadze wrote to the prosecutor general complaining about the harassment of himself and his colleagues. Even as he was photocopying the letter to the prosecutor, he noticed a cameraman filming him through the window of the shop. The instances of harassment which Gongadze listed in his letter were:

1) On July 10th, a police officer had attempted to frame him for a shooting in Odesa;

2) Undercover men had kept surveillance for several weeks near his apartment and office in a Zhiguli car with the license plate no. 07309 KV;

3) Uniformed police had stopped three employees of pravda.com to check their identities and ask questions;

4) A state security service or police agent pretending to be a Lviv city official had asked his mother and neighbors in Lviv for personal details on him.

(Source: See Gongadze's letter to Prosecutor General in Appendix 1)

Gongadze ended his letter with the following statement:

As all the evidence about my involvement in a crime is absolutely absurd, I reserve the right to see these actions as a planned provocation, with the aim at the very least of scaring me, and at the most – of stopping my activities. I therefore demand that you stop this persecution and defend me from moral terror, and also discover and punish the people responsible for organizing this.

(Source: Ibid.)

On July 28, 2000, the Kyiv city council sponsored newspaper, *Khreshchatyk*, published an article about Gongadze's complaint to the prosecutor general under the title – "Stitching up Georgi Gongadze with a crime".

According to Moroz, Gongadze went to the Kyiv city interior ministry headquarters to complain and to provide the license number of the car, a Zhiguli, that had followed him. Acting on his complaint, the deputy head of the Kyiv city police, Petro Opanasenko, launched an investigation (this was verified by a Melnychenko recording made on September 11, 2000 of a discussion between Kuchma and Kravchenko on Opanasenko's investigation).

Ukraine's Prosecutor General Mykhaylo Potebenko cynically forwarded Gongadze's complaint to the prosecutor's office in Lviv, where he and his mother were officially resident, though he was being shadowed in Kyiv. The Lviv prosecutor's office replied that the names of the places and the streets where he had followed were 'unknown in Lviv'.

After Gongadze submitted his letter and went to Kyiv's interior ministry, the overt surveillance stopped. For the remainder of July and until he disappeared on September 16, 2000, Gongadze didn't notice anyone following him, according to his friends.

Kravchenko's "eagles without morals" failed to link Gongadze to Chechens. Their noticeable surveillance suggested that they were trying to terrorize him and his staff to stop the critical articles appearing in pravda.com. It seemed that Kravchenko didn't quite have the nerve to do what Kuchma wanted, at least not in the first instance.

The "eagles" were, alleged the journalist Oleh Yeltsov, a four-man police under-cover team led by Volodymyr Yaroshenko, which included Serhiy Chemenko, Salashenko, and Nazarchuk. All apparently were recent graduates from the Interior Ministry Academy. Their handler was Mykhaylo Pustovit from the first division of the Criminal Investigation Department of Kyiv's police. Later it transpired that Chemenko's father was Police-General Oleksandr Chemenko, the police chief of the Kyiv Oblast.

After Gongadze's letter to the prosecutor-general and complaint to the Kyiv police, Kravchenko seemed at a loss on what to do about him. In the meantime, he came under heavy pressure from Kuchma on two occasions to carry out his orders have him taken to Chechnya.

On August 30, Kravchenko saw Kuchma, who immediately asked if Gongadze was taken care of. The interior minister reassured the president that he would be silenced within two days – "After tomorrow, … after tomorrow":

[Kravchenko] Leonid Danylovych, well, what is new, that is…

[Kuchma] What about Gongadze?

[Kravchenko] After tomorrow, … after tomorrow …

[Kuchma] OK.

(Source: IPI, Gong01.wav, part 7.)

To further please the president, Kravchenko also promised to sort out the president's other critics like the MP Serhiy Holovaty, the newspaper publisher Oleh Lyashko, and the crime investigator, Oleh Yeltsov:

[Kuchma] Are you looking after [the MP Serhiy] Holovaty?

[Kravchenko] Yes, I'm looking. Found two or three of his contacts. The same one I want to grab during … when they meet … the two boys. We have followed him. I just simply want to grab him in the act. That will be the simplest variant. ….

[Kuchma] Yes!

[Kravchenko] … Everything that has been set up is working. Well, I think that Gongadze will be sorted out within a few days. How it comes out we will see. I have looked at his materials from the Internet. This is him. There is a Yelisyeyev [Yeltsov] … *Svoboda* – [*Svoboda's* editor Oleh] Lyashko. And then …

[Kuchma] ?

[Kravchenko] For me Lyashko is next in line. We have studied Lyashko well

[Kuchma] Will everything be under control?

[Kravchenko] Everything will be.

(Source: Ibid.)

Though promising the president immediate action against Gongadze, his "eagles" took no action. Soon after his discussion with

Kuchma, Kravchenko left for Cholpon-Ata in Kirghizia to attend the September 6, 2000 CIS (Commonwealth of Independent States) conference of interior ministers. Meanwhile Kuchma attended the UN millennium conference of 150 heads of states in New York City September 7-9.

Kuchma, upon his return from the millennium conference, heard about an article on his close confidant, the MP Oleksandr Volkov, in pravda.com. This reminded him that Kravchenko had not disposed of Gongadze as he had promised on August 30.

The article in question was by Ivan Stepanov (a pseudonym of Oleh Yeltsov) and called "Everything about Oleksandr Volkov" and published on September 5, 2000, in pravda.com.ua. It was a shortened version of "A wolf in a sheep's clothing", which appeared on the Russian web site, flb.ru. (The word Volkov derives from wolf.)

What was new in the article was that it charged Volkov with having a criminal past. It claimed that by the time of the collapse of the USSR, he had become rich from criminal activities with, among others, his boyhood friend and Kyiv mafia boss, Kisil senior, Volodymyr Kyselev. The article brought together known information about Volkov's illegal enterprises and his rise to the heights of Ukraine's elite on the back of his relationship with President Kuchma.

Ukraine's journalists, fearing reprisals in Ukraine, had got into the habit of writing critical articles for the Russian media under pseudonyms, and then having them republished on Ukrainian web sites. Kuchma felt the need to tell Ukraine's journalists off for doing this. In a conversation on September 11, 2000 with an unidentified adviser, most likely Volodymyr Lytvyn, the head of the president's office , Kuchma expressed the worry that maybe the Russian president, Vladimir Putin, was behind these articles:

> [Kuchma] Now listen, I have on the nineteen [Sept. 19] a press conference. I am obligated to say that some of the mass information media exploit the Russian [media] as a dumping ground – the fuckers – so that they can reprint dirt in Ukraine. Yes?
>
> [Unknown - probably Lytvyn] …

Nov. 15, 2001 – Volodymyr Lytvyn, head of the president's office (UNIAN)

[Kuchma] What? But what should I say? Maybe. I think I could say that I am surprised that during President Yeltsin's time such things didn't occur, and that it has taken place since the election. Does this mean that someone in Russia is interested in worsening the situation in Ukraine?

[Unknown] Putin …

[Kuchma] Putin, so what?

[Unknown] …

[Kuchma] Hum?

[Unknown] Though in reality … in the last period.

[Kuchma] … Not to say this about Yeltsin, I think. Earlier this did not occur. It's happening recently.

[Unknown] Yes

[Kuchma] Even during the election campaign this didn't happen.
(Source: IPI, G1109p3.dmr, 0:28:45-31:45, Sept. 11, 2000)

The article on Volkov made Kuchma acutely aware that Kravchenko had failed to get rid of Gongadze as he had promised on August 30. In the same September 11, 2000 conversation with the unidentified adviser – probably Lytvyn, Kuchma said he would once again remind Kravchenko to get rid of Gongadze:

[Unknown probably Lytvyn] that about Volkov, about Volkov, did you read it?

[Kuchma] … They say an article has appeared. Volkov himself has read it.

[Unknown] …

[Kuchma] There is a name Derkach gave me. It is the Georgian's group.

[Unknown] Who, Gongadze?

[Kuchma] Gongadze!

[Unknown] What about Kravchenko? He was supposed to take care of him?

[Kuchma] What! What did he take care of … Not a dick connected. … I will tell him to quickly … there is a separate article on him [Gongadze's Sept. 9th article, "The Political Manager", called Kravchenko "the general in a 'SS' uniform" groomed to replace Kuchma as president]

(Source: Ibid.)

On the same day, the interior minister came to see Kuchma. The meeting had scarcely begun when the president told him off for not getting rid of Gongadze.

[Kravchenko] Good day!

[Kuchma] Welcome! Everything OK? So I don't forget; Gongadze is continuing to mouth-off.

[Kravchenko] I'm reporting to you. Here we made a bit of a mistake.

[Kuchma] He's got a team headed by that surname [the editor Olena Prytula?] – which that shit told to me.

[Kravchenko] Look, he wrote a complaint to the prosecutor general. Well, I think.

[Kuchma] Who?

[Kravchenko] Him.

[Kuchma] So!

[Kravchenko] I made a bit of a mistake here. Now I'm thinking why did I fail. Now I'll tell you. I came across the deputy head of Kiev city's police, [Petro] Opanasenko. Thinking what Opanasenko did to the undercover group. Opanasenko attempted through his people to get to the bottom of what kind of car it was and [Gongadze] wrote to [prosecutor-general] Potebenko, that is, a complaint.

[Kuchma] Who, Opanasenko?

[Kravchenko] No, no, Gongadze.

[Kuchma] Aha

[Kravchenko] Well, he gives a [license plate] number here that was cancelled a year ago. I 'm changing tactics here a little because – I want to get rid of that Opanasenko. Doubts rose in my mind when they reported to me all the way in Kirghizia that Opanasenko is interested in the numbers; so I said wait, so that I'll do it. I come back and they tell me there's been a complaint. I will take care of him, Leonid Danylovych. I will do it. I simply, so that it doesn't fall through any-where. So, he will be sorry. He writes here that this could be on my account, and so on. …

(Source: IPI, G1109p2.dmr, 0:12:47-0:14:41, Sept. 11, 2000)

Kravchenko clearly was worried that he might be connected to any kidnapping of Gongadze after the letter to the prosecutor general and Opanasenko's intervention. He changed the discussion to his report on the state of crime in the Mykolaiv and Vinnytsya Oblasts and in Kyiv, and how to curtail the political influence of the oligarchs Medvedchuk and Surkis in the capital and the Transcarpathian Oblast. The interior minister then digressed to a long personal account of his trip to Kirghizia on September 6th to attend a CIS conference of interior ministers. "We should pray to your politics and to you that Ukraine, thank God, has not had that experience [a civil war like those that took place in Russia and Central Asia]." He also expressed the fear that Islamic militancy would appear in Ukraine. "I don't know if SBU [the state security service] knows – our (Crimean) Tatars also go to Kirghizia to become extremists."

Kravchenko ended his presentation by promising once again that he would take care of Gongadze:

> [Kravchenko] I won't let Gongadze go. Simply it is also important for me … There are vehicles … contacts … I have thrown on suitable surveillance. I want to learn some contacts of his. That is.
>
> [Kuchma] Does Gongadze have a team … all these names, like [Viktor] Nikazakov [the lawyer who advised Gongadze by e-mail on July 12, 2000 how to deal with the police surveillance, see pravda.com, March 16, 2001] … Who writes this dirt?
>
> [Kravchenko] There are three of them [the three employees at the time were Olena Prytula, Konstantyn Alaniya and Serhiy Korniyenko.] I have them. I have them all. But I want to start with him. I want to see how the General [Prosecutor's Office] will react. There are no number plates, I don't know. Here he writes … that they might be ….
>
> [Kuchma] But what does the General [Prosecutor's Office] have to do with Gongadze?
>
> [Kravchenko] They received this complaint. It is official.
>
> [Kuchma] So what?
>
> [Kravchenko] The request is official. I will wait and see what happens.
>
> [Kuchma] So, what if every shithead writes to the Prosecutor General.
>
> [Kravchenko] Leonid Danylovych!
>
> [Kuchma] He can send it to a district prosecutor.
>
> [Kravchenko] But how can I know what the prosecution will say? This is the prosecutor … but who controls the money? (they both laugh).
>
> [Kuchma] I wish you all the luck.

[Kravchenko] Thanks

(Source: IPI, G1109p2.dmr, 0:36:41- 0:37:50, Sept. 11, 2000 and IPI, Gong06.wav, and Moroz 4c)

Kravchenko left Kuchma's office with the promise that this time he would carry out the president's order to have Gongadze kidnapped and dropped in Chechnya. The interior minister, who had been pre-varicating for weeks, would finally carry out Kuchma's order to get rid of Gongadze, but it will not take place as planned.

Derkach not told about the kidnapping?

Also on September 11, the spy chief Derkach came to see the president. As always, Derkach came with lots of telephone transcripts and surveillance reports. Significantly, their discussion only touched once on Gongadze. As in previous conversations, the president was keeping from the spy chief the order he gave to Kravchenko to kidnap Gongadze.

Derkach's meeting focused almost exclusively on transcripts of spy reports on various people, including the prime minister, Viktor Yushchenko, the deputy prime minister, Yuliya Tymoshenko, the deputy speaker, Viktor Medvedchuk, the MP Taras Chornovil, Radio Liberty's director Roman Kupchinsky and others.

They also discussed a report that some aged members of the Union of Soviet Officers were planning to stage a coup. Kuchma ordered their arrest and Derkach promised to have them arrested on September 21.

Ihor Bakay the former head of Naftohaz Ukrayina was supplying information to the Kyiv journalist Oleh Yeltsov for his articles, Derkach told Kuchma. It wasn't clear from the recordings whether Bakay had supplied the information for Yeltsov's article on Volkov.

The only reference to Gongadze in this meeting was when Kuchma suddenly read out loud from a report: "*Ukrayinska Pravda* newspaper has been bought by Medvedchuk!" Was it true that Viktor Medvedchuk – oligarch, leader of the Social-Democrat United Party and first deputy speaker – had purchased Gongadze's internet publica-

Sept. 14, 2000 – President Leonid Kuchma
with President Jacques Chirac in Paris (UNIAN)

tion? Or was Derkach making it up – saying what the president
wanted to hear? Derkach had previously reported that the owner was
the oligarch Mykhaylo Brodsky.

What was clear from this meeting was that the president did not tell
Derkach that he had ordered the interior minister to kidnap Gongadze
and dump him in Chechnya. Was it possible that the spy chief did not
know about the president's secret, considering his extensive surveillance network, maybe even recording in the president's office?

After giving his final order on Gongadze, Kuchma left on more state
visits. On September 14, he was in Paris with President Jacques
Chirac. The following day he attended a EU summit. On the
September 16 he returned to Kyiv. While he was away, did
Kravchenko carry out his order to get rid of Gongadze?

12

Gongadze's last day

Undated – Georgi Gongadze (Irex-ProMedia)

On the fatal Saturday, September 16, there was nothing to forewarn Gongadze that this would be his last day. In the morning, his wife Myroslava, the twins and nanny said good-bye to him. They went to Pushcha-Ozerna – a resort outside Kyiv, where Myroslava was to lecture on public relations at a business seminar.

At 11 am, Gongadze and the *Ukrayinska Pravda* editor Olena Prytula met the presenter of Epicenter, Vyacheslav Pikhovshek, at his office in the town center. After a half-hour discussion, Georgi and Olena made their way to the office to publish the day's issue. They were joined by Koba Alaniya and another employee, Serhiy Korniyenko.

At 1 pm Myroslava called Georgi to say that she would not be staying the night at Pushcha-Ozerna but would return that evening. Around 4 pm, she telephoned to ask her husband to be at the apartment at 11 pm because she had forgotten her keys.

That day Gongadze helped prepare three articles for pravda.com.ua. At 3:39 pm, *Pravda's* first unsigned article was placed on the web site. It was about how the Russian press viewed the recent attempt by parliament to impeach President Kuchma. It was the type of article President Kuchma disliked as it spread "dirt" about him from Russia to Ukraine. It reported the Russian newspaper *Vremya Novosti* as making the startling assertion that the oligarchs Hryhoriy Surkis and Victor Medvedchuk and his National Security Council secretary Yevhen Marchuk were secretly sponsoring the "anti-mafia" MP group to have the president impeached. It also detailed the impeachment charges laid out against the president by the group. (On September 14, the Yermak-Omelchenko bill fell far short of the minimum 226 votes needed to begin the process of impeaching the president.)

At 5:22, Gongadze placed on line an article on the head of the presidential administration, Volodymyr Lytvyn, and the leader of the Social Democratic Party United (SDP(U)), Victor Medvedchuk. They had appeared together the night before on the national TV channel Inter – owned by SDP(U) supporters like Medvedchuk and Surkis, and the Russian oligarch Boris Berezovsky.

This article said that Lytvyn and Medvedchuk's reason for appearing together was to quash the rumors that there was a rift between the president and the SDP(U). In the program they had denied the claim made by the journalist Serhiy Rakhmanin (*Zerkalo Nedeli*, Sept. 9, 2000), that there was a confrontation between the two sides. Gongadze commented that their appearance only underlined the divi-

Undated – Georgi Gongadze with Vadim Hetman,
former head of National Bank of Ukraine,
assassinated in Kyiv on April 22, 1998

sion because Medvedchuk kept emphasizing that politics should represent the will of the voters, while Lytvyn stressed the will of the president.

Gongadze was pleased that the two had appeared on TV because on September 12 he too had written about the rift for his web site. He wrote that Lytvyn – the "gray cardinal" – was attempting to separate Medvedchuk from Surkis to improve his bid for the president's office in the next election. In the article Gongadze suggested that Lytvyn could achieve his goal if he made his main competitor – the interior minister Yuriy Kravchenko – the prime minister, as this post was normally a graveyard for would be presidential hopefuls.

At 6:23 pm, Gongadze placed his last article, "Oligarchs 'beat' Yushchenko, at least that is how the our readers see it".

These were to be Gongadze's last articles. Within four hours he was to disappear and the search, the discovery and accusations against the president would change the history of Ukraine for ever.

Last hours

At about 7:30 pm, Georgi and Olena left the pravda.com office at 86 Volodymyrska Street for the Taj Indian restaurant on 25 Litnya Street, a 20 minute walk or 5-10 minute car ride. After supper. they left for the 15 minute walk to Prytula's apartment on Lesya Ukrayinka Boulevard, arriving between 9 and 9:15 pm. The concierge saw them enter the building.

At about 9:20 pm, the TV producer Lavrenti Malazoni telephoned the apartment to invite Georgi to a birthday party for their mutual friend, the broadcasting journalist, Lyudmyla Dobrovolska. At 9:47 pm Georgi telephoned Koba, Konstantyn Alaniya, to discuss setting up the sports Internet site that was being negotiated with Surkis through Malazoni.

Gongadze had been negotiating with the oligarch Hryhoriy Surkis through Malazoni to sponsor his planned sports web site. Malazoni was a well-established TV producer at Kyiv's TET channel, which specialized in entertainment. According to Malazoni, Gongadze never reached an agreement with Surkis.

Georgi telephoned Koba again at 10:04 pm and said that if Myroslava telephoned the office (where Koba lived), Koba was to tell her he was on his way home. Before going home, Georgi went out to buy "Kit-e-Kat" for Olena's cat (named Martyn after the President's press secretary Martynenko). He went shopping for the cat food with a single $100 note. After about 20 minutes, he returned with the cat food and immediately left the apartment. It was just before 10:30 pm. On his way out, he took two bags of rubbish to drop in the waste bins located in the building's courtyard.

The concierge sitting near the building's door said she didn't see him go out. She told investigators that between 10:00 – 10:30 pm she was not near the building. Since she had no access to a toilet in the building, she had to go to a wooded area not far from the apartment to relieve herself.

It normally took Gongadze about three minutes to get down to the ground floor and out of the building from where he would wave to

Prytula standing on her balcony. She stepped out on the balcony, waited but didn't see him and assumed she had missed him.

He probably never got out on to the street. Two people heard a male scream from the direction of the building's courtyard between 10:00-11:00 pm on that fatal night.

> One of the witnesses was walking her dog when she heard what sounded like a male scream. The woman told us she immediately returned home and looked out of her apartment window into the courtyard but did not see anything suspicious. She said she did not think about it again until the police starting asking neighbors questions about three days later. The other witness was an elderly man who said he was in his kitchen, which faced Prytula's courtyard, with the window open when he heard a male voice scream 'Save me!' The man said he heard only one scream. He also said he did not hear any cars leave the area after the scream, nor did he see anything suspicious. Both witnesses said they did not call the police.
>
> (Source: Kroll)

It seems that when Gongadze walked into the courtyard to place the rubbish bags into the bins, he was attacked and quickly silenced and not seen again alive.

The only material evidence as to who might have kidnapped Gongadze comes from the Melnychenko recordings. President Kuchma had on four occasions ordered the interior minister Kravchenko to kidnap Gongadze. His "eagles" certainly could seize Gongadze, knock him out and remove him quickly from a semi-lit courtyard, as they did when they snatched Oleksiy Podolsky from a square in the capital's center. However, Podolsky came out alive from the kidnapping despite being hit over the head and beaten violently.

What happened to Gongadze?

The available forensic evidence suggested that Gongadze was killed soon after his kidnapping, and the head severed much later. The first autopsy, which was carried out by a coroner in Tarashcha (November 4-6, 2000), found that bits of his last meal – potatoes, watermelon seed, and cabbage – were still undigested in the stomach. This was strong evidence that he died within six hours after digesting this food. The coroner's autopsy suggested that his death occurred 50 days earlier – about September 16 or very soon after he disappeared. Hence there is evidence that Gongadze was killed during or soon after his kidnapping.

The autopsy also concluded that Gongadze died from some kind of head injury, as there were no wounds on the headless corpse, except for two cuts just below where the head was severed. There was also evidence that the head was severed well after death, as there was very little blood around the neck. Finally, as the head was missing, it could not be determined what kind of head injury he died from.

The reason why Gongadze's body was beheaded – an act normally not associated with Ukraine – was not clear as a DNA test could quickly establish if the body was his. It might have been due to the sadism of the killers. As the first autopsy will show in chapter 16, the killers not only cut off the head of a dead body, but stripped the skin from the legs and buttocks.

The state of the corpse on discovery suggested it had been kept in low temperatures and out of the ground before it was found. When discovered it was in perfect condition without any major decomposition and without maggots. For the body not to be invested suggested that it was kept refrigerated before being buried soon before it was found on November 2.

The evidence suggests that the kidnapping ordered by Kuchma didn't go according to plan. Gongadze was snatched, but not taken to Chechnya. Instead he was murdered almost immediately after the kidnapping, and his body kept refrigerated and then almost two months later dumped, as we shall see, in the parliamentary constituency of Oleksandr Moroz – Tarashcha. Once again, like in the grenade-throwing incident, a major provocation was committed against Moroz. And again, like in the STB, Yelyashkevych and Podolsky crime incidents, the Gongadze kidnapping showed a strong correlation between a discussion in the president's office and a crime.

13

Suspects lead the search

An hour after Gongadze's disappearance on September 16, 2000 at 11:30 pm, his wife, Myroslava, and the twins had arrived at their apartment expecting him to be there. They returned along with Genyk Hlibovytsky, a journalist with Epicenter, and godfather to the twins. Like Myroslava, Genyk had also lectured at the business conference. As Georgi was not at the apartment as he had promised with the keys, Myroslava used Genyk's mobile to call Koba, who was surprised that he had not yet arrived. He came right over to open the apartment with a set of spare keys.

From Myroslava's apartment, Koba telephoned Olena Prytula, who, immediately fearing the worst, began telephoning his friends and acquaintances asking for his whereabouts. Failing in her inquiries, Olena called the local police stations, ambulance services, hospitals and city morgues, only to also get negative replies.

At 3 am on Sunday, in desperation Olena called her friend, the president's press secretary, Martynenko, to ask him if he could use his influence to get the police to search for Georgi. Normally, the police don't search for missing persons until three days after their disappearance. He told her that it was still too early for the police to get involved, but to call him again if Georgi wasn't found by the morning. At 10 am, Prytula telephoned Martynenko again asking for his help. He contacted a deputy interior minister asking that a search should begin sooner than the required time of three days because Gongadze was "an opposition journalist".

At 11 am on Sunday, September 17, Prytula announced on pravda.com.ua that Gongadze was missing. By the evening, journalists and friends had gathered around Prytula to launch a massive publicity campaign with the slogan "Find the journalist".

On Sunday, Prytula also got in contact with Yevhen Lauder, one of Georgi's acquaintances. He was a former doctor, now a businessman, who worked as a mercenary in Africa. He arrived on Sunday afternoon at Prytula's apartment with a posse of armed friends from the "Golden Eagles" (or Berkut) – a paramilitary police unit. They searched the building and the surrounding area and failed to find any trace of Georgi, except for one of the rubbish bags that he had taken from Prytula's apartment on his way out, which was found in the rubbish container in the courtyard. The police reacted to Lauder's vigilante initiative by taking him into custody for ten days and treating him as a suspect.

That Sunday evening, after Lauder and his "Golden Eagles' " had left, the police arrived to search Prytula's apartment, the building and the surrounding area. They also found no trace of Gongadze. Surprisingly, they didn't question the residents until two days later, on September 19. As required by the law on missing persons, on that day the police visited the residents of the building and heard from two of them that they heard a male scream between 10:00-11:00 pm on Saturday, September 16.

September 18

On Monday, President Kuchma informed the public through his press secretary Oleksandr Martynenko that he had heard of Gongadze's disappearance the day before, and that it had "upset him very much". The president said he had ordered the interior minister Kravchenko to take personal control of the search for Gongadze.

The authorities will bill the search for Gongadze as the biggest ever for a missing person in the history of Ukraine. The irony will be that the two chief suspects responsible for his disappearance, President Kuchma and Interior Minister Kravchenko, will take charge of the search. Their main goal will be to make sure that no evidence links them to the crime.

The first people accused of being responsible for Gongadze's disappearance were Kravchenko, Volkov and Kisil. On September 18, the

Georgian ambassador, Malkhaz Amiranovych Chachava, issued a statement that an anonymous telephone caller had phoned the embassy's private number with the message that this trio were holding Gongadze in Kyiv's Moscow district near Feofaniya (a hospital surrounded by a large forest on the edge of the city). The caller spoke in Russian with a heavy Caucasian accent, said the Ambassador

What was interesting about the telephone call to the Georgian embassy was the linkage of Kravchenko and Volkov to Kisil. As has been mentioned, Ivan Stepanov (a pseudonym of Oleh Yeltsov) had linked Volkov to Kisil in an article published in pravda.com.ua on September 5. At the end of this chapter, a TV documentary broadcasted on September 15 and 16 would link Kravchenko and Kisil. The question has to be asked was whether all three links, which appeared in a short space of time, were part of a plot or just coincidental.

Kuchma, as the Melnychenko recordings showed, played the innocent from the first day of Gongadze's disappearance. He got angry with the Georgian ambassador for blaming his closest political allies, Volkov and Kravchenko, for the disappearance of Gongadze and linking them with the crime boss Kisil. In discussion with Lytvyn, he demanded that the ambassador either immediately issue a denial or be replaced.

> [Lytvyn] The mass media is reporting an official statement by the Georgian Embassy of an anonymous telephone call received by the embassy that Gongadze should be looked for in the Moscow district [of Kyiv] and that Volkov, Kravchenko and Kisil are involved in this affair. They are distributing this. I called them and said how can an embassy interfere in such a delicate question and stoke the affair. This is unforgivable.
>
> [Kuchma] The Ambassador should be summoned.
>
> [Lytvyn] I agree – and should be given some kind of note or warning.
>
> [Kuchma] A telephone call must be made to get rid of him – to hell with such an ambassador.
>
> [Kuchma speaks on the intercom]
>
> [Koval?] –I'm listening

[Kuchma] Koval, it looks like you may be sacked. Have you dealt with the Georgian Embassy?

[Koval?] We'll do it now.

[Kuchma] And summon him, bastard, let him issue a denial, or I shall call [Georgian President Edward] Shevardnadze to recall him on his ass.

[Koval?] All right, all right, I am calling him right now.

(Source: IPI, Gong01p8.wav, 0:10:22-0:11:58, September 19, 2000.)

The Georgian ambassador, who knew Gongadze, had over-stepped his position when he issued the contents of the telephone call, so it wasn't surprising that he was replaced. On November 28, 2000, a new Georgian ambassador presented his credentials to President Kuchma.

By Monday, two days after Gongadze disappeared, Kuchma must have had discussions with Kravchenko on what happened during the kidnapping of Gongadze. However, Melnychenko had not made available a single conversation between the president and the interior minister after Gongadze's disappearance. He has not explained the reason for this, causing suspicion that either he is hiding something or waiting for the right moment to release them.

September 19

Tuesday, September 19, was a busy day for Kuchma, judging from his public appearances and the Melnychenko recordings. He began with a morning press conference for the regional press. Prytula took advantage of it to hand him a petition signed by 87 journalists demanding a full investigation into the disappearance of Gongadze. Kuchma responded that he had instructed all law enforcement agencies to provide him with a list of all criminal attacks on journalists. His concern for journalists was featured on all TV news programs that day. While in public he was defending press freedoms and journalists, in private, he showed his traditional hatred of journalists.

On Tuesday, Prytula, Myroslava Gongadze and a number of prominent journalists held a press conference to publicize Gongadze's disap-

Sept. 19, 2000 – The mother and wife of Georgi Gongadze, Lesya and
Myroslava (Photo by Vasyl Artyushenko / Irex-ProMedia)

pearance. Kuchma and the head of the president's office, Volodymyr
Lytvyn, saw a TV news report on it. Their conversation illustrated not
only Kuchma's duplicity but Lytvyn's as well. Neither mention
Kravchenko taking care of Gongadze as they did in earlier discussions.
Instead, Lytvyn played up to Kuchma by saying that the disappearance
was probably a ploy by Gongadze and his wife to gain publicity:

> [Lytvyn] It has become known that Gongadze's wife works as the press
> secretary for the Reform and Order Party.
>
> [Kuchma] Yes.
>
> [Lytvyn] Today I had a discussion with [the president's press secretary]
> Martynenko. It seems to me that journalists themselves are worried
> that this might be a provocation – that he [Gongadze] will turn up

later and say, Leonid Danylovych, I did this to secure my future. If he was dead, then his wife would be distraught and not give interviews right and left. He must have given her permission to do this.

(Source: IPI, Gong01.wav, 15:30-17:06, Sept. 19, 2000)

Why would Lytvyn tell Kuchma that Gongadze's disappearance might have been self-initiated with the connivance of his wife to gain publicity? Surely he must have suspected that Kravchenko had carried out Kuchma's orders. After all, on July 3 he had proposed to Kuchma that Kravchenko should take care of Gongadze. Maybe Lytvyn was attempting to discover what had happened to Gongadze, as Kuchma had not told him how the orders were carried out.

Kuchma and Lytvyn continued to watch the news broadcast:

[Kuchma] Look [a TV news item of the press conference by Myroslava Gongadze and Olena Prytula] who is sitting alongside this woman …

[Lytvyn] It is that Olena Prytula.

[Kuchma] Olena!

[Lytvyn] Yuliya Mostova [from *Zerkalo Nedeli*], Natasha (Nataliya) Kondratyuk from ORT [Russian TV station].

[Kuchma] This 1+1 [TV channel] fucker shows me with [Gongadze]

[Lytvyn] ?

[Kuchma] What?

[Lytvyn] Yes.

[Kuchma] They say that something about Volkov has appeared.

[Lytvyn] It is said that someone telephoned the Georgian Embassy and said that three people are connected to his disappearance – Volkov, Kisil and Kravchenko.

(Source: Ibid.)

In response to Gongadze's' disappearance, Lytvyn devised a propaganda campaign to devalue its importance. On September 22, he suggested to Kuchma how to make Gongadze's disappearance seem insignificant. He said that 7-Days, Ukraine's flag ship weekly TV news program, should present Gongadze's disappearance in the context of statistics showing that many people disappear annually in Ukraine and nobody takes any notice. It should also say that a journalist's job was not as dangerous as a miner's, for example.

Also on September 19th, President Kuchma had a long meeting with his prime minister, Viktor Yushchenko, to discuss the state of the economy. Following his presentation, Yushchenko brought up allegations published in the Russian and Ukrainian media that his American wife, Kateryna Chumachenko, was a CIA spy. He placed a newspaper article in front of the president and asked him if he had read it. Nervous laughter could be heard from Kuchma and the others present. Instead of answering the question, Kuchma went into a diatribe on how he too was a victim of the media but didn't respond to their attacks.

[Kuchma] ... Don't ask what they write about me. ... [I tell them], don't write about me, I don't read it. Through the Internet they spread it to Russia. ... Such vile things are written about me. ... (MP Hryhoriy) Omelchenko wrote such awful things on the impeachment of the president ...

[Unknown] [Omelchenko] he is a sick person

[Kuchma] Through Russia they throw this. Who stands behind this? ... They grind this about the president across Russia and spread it not only through the Internet, but also in [the Russian newspapers] *Nezavisimaya Gazeta, Izvestiya*

[Yushchenko] Why do they bother you? I don't know ....

[Kuchma] The newspapers are full of this..

[Unknown] Brodsky Mykhaylo

[Kuchma] Brodsky – he is the main person behind this ... Brodsky

[Yushchenko] ... you should issue a statement ...

[Kuchma] ... I don't take revenge; I keep silent and don't say anything to anyone and just accept it as I accept the parliamentary opposition (Source: IPI, ZL1909.)

Kuchma's statement – "I don't take revenge" against the media – showed what a brilliant actor he was. He had just taken his revenge against two journalists: Gongadze and, as it will be shown in the next chapter, Lyashko and Yeltsov. The prime minister, too, played his part well in the charade, when he said he couldn't understand why journalists bothered criticizing Kuchma. The truth of the matter was that there is evidence that Kuchma instigated the rumor that Yushchenko's wife a CIA agent. In an affidavit, Mykola Melnychenko, stated that Kuchma had ordered Derkach to give untrue information on Yushchenko's wife being a American agent to *Kievskie vedomosti*. This was repeated, as we shall see by the then correspondent of London's *Financial Times*.

Yushchenko also showed his concern about what had happened to Gongadze. His press secretary announced on September 20 that he had asked the police and security service to inform him daily on their investigation into Gongadze's disappearance. The prime minister had also assigned his deputy Mykola Zhulynsky (whose wife had approved a Turbota Credit Union loan to Gongadze) to investigate the state of the mass media so that it could function normally. After his headline-catching statement, the prime minister's actions never produced any results.

One of the president's opponents attracted the media spotlight on September 19. The MP Hryhoriy Omelchenko of the "anti-mafia" faction told the UNIAN news agency that Gongadze's disappearance might have been linked to documents he had given him. Some time later, he revealed that they dealt with Kuchma's money-laundering, which he had prepared for his failed impeachment resolution.

Parliament's Gongadze committee

On September 21, parliament, under pressure from journalists, voted by 232 votes – well over the 226 votes required – to set up a 15-strong committee to look into Gongadze's disappearance. Oleksandr Lavrynovych, from the wing of the national democratic Rukh Party led by Henadiy Udovenko, was voted head of the committee. Journalists accredited to parliament had lobbied for his appointment because they felt he would be the most suitable and impartial candi-

Oct. 10, 2000 – Olena Prytula and Oleksandr Lavrynovych
the head of parliament's Gongadze committee
(Photo by Vasyl Artyushenko / IREX-Promedia)

date for the job.

The committee's work was hampered from the start because parliament did not have the right to set up committees with powers to subpoena witnesses and use law enforcement agencies to investigate. This was because the president had not signed into law the relevant legislation. The Gongadze committee soon discovered that the president and his subordinates refused to cooperate with it, claiming it was illegal. Without investigating powers, the committee was doomed to failure.

In addition, the head of the committee, Oleksandr Lavrynovych, proved to be less than enthusiastic about investigating the president and the security services. He did his best to sabotage any parliamentary resolution from the committee to impeach the president. Also, only eight of the committee's 15 members attended meetings regularly, and if one was absent the meeting would be cancelled because of the lack of a quorum. The seven regular absentees came from the pro-presidential oligarch factions. Nevertheless, individual members of the committee made headway in the investigation, especially the former prosecutor general of Ukraine Viktor Shyshkin, the former justice minister Serhiy Holovaty, and the former state security service agent

Oleksandr Zhyr. In the autumn of 2001, Zhyr took over the committee from Lavrynovych, who resigned to take up a job in Kuchma's government.

Kuchma accuses Derkach of a plot

In the week after Gongadze's disappearance, Kuchma suspected that Derkach was behind plot to discredit Kravchenko. In an undated discussion, but which took place after Gongadze's disappearance – most likely on Monday, September 18, Kuchma angrily accused Derkach of being a plotter.

The conversation was about a TV documentary program called Pohlyad (Viewpoint), presented by Yuriy Nesterenko. An unscheduled showing was broadcast on Friday, September 15, 2000, and it was repeated in its normal slot on the first state channel (UT1) the next day – the day Gongadze was kidnapped.

The program was produced by a company owned by the son of the spy chief, Andriy Derkach. It was shown on the morning slot on UT1 allocated to ERA, a company owned by young Derkach and Vadim Rabinovich.

Viewpoint presented a flattering portrait of the alleged Kyiv crime boss, Mykhaylo Kyselev, who is better known by his nickname Kisil. The program makers pretended to secretly follow him to discover what he actually does. It showed him as a local councillor in Kyiv's Moscow district, and as a respectable and charitable citizen with many prominent friends, including the former American basketball player, Oleksandr Volkov – no relation to the MP Oleksandr Volkov. What caused offense to Kuchma was showing Kisil's relationship with Kravchenko in the form of their shared sponsorship of the Olympic weightlifter, Denis Gotfrid.

The weightlifter's had won an Olympic bronze medal in Atlanta, and was expected to get a gold in Sydney. But in the Olympic competition held on September 25, 2000, Gotfrid failed to win any medals.

What also caused Kuchma's to suspect the state security chief Derkach was the timing of the documentary. It was broadcasted on the same weekend as Gongadze's kidnapping. Maybe an additional paranoia crossed Kuchma's mind, as it was the security chief who motivated him to punish Gongadze over an article suggesting that young Derkach wanted to take Kuchma's place as president. Whatever the reason for the making of this documentary and showing it on the same weekend that Gongadze was snatched, it caused Kuchma to burst out with profanities at Derkach senior:

[Kuchma] Listen! Did you see on Saturday on ERA, not on ERA but by [Yuriy] Nesterenko the journalist, in the past, (pause) he had this program.

[Derkach] Well I …

[Kuchma] (...)

[Derkach]: Pohlyad [Viewpoint]?

[Kuchma] Yes, "Pohlyad"? So did you see it or not?

[Derkach] About Kisil?

[Kuchma] Yes!

[Derkach] I did.

[Kuchma] What are you doing giving such material – you bastard – giving it to Derkach junior?

[Derkach] I did not.

[Kuchma interrupting] There was this guy – that fucker – and Kravchenko.

[Derkach] On Kravchenko I did not give them anything, nothing.

[Kuchma shouting] You did not?

[Derkach] (...) Didn't give it.

[Kuchma] This is Andriy's program. Do you want Kravchenko to tell you to fuck off once again, and not speak to you or what?

[Derkach] Leonid Danylovych! What about me and about Kravchenko? I have good relations with Kravchenko!

[Kuchma] Good relations, until your son showed, showed materials like this. What is he doing? Are you fucking crazy or what!

[Derkach] I told them to cut it out.

[Kuchma shouting] So why did they show it on the fucking Ukrainian television? On the state channel! Fuck your mother! I have told him off him before, this Derkach junior, because of such activity! And you have done it again! [The UT1 director Vadim] Dolhanov wasn't there to be in charge, but his deputy. They fucking grabbed me by the throat! You had no right to show that! I came back [Kuchma was out of the country on state visits] and people asked me what was going on? If they show Kisil on a state channel together with Kravchenko, they can just show anyone! It's just awful. What will the nation say that the president is keeping a minister who is hugging criminals? Well, where does [Yuriy] Nesterenko get cassettes about Kisil?

(Source: IPI, Gong07p1.wav.)

Derkach denied he gave his son the materials to make the documentary and said he would find out where they came from and report back. Kuchma, still shouting, accused Derkach of a serious failure.

This TV documentary was fodder for the making of a great conspiracy theory. Was there a connection between the TV documentary and the anonymous telephone call to the Georgian Embassy? Why was the name Oleksandr Volkov included in the documentary? Was the documentary and the embassy telephone call connected to the article about Volkov's past criminal relationship with Kisil senior? Why wasn't Leonid Derkach's name mentioned in the telephone call, given that the secret police and not the police be expected to have kidnapped Gongadze?

Then there were another set of unanswered questions. Why would the son of the state security service chief promote an alleged criminal godfather? Maybe the film makers made an innocent TV documentary whose importance was overblown by Kuchma following Gongadze's murder?

14

Kuchma's duplicity

Kuchma's duplicity was best expressed by his statement at the September 19, 2000 press conference. He said he would ask the security services to provide him with a list of all the journalists who had been attacked. This must have been a bad joke, as he had orchestrated many of these attacks. Just in one of the conversations recorded by Melnychenko in September, Kuchma had ordered Kravchenko to punish, besides Gongadze, the crime journalist Oleh Yeltsov, and the editor of *Svoboda*, Oleh Lyashko.

Also as he was speaking at the press conference, and for the next three weeks, Kravchenko's agents prevented Lyashko's newspaper from being printed. They ordered the state printing house in Zhytomyr not to publish *Svoboda's* September 19 issue. Lyashko then signed an agreement with *Desnyanskaya Pravda* in Chernihiv to print his September 26 issue, which was also stopped. In vain, Lyashko approached Tyrazhya printers in Kyiv to publish the October 3 issue. Once again the officials successfully intervened. After three weeks of not appearing, *Svoboda* came out on October 10, but in a self-published format. Lyashko had gotten hold of an A3 size printing machine and produced a newspaper by printing both sides of four A3 sheets and then stapling them together. This was how the newspaper appeared for the next year.

Kuchma had had enough of Lyashko and got a court in Kyiv on July 7, 2001 to ban him from publishing a newspaper for two years. Maybe as a joke, the court handed out the punishment on Ukraine's official day to honor journalists. The ban came after four years of almost continuous harassment of Lyashko by the courts, the tax police, the security services. When he ignored the court order, he was jailed in 2002 and then released, only to be repeatedly harassed again. His punishments from the authorities are far from over.

Threatening Yeltsov

As promised by Kravchenko, an attempt was made to punish Yeltsov. The threats against him began on September 15, the day before Gongadze's disappearance. At 8 pm that day, Yeltsov answered his telephone to hear:

> "Oleh Dmitrievich [Yeltsov], shut your mouth and listen up. Your articles on the internet [his site – Criminal Ukraine – cripo.com.ua] are disturbing influential people, who are fed up with your secret service pretensions. Your time is running out ..."

Yeltsov immediately reported this threat to the local police. The next morning at 10 am, Yeltsov had another menacing phone call. "OK, smart aleck, so you called the police..." and then the caller hung up.

Yeltsov had planned to leave Kyiv that day with his daughter to visit his mother in southern Russia. But before he left for the station, he took the precaution of telephoning the UNIAN news agency with the details of the threatening telephone calls, and giving them the license plate number of a green Zhiguli parked in front of his apartment building with men watching him.

At 4 pm on September 16, Yeltsov and his daughter boarded a train bound for Armavir in southern Russia. On the way to the Russian border, police and security agents twice boarded the train to harass him and check his identity and belongings.

It was probably Yeltsov's luck that he had decided to leave Ukraine with his daughter to see his mother. If he had stayed in Kyiv that weekend something awful might have happened to him.

On Tuesday or Wednesday, September 19 or 20, (again Melnychenko failed to provide the date of the recordings) Derkach came to Kuchma to report on how Kravchenko's men had punished Yeltsov. Also present in the president's office was the MP Oleksandr Volkov, who had a score to settle with Yeltsov for the September 4th article, "A wolf in a sheep's clothing", which appeared on the Russian web site, flb.ru. What was interesting was that Derkach's security service had monitored Kravchenko's men intimidating Yeltsov.

[Kuchma] What's up with Yelkovich?

[Derkach] Yeltsov?

[Volkov] Yeltsov.

[Derkach] I already told him . Today I have given him a report.

[Kuchma] I see that in your report.

[Derkach] Well, they [Kravchenko's men] scared him. They telephoned, that is, they said his head would be cut off. And he fled to Armavir to his mother and is there now.

[Kuchma] So he's on the run, you could say.

[Derkach] Now, from Armavir he telephoned a number of times to his wife and told her: 'I don't know when I'll be back, maybe in a week or so. I'm not sure because of the Gongadze scare.' We gave FSB [Russian Federal Security Bureau – the former KGB] a note on him directly to Krasnodar, and about [flb.ru editor Sergei] Pluzhnikov.

[Volkov] There is a note to [FSB chief Nikolai] Patrushev to kick his ass.

[Derkach] They interviewed Pluzhnikov [who published Yeltsov's article on Volkov] and told him that if he continues to involve himself in scandals, they will [interrupted]

[Kuchma] Were there any mistakes?

[Volkov] Did you say this ...

[Derkach] I didn't simply say this, I sent a telegram. As I said before, send a telegram so that there is an official document. And that little pike, he fled there. He received a telephone call, "if you don't keep out of everything we will cut your head off". After this, in five minutes, flat, as he told his wife on the telephone, he fled to the station, bought a ticket and left. Well, we will sort him out. At the moment we are investigating and stopping his activity. I, I think he will not stop – I heard somewhere he is not short of money.

[Kuchma] Listen, is the whole internet disconnected?

[Derkach] The whole internet is disconnected.

[Volkov] Did you hear that Gongadze was in the pay of [the deputy prime minister] Yuliya Tymoshenko?

(Source: IPI, Gong07p2.wav, 0:08:07-0:10:20)

Derkach's report lacked accuracy. Yeltsov had not run away. The train ticket was purchased earlier to travel with his daughter to his mother's place in South Russia. Yeltsov said he was threatened with the words "your time is running out" (Peter Byrne, "Kyiv journalist caught up in case of vanished reporter", *Kyiv Post*, Sept. 29, 2000), while Derkach told the president it was "your head will be cut off". As to the choice of words used by Derkach, all one can say is that it is interesting considering that Gongadze was beheaded.

This conversation exposed Kuchma's ignorance about the internet, when he asked – "Listen, is the whole internet disconnected?", Derkach, always ready to please the boss, replied that it was. The "whole internet" could be disconnected only if Ukraine cut off all telephone lines and satellite links to the outside world.

Gongadze involved in "dangerous business"

As mentioned earlier, listening to Derkach's report on Yeltsov was the the MP and oligarch Volkov. Kuchma might have invited him so he could hear how Yeltsov was punished for the article he had written about him.

Volkov had taken his revenge on Gongadze for that article which was republished in pravda.com on September 5, under the name of "Everything about Oleksandr Volkov". On September 14, guards at the door to his and Bakay's press conference at the parliament building had barred Gongadze from entering.

Gongadze replied on the same day with a scathing article about Volkov in his internet publication. He said that until that day, only the Progressive Socialists – Nataliya Vitrenko and Volodymyr Marchenko – had excluded journalists from their press conferences. He suggested that Volkov read a few more articles about himself on his web site, including an article on how a list of signatures to hold the April 2000 referendum had been faked in the city of Lviv ("Oleksandr Volkov

Jan. 18, 2000 – Oleksandr Volkov at impromptu press conference in the
parliament building (Photo by Vasyl Artyushenko / Irex-ProMedia)

Angry at *Ukrayinska Pravda*", pravda.com.ua, Sept. 14, 2000).

Yeltsov's Volkov article was reminded Kuchma that Gongadze had
not been dealt with by Kravchenko as he had promised earlier. On
September 11, on his return from the UN millennium heads of states
meeting in New York and just before he went to meet with President
Chirac in Paris, Kuchma had a discussion about the Volkov article
with someone in his office, probably his chief of staff, Volodymyr
Lytvyn. They discussed Kravchenko's failure to take care of Gongadze
and the possibility that maybe the Russian president, Vladimir Putin,
might be behind articles intended to embarrass him. Kuchma saw
Kravchenko that day, who promised to carry out his orders on
Gongadze.

Before the arrival of Derkach to give his report on Yeltsov, Kuchma
and Volkov had an important and revealing discussion on Gongadze
and the need to control the news on his disappearance. It began with
Kuchma and Volkov discussing the previous day's news on 1+1 TV,
which had reported the telephone call to the Georgian embassy implicating Volkov, Kisil and Kravchenko in the kidnapping of Gongadze.

Volkov began by asking Kuchma what happened to Gongadze, to which he didn't receive an direct answer. The discussion continued with Volkov complaining that he had been unfairly blamed for Gongadze's disappearance. Kuchma countered that the attacks actually were being aimed at him. The conversation also revealed Volkov's power over Ukraine's second TV channel, 1+1, where he had appointed a "commissar-chief-editor" to manage all future news on Gongadze. Both discussants peppered their references to the general director of 1+1 TV channel, Oleksandr Rodnyansky, with anti-Jewish remarks.

[Volkov] Leonid Danilovich [Kuchma], I don't understand what is happening

[Kuchma] What?

[Volkov] With this Gongadze ... You understand I'm not that kind of man. That bastard I have never seen before in my life.

[Kuchma] They're after me, motherfuckers! Did you read this? It's not against you! Everything is directed against me.

[Volkov] You look a bit further down.

[Kuchma] Did you watch TV last night?

[Volkov] Yes.

[Kuchma] You should have made [the news?] on Gongadze yourself. Did you see?

[Volkov] Yes, I saw. Today, I asked to be brought the newspapers.

[Kuchma] Who told you?

[Volkov] I saw it with my own eyes.

[Kuchma] I wasn't going to tell anyone. They can't be so stupid as not to understand? ...

[Volkov] Yes. This morning I got the [video] cassette and called [Oleksandr] Rodnyansky [general director of 1+1 TV channel] and ...

[Kuchma] Jew, fucker, scum, fucker.

[Volkov] I got them together and said: "Boys, I'm fed up with this. I'm paying you $90,000 a month. I pay your salary. I pay for your news.

114

I'm the one that puts out the news." [Volkov goes off the subject on how he paid for a film crew to go to Kazakhstan and Kirghizia] I have appointed [Voinolovich ?] as chief editor – commissar-chief-editor. He will do everything there.

[Kuchma] I told him [1+1 TV general producer, Oleksandr Rodnyansky] today: "You – I told him – you have simply fucked things up, fucker. You're absolute scum. You've no conscience, fucker, none whatsoever." If I let you read a few of his conversations about you, you'd have long ago [not understood]

[Volkov] What shall we do?

[Kuchma] What are we going to do? What are you going to do?

[Volkov] Take no notice?

[Kuchma] Of course.

[Kuchma] We asked that one.

[Volkov] The Russians.

[Kuchma] Yes, Russians to help us. Yes. I just now was told by –

[Volkov] Derkach

[Kuchma] Yes, Derkach. Let him work on this.

[Just then Derkach walks into Kuchma's office]

(Source: "Kuchma after Gongadze's disappearance", www.5element.net)

After Derkach presented his report on Yeltsov, the three of them bantered about Gongadze. Volkov started with: "Did you hear that Gongadze was in the pay of Yuliya Tymoshenko"? If this was true, Tymoshenko would be the third person to have sponsored Gongadze in the space of four months, after Brodsky and Medvedchuk reportedly gave him money.

Volkov attempted to impress Kuchma and Derkach with details about Gongadze's personal life and made sexual innuendos about him and Olena Prytula. He seemed to have been better informed about Prytula than Kuchma and Derkach. As Volkov didn't know Gongadze of Prytula personally, it would be interesting to know who was his informant. For example, he knew, as opposed to Kuchma, when she had left her job as Interfax-Ukraine correspondent to the president's office.

Derkach contributed by alleging that the US embassy press attache (Peter Sawchyn) had been attempting to "stir things up" over Gongadze among journalists. Kuchma agreed that the Americans were "trying to use" Gongadze's disappearance to "pressure us".

What Volkov and Derkach wanted to know from Kuchma was what had happened to Gongadze. All what Kuchma would say that Gongadze had got himself involved in "dangerous business, not journalism, but dangerous business". He said this in such a way that it suggested that something very serious had happened to him.

The conversation ended with Kuchma being pleased to hear from Derkach that repressive actions were also being taken against the newspaper *Svoboda*. "OK. Good" replied Kuchma.

The significance of this conversation was that Kuchma didn't take Volkov and Derkach into his confidence and tell them exactly what happened to Gongadze. But if Derkach's security service could monitor Kravchenko's "eagles" hounding Yeltsov and Lyashko, what was stopping them from doing the same on Gongadze?

15
Kravchenko fakes a search

The interior minister, Yuriy Kravchenko – the person who had repeatedly promised to get rid of Gongadze from Ukrainetook charge of the search for Gongadze. On September 20, 2000, he opened the first police press conference on his disappearance. Flanked by his deputies, Kravchenko said that an unprecedented effort was being made to find Gongadze. To give the search the highest status, said Kravchenko, it was being carried out under the criminal law for first-degree murder – statute 94.

The police chief for Kyiv, and future Interior Minister, Yuriy Smirnov, introduced the possibility that Gongadze was alive, and this became the police refrain for the rest of the investigation until five months later a DNA test concluded that a discovered headless corpse belonged to Gongadze. Smirnov began by saying that the police didn't know if Gongadze was alive or dead, and this was why they were focusing on possible causes for his disappearance that included marital, professional, or other conflicts. Kravchenko added that his disappearance could have been due to business or financial problems. The police chiefs avoided mentioning Gongadze's complaint about being threatened made in his July 14 letter to the prosecutor general.

The focus on Gongadze's personal problems was a convenient diversion for Kravchenko. It was no secret that the married Gongadze was having an affair with Olena Prytula. She had told an interviewer within two days of Gongadze's disappearance that he was with her "seven days a week" (part.org.ua, Sept. 18, 2000). Meanwhile, his wife Myroslava said he made a point of seeing his children every day. For at least a year before his disappearance, friends and acquaintances had known that the affair had created tension between Gongadze and his wife.

Despite the president's announcement that the interior minister would take responsibility for the search, Kravchenko announced at the first police press conference, that one of his deputies, Mykola Dzhyha, who headed the interior ministry's department fighting organized crime, would take charge of the Gongadze case. Soon Dzhyha would be appointed as Kravchenko's first deputy, replacing Leonid Borodych, who died in a plane crash on September 16 – the day Gongadze disappeared – while performing aerobatic maneuvers at the Kyiv air show.

The disinformation supremo

Dzhyha proved to be vigorous and aggressive in denying any police or state involvement in the disappearance of Gongadze, while emphasizing his financial problems and sightings of him across Ukraine and Russia. A close friend of Kravchenko's, he became the official spokesman on the search from the end of September until early December when the prosecutor-general's office took over the Gongadze case. His information became a by-word for disinformation.

Even before he was officially appointed to head the inquiry into Gongadze's disappearance, he set out the official criterion on which the case would rest until February 2001. On Sept. 19, less than 48 hours after Gongadze's disappearance – even before the police inquiry officially began and before his appointment to head the inquiry was announced, Dzhyha told Inter TV that he rejected a political motivation for the disappearance and that Gongadze might have simply "run away".

At his first press conference on September 21, Dzhyha was asked about Gongadze's July 14 letter complaining about being followed and harassed. Dzhyha categorically dismissed any involvement of state agencies in Gongadze's disappearance. "I do not believe there were political motives, because he was not a political or a civic figure, who could have influenced politics … I do not believe that special services [undercover units] had anything to do with the disappearance of Georgi Gongadze, because he was not a danger for the state." Dzhyha added that if the police had followed him, Gongadze would never have noticed. "As to Gongadze, no approaches of a secret character were ever carried out [against him]. He did not pose any criminal interest for us." A state security service or SBU official at the press conference said the same on behalf of his organization.

As to the Zhiguli that followed Gongadze, the police gave contradictory answers. Kyiv's deputy police chief, Yuriy Cherkasov, said that the car's license plate number had not been identified, as it probably was "created by someone". Later the police changed the story. They said the license plate was stolen several weeks before Gongadze first believed he was being followed.

At the October 3 press conference, Dzhyha was asked about the police officer who accused Georgi and Koba of participating in the shooting in Odesa. Dzhyha denied that any police officer had come to Radio Continent to make this accusation.

However, at this time the police had failed even to interview the two witnesses who met this police officer at Radio Continent – the director Serhiy Sholokh and his employee. Sholokh recalled that he was never interviewed by the interior ministry. It wasn't until the prosecutor general's office took over the case in December 2000, was he interviewed, and it was unsatisfactory:

> On December 7 or 8, Hryhoriy Harbuz (the investigator into the disappearance of Gongadze at the prosecutor general's) called me to his office to identify the police colonel from photographs. I was sure I chose the right photo, but Harbuz told me I selected the wrong one! On Harbuz's desk I saw a letter from the Odesa police that was difficult to read upside down. It said that they have an officer called police deputy-colonel Oleksiy Volodymyrych Bagrov, Bahrov or Badrov. ... I then was surprised to hear from [Prosecutor General] Potebenko's report on Gongadze in Parliament [Jan. 10, 2001] that I was the only person who saw this colonel and that I couldn't identify him. I had told the Prosecutor's Office that besides me, Radio Continent's engineer Oleksandr Novikov also saw him.
>
> Source: Interview with Serhiy Sholokh by the author, Feb. 20, 2001)

Also at the October 3 press conference, Dzhyha emphasized that Gongadze's debts were an important factor in his disappearance. He claimed Gongadze owned a total of $5,000, which included the money owed to a Turkish car rental firm for an accident he and his family were involved in on holiday.

Witnesses see Gongadze

Dzhyha specialized in making up eyewitness sightings of Gongadze. At his second press conference on September 25, Dzhyha made the dramatic announcement that Gongadze was seen on September 17 – the day after he disappeared – in Kyiv's Eric's Bar, a popular watering hole for expatriates, "new Ukrainians" and foreign journalists. He promised to provide further details in the future.

After keeping the hacks in suspense for a week, on October 3, Dzhyha, provided the details. A taxi driver parked near Eric's and Eric's employees saw Gongadze the day after he disappeared. The taxi driver said he saw a person resembling Gongadze along with someone much shorter. At Eric's, an employee saw Gongadze talking to someone between 8 and 9 that Sunday evening.

This report of Gongadze being seen such a popular bar immediately aroused suspicion, as many journalists were in the bar that night. As a matter of fact, at the time of the alleged sighting – 8 to 9 pm – two of Gongadze's professional acquaintances – Vyacheslav Pikhovshek, the Epicenter presenter, and Katya Gorchinskaya, a reporter from Kyiv Post – were at Eric's and didn't see him there.

It transpired that the police had shown Gongadze's photograph to two Eric employees, a barman and a bouncer on September 24. They responded that a week earlier that they might have seen the person in the photograph. One of the employees told an inquiring journalist that he had never met Gongadze. The police conveniently ignored the fact that two people who knew Gongadze and were aware of his disappearance didn't see him at Eric's that night.

The news of the sighting of Gongadze at Eric's saturated the mass media and was soon followed by more sightings, which when investigated also proved to be flawed. Kravchenko's purpose was clear – to show that Gongadze was on the run from marital and financial problems and in this way to divert any attention that its special units might have been behind his disappearance.

The security service chief, Leonid Derkach, backed the mis-information the internal ministry was churning out. He announced on October 17, 2000, that Gongadze was alive because he was seen at Eric's on September 17!

Soon Dzhyha came up with another sighting. This time Gongadze had been seen in Lviv, 525 km from Kyiv, the day after the sighting at Eric's. A teacher of foreign languages named Roik said she had seen Gongadze on Monday, September 18, on Kosziuszko Street at about 3:30 pm. Soon Dzhyha reported that Gongadze might have been in Moscow on September 21, as a person with that name purchased a train ticket on that day to go from Moscow to Smolensk. Later it was discovered that the Gongadze who purchased the ticket had a different first name.

After the report of the Moscow sighting, Dzhyha told the press that Gongadze probably was not in Kyiv or even in Ukraine, because the unprecedented police search – the biggest ever – would have found him by now. "Such complete search efforts for an individual in Ukraine were not utilized at the time of the search for Mykhaylo Boychyshyn," said Dzhyha. (Mykhaylo Boychyshyn, the very able organizer for Rukh, the political party led by Vyacheslav Chornovil, disappeared in 1994 in Kyiv. His body was never found.)

A public relations exercise

On October 6, Kravchenko reported to parliament how the police were pursuing the search for Gongadze with unprecedented resources, and that it had become an international search. They were following three lines of inquiry – personal problems, professional activities or a victim of crime.

As for the people who stalked Gongadze and their car, Kravchenko told parliament that some of them had been identified and the owner of the car with the self-made license plate number had been partially identified. (In the September 11, 2000 Melnychenko recording, Kravchenko told Kuchma that his team of "eagles" had used an expired license plate number.)

The interior minister told parliament that to create a climate of confidence in the police investigation, an unprecedented goodwill gesture had been made. Gongadze's wife Myroslava and the editor of pravda.com Olena Prytula would be made part of the police investigation team. Kravchenko highlighted this as a privilege never before extended to civilians.

This was just a public relations exercise. For example, the police never told Myroslava or Olena that two witnesses heard a male scream around the time that Gongadze left Olena's apartment. As it will be shown later, Kravchenko failed to inform either of them that a local police force had reported that they suspected a headless corpse to be Gongadze's.

In response to questions by the MPs about the telephone call to the Georgian Embassy linking him, Volkov and Kisil to a kidnapping of Gongadze, Kravchenko replied that the Georgian ambassador had apologized for distributing this information.

Kravchenko assured parliament that the police were using all their resources to Gongadze, though it seemed he had run away from his marital and financial problems. He then proceeded to ask whether it was fair to use such huge resources at the expense of thousands of similar cases. In the previous year, he said, the police had searched for 35,000 missing people.

Also Kuchma was supposedly following the investigation closely. On September 27, the president's press secretary Martynenko said that the President had taken personal control of the search for Gongadze and had asked the internal ministry and security service to report to him daily on the affair. But when a corpse fitting Gongadze's description was found on November 3, both fell uncharacteristically silent.

16

The headless corpse

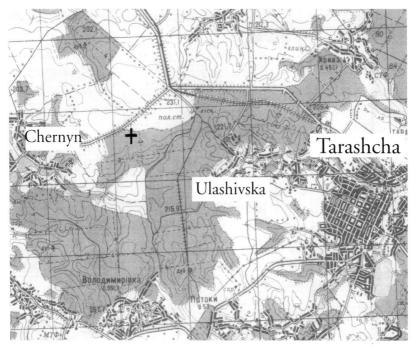

Map 1 - The cross marks the spot where the headless body was discovered
on Nov. 2, 2000 near Tarashcha, Kyiv Oblast

In the late afternoon of Thursday, November 2, 2000, two farmers
came across a hand sticking out of the ground. The discovery of the
hand and the body attached to it would not be welcomed by the interior minister and the president. Their subordinates would attempt to
get rid of the body, while the president would later claim that no one
was interested in it.

The farmers on their horse-drawn cart were coming from the Chernyn flour mill to their village, Ulashivka, located on the edge of Tarashcha – a district town 140 km south of Kyiv. As the cart meandered along a dirt track through a thickly wooded beech forest, 58-year-old Volodymyr Shushko and his 21-year-old son Serhiy saw a BMW with dark tinted windows parked off the track. They took no special interest in the car as people often parked in the woods for a picnic or an amorous activity. About 100 meters further, at a fork in the road, Serhiy, who was now walking alongside the cart, noticed a pile of fresh earth under a fallen tree. (Map 1 shows where the corpse was found.) If it had been a normal winter Serhiy would never have seen the fresh earth, as snow would have covered it, his father said. But the weather in early November 2000 was unusually warm and dry.

Serhiy looked under the tree and to his horror saw a hand sticking out. His father came over, picked up a stick, and poked to see what, if anything, was attached to the hand. The poking revealed a rib cage with skin hanging off it. Shocked, they jumped back on the cart and drove to the police station in Tarashcha. Later they surmised that an animal, perhaps a fox, attracted by the smell, might have dug the hole and pulled at the hand.

The policemen on duty in Tarashcha, upon hearing their story, roared with laughter, but the local police chief took them at their word. He told them that as it was getting dark, he would call upon them in the morning to show him where the burial site was. But as soon as father and son returned to their village, a policeman arrived in a car and had the father direct him to the spot.

The exhumation

Next morning, Friday, November 3, a party of officials along with a group of locals with shovels and a lorry came to exhume the body. The officials included the Tarashcha district prosecutor, investigator, coroner and police chief. As stipulated by law in criminal cases, the local prosecutor was in charge of the exhumation.

The exhumation revealed a body stuffed in a hole originally created by a fallen tree but subsequently enlarged, and covered with less than a meter of earth. While the earth above the corpse was loose, maybe due to the digging by an animal and certainly by the farmers, the earth around it was settled. This suggested that it had been buried in that spot for more than a day, but its "freshness" suggested it wasn't in the ground for more than a few days.

The discovery of jewelry

No jewelry was seen on the corpse at the place of discovery. Still covered with earth, the corpse was taken to the Tarashcha morgue, which was located in the grounds of the district hospital. After cleaning the dirt off the body, the coroner Ihor Vorotyntsev found a white metal ring and bracelet on the right hand. "I personally removed them. The bracelet was from a heavy white metal, quite heavy. It had a flowery, interesting fastener with a clasp. The ring was also made from a white metal with an unusual shape." He handed the two items over to the police late that Friday afternoon.

On the next day, Saturday, November 4, the investigator from the prosecutor's office and the police found a necklace with a white metal hanging ornament in the shape of a half moon in the burial site.

A search around the burial site within a radius of 150 meters revealed an enormous amount of rubbish, as the area was used for picnics. It included all sorts of bottles, plastic cups and even condoms. None of the rubbish was connected to the corpse at the time, though later, the general prosecutor in his report to parliament on the Gongadze case, said that a shovel without a handle, a champagne bottle and a broken wine glass had been found at the burial site. He was suggesting that the killers had had a celebration at the site.

Autopsy – headless body Gongadze's

The Tarashcha coroner, Ihor Vorotyntsev, began the autopsy on the body on Friday, the day of discovery, and had it ready on Monday, November 6. By law, the local prosecutor should have witnessed the autopsy, but he was not present. After the coroner hosed and cleaned the earth off, he found a relatively fresh, headless, naked, partially skinned body, decaying on the extremities of the fingers and toes. While decay on the extremities was normal for a fresh corpse, the skinning of the legs and forearms shocked him. "The skinning revealed the leg muscles like in an anatomical illustration, and suggested that sadists had been at work," he surmised.

His post-mortem examination concluded that the body belonged to a young man, aged about 30, well built and muscular, 162 cm in height, without the head. The watery fetid discharge fluid in the chest indicated the body had been dead for about 50 days. The food found in the stomach resembled potatoes, water-melon seeds, and long white cabbage threads. The undigested food suggested that death occurred within hours after the victim had eaten it.

The decapitation occurred well after death because there was very little blood around the neck. Also, the lack of injuries on the body and especially on the wrists and ankles – suggesting he was not restrained – backed up the conclusion that he died from a head wound and the severing took place after death. As the wounds below the neck were deep, it was assumed the killers used an axe to sever the head.

As the head was missing the cause of the death could not be determined. It could have been anything from a bullet wound to a head injury.

Vorotyntsev's autopsy approximated the profile of Georgi Gongadze who had disappeared 50 days earlier, was about 193 cm in height and 31 years of age. Already on Monday, November 6th, the Tarashcha police, basing themselves on the missing person's report and comparing it to the coroner's report, had concluded that the body fitted the description of the missing journalist Gongadze.

Their information would have first gone to the Kyiv Oblast interior ministry headed by Police General Oleksandr Chemenko, and then to the national office headed by Yuriy Kravchenko, and end up on the president's desk. Chemenko's son, Serhiy, was said to be a member of the "eagles" under-cover group organized by the interior minister who stalked, and may have kidnapped and murdered Gongadze.

126

The cover-up of the corpse begins

The president and the interior minister, who must have known about the discovery by November 7, kept it secret from the public and the relatives. The interior ministry did not inform Myroslava Gongadze and Olena Prytula of the discovery, though they were part of the police team investigating the disappearance. Instead, top officials were sent to Tarashcha to get rid of the body, while others created a rumor that it wasn't Gongadze's. So began the official cover-up of the corpse that would not end until February 2001, when a Russian DNA test confirmed the Tarashcha police's conclusion that the corpse was Gongadze's.

This cover-up began with a leak of information. On Monday, November 6, the police detective, Hryhoriy Harbuz, telephoned Gongadze's wife and Prytula to ask what kind of jewelry Gongadze wore. Prytula told the investigator about Gongadze's pendant with a half moon, and that she wore a matching pendant with the other half of the moon. He also had asked what Gongadze ate before he disappeared. Prytula told him, among other things, potatoes, cabbage and water-melon, the very food that the coroner had found.

But the detective didn't tell either of them that a corpse matching Gongadze's description had been found. Nor did he tell both women that their description matched the jewelry found in Tarashcha, or ask them to come and identify the corpse or the jewelry. He failed to follow up his telephone call with an interview to see Prytula's pendant. He would have found, after comparing the two, that they fitted together to make a moon. (Only six weeks later, on December 18, after a great deal of public pressure, did Prosecutor General Potebenko allow Myroslava to see the corpse and jewelry, which she identified as her husband's.)

If the first sign of an official cover-up was the president's and the interior minister's silence, the second was the decision by Kravchenko – as he was in charge of the investigation – not to transfer the body to a Kyiv city morgue, where it could be preserved. The Tarashcha morgue did not have cold storage facilities. It was just a shed for

127

preparing bodies for funerals. It, and its hospital, lacked the equipment and expertise for more sophisticated analysis, like DNA tests, to confirm the body was Gongadze's, and maybe even to discover if the killers had left their DNA behind. Leaving the corpse in Tarashcha meant that it would quickly decompose and vital evidence would be destroyed.

Instead of getting the corpse brought to Kyiv, on Wednesday, November 8, Ukraine's chief coroner, Yuriy Shupyk, in the company of the Kyiv Oblast Prosecutor, Volodymyr Babenko, came to Tarashcha. After hearing Vorotyntsev's report, Shupyk took all the internal organs that the coroner had used for his autopsy – the heart, lungs and stomach, ordered the coroner to dispose of the corpse, and left. Shocked and confused, Vorotyntsev sought advice from colleagues at the hospital, the local police chief and prosecutor. The collective advice was to hold on to the corpse and await further developments.

When Kuchma was asked what he knew about the discovery of the body by the CBS 60 minutes TV program, broadcast on April 29, 2001, he replied that "law enforcement agencies originally thought it was a homeless person and paid no attention to the corpse at all". This was absolutely untrue. Local and national officials paid a huge amount of attention to it. All the relevant local officials - the prosecutor, investigator, coroner and police chief – were present at the exhumation. After the local coroner had made the postmortem, the local police, prosecutor and investigator concluded that the body probably was Gongadze's. The chief coroner of Ukraine and the regional prosecutor came to Tarashcha to view the corpse and hear the local coroner's autopsy report. As no one else has ever mentioned this story of a homeless person, it can safely be assumed that Kuchma made it up on the spur of the moment.

In retrospect, it can be assumed that from November 6, the president, the interior minister, and the prosecutor general knew about the discovery. It can also be assumed that the decision to dispose of the corpse only could have come from the highest authority – the president. No one else but Kuchma could have made such a controversial decision as getting rid of evidence of murder.

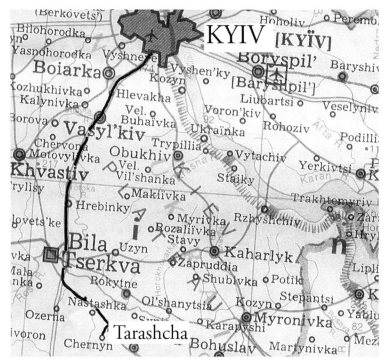

Map 2 – The town of Tarashcha, 140 km south of Kyiv

The corpse – another provocation against Moroz?

Why was Gongadze's headless corpse buried near Tarashcha? To get there, the killers had to transport it from Kyiv – some 140 km – over three different main roads and past two major permanent police check points (see Map 2). They buried it in a small forest in the middle of hectares of farmland, when within 30 kilometers of Kyiv there are massive forests without any open spaces. And why was the head severed?

Their choice of burial place undoubtedly had something to do with the fact that the district was in the parliamentary constituency of Oleksandr Moroz, the socialist leader. This was the same politician whom the authorities had linked to the grenade attack on the candidate Nataliya Vitrenko in the 1999 presidential campaign.

Within days of the discovery, Moroz and his supporters in

Tarashcha came to the conclusion that the corpse was intended as another provocation to discredit him. In Tarashcha, he was a very popular figure, the local boy who had done well. He was born, went to school, and worked in the Tarashcha district, and went on to lead the Socialist Party and head Ukraine's parliament from 1994-8. Given his local connections, it was not surprising that Moroz was one of the first people in Kyiv to hear about the discovery of the corpse. His constituency members informed him on Sunday, November 5, only two days after the corpse had been exhumed. On Tuesday, November 7, Moroz's constituency agent and the head of the Tarashcha hospital, Dr. Volodymyr Musiyenko, telephoned him with the news that the local police and the coroner had concluded that the corpse fitted Gongadze's description.

Moroz surmised that the corpse was meant to be "discovered" much later at an opportune moment to undermine his and his party's chances in the March 2002 parliamentary elections, when its "discovery" would have had as detrimental a political effect as the grenade-throwing incident had had during the 1999 presidential elections. It could be further surmised that the president and the internal minister wanted to keep the corpse a secret and get rid of it as it had been found too early to serve any political purpose.

The socialist leader had another worry on his mind. In mid-October, he had met in great secrecy the presidential guard Mykola Melnychenko who gave him a selection of excerpts from recordings made in President Kuchma's office. They contained discussions in which the president repeatedly ordered the interior minister to have Gongadze kidnapped and deported to Chechnya. Now, with the discovery of Gongadze's corpse in his constituency, Moroz had to decide how to publicize this information against Kuchma, while making sure no harm would come to its source.

17

Journalists uncover the corpse

As the rumor spread to Kyiv that Gongadze's beheaded corpse had been discovered in Tarashcha, the authorities countered with a misinformation campaign. One of Kyiv's major newspapers, *Segodnya*, reported it on November 10, 2000 that a corpse had been found in Tarashcha, but it was not Gongadze's because it did not match his physical characteristics or the time of his disappearance, as it had been buried for at least three years.

Moroz, watching the official cover-up unfolding, decided how to respond to the situation. He would let the public know that Gongadze's corpse had been found – by telling the editor of Gongadze's internet publication, Olena Prytula, to go to Tarashcha and view the body. He would get the presidential guard Melnychenko and his wife and child out of the country, and then present to parliament the evidence that the president was responsible for Gongadze's disappearance.

Prytula, tipped off by Moroz, and undeterred by the denials in *Segodnya* decided to go to Tarashcha. She was accompanied by the TET TV producer Lavrenti Malazoni, the 1+1 TV presenter Lyudmyla Dobrovolska, and Gongadze's lifelong friend Koba Alaniya. They drove to Tarashcha on November 15 in Malazoni's Cherokee jeep. What the journalists discovered blew the lid off the official conspiracy to destroy and cover up the corpse.

Moroz's constituency agent, Dr Volodymyr Musiyenko, facilitated their visit by making the arrangements with the coroner, Ihor Vorotyntsev. Following the journalists' visit, Musiyenko lost his job as acting head of the Tarashcha hospital.

Nov. 15, 2000 – The Tarashcha coroner and the corpse

The journalists viewed the corpse but could not identify it. After two weeks without refrigeration, the initially fresh corpse was now rotten, being eaten by maggots and stinking unbearably. The body was in such bad condition that the coroner had to decide either to bury it or, as the visitors wanted, hand it over to them.

Prytula contributed three important pieces of evidence that hardened the coroner's conclusion that the corpse was indeed Gongadze's. The food she described Gongadze as having eaten before his disappearance matched what he had found. She showed him the other half of the pendant she wore, which matched what Vorotyntsev had handed to the police. He decided to discover whether there was shrapnel in the right hand, which would have been one of the 26 pieces Gongadze received from the explosion in Abkhazia in 1993. He cut off the right hand of the decomposed body and took it to the nearby hospital where the shrapnel appeared on the X-ray. The hand was cut off because the smell and decay of the corpse was such that it couldn't be taken to the X-ray room.

When the journalists asked if they could take the corpse back to Kyiv, the Tarashcha coroner readily obliged. Otherwise he would had to bury it as maggots were devouring it rapidly. He issued a death certificate in Georgi Gongadze's name and handed it to Prytula, which

Nov. 15, 2000 – Headless corpse discovered on Nov. 2, 2000

gave her the right to take charge of the corpse. Though Ukraine's law allows for a death certificate and the corpse to be given to a non-relative, the handover has to be witnessed and signed by a police officer. In this case, the coroner was breaking the law, as no police officer was present. But given that everyone in Tarashcha suspected there was some form of official cover-up, the procedure safeguarded the primary evidence that a murder took place.

By handing over the corpse to journalists who would publicize it, Vorotyntsev was taking a personal gamble with his job if not his life. But he didn't have much to lose as he had already ignored instructions to bury the corpse.

Later, Prosecutor General Potebenko – who had instructed his oblast prosecutor Babenko along with the chief coroner Shupyk to order Vorotyntsev to dispose of the corpse – blasted Vorotyntsev in parliament on January 10, 2001 for "issuing a death certificate in the name of Gongadze", claiming that it "was absolutely without foundation as the investigation had not determined the identity of the corpse". The leading prosecutor forgot to mention that he was responsible for not safeguarding the headless body – prime evidence in a criminal investigation – and attempting to destroy it by ordering the coroner to get rid of it. Thanks to the coroner, the body was available for a DNA test. If the authorities had had their way, the body would have disappeared, a test might never have taken place, and everyone would have believed the official line that the Tarashcha corpse was not Gongadze's body.

From Tarashcha, Prytula had telephoned the interior minister's office with the naive belief that they might be interested to hear that Gongadze's corpse had been found. Neither Kravchenko or Dzhyha nor any other official wanted to speak to her. This was hardly the response expected from officials who said they were conducting the biggest man hunt ever to find Gongadze. So much for Kravchenko's October 6th statement to parliament that he would allow Prytula and Gongadze's wife to be part of the police investigation in order to create a climate of public trust.

But Kravchenko's office did react to Prytula's telephone call by ordering the local police to seize the corpse. As the journalists looked for a casket and transport to take the corpse to Kyiv, and as Vorotyntsev waited in his office for their return not far from the morgue, the police sneaked into the morgue and took the corpse. When the journalists heard that the corpse was missing, they went into a state of shock. "Gongadze" had been kidnapped again!

The prosecutor general's office later said that the Tarashcha corpse had been taken to the Kyiv city morgue located at 9 Oranzhereyna street. It failed to explain how the police could take a corpse from a morgue without the coroner's permission.

Malazoni, who was the first to return to the morgue, saw for himself that the corpse was gone. He asked the coroner for any remaining body parts. The coroner gave him a piece of tissue left from when he cut off the right hand to take the X-ray for the embedded shrapnel. (On March 20, 2001, the German laboratory Genedia said this tissue did not match Gongadze's DNA when compared to a drop of his blood on a medical card and his mother's blood. However, Russian and American DNA tests on the bones of the corpse concluded that the Tarashcha corpse was Gongadze's. See the results of all three DNA tests in chapter 22)

The journalists returned to Kyiv on the evening of November 15 and raised the alarm in the media that Gongadze's corpse had been stolen. Late that evening, Interfax-Ukraine released a long, detailed press release from Prytula about the journalists' trip to Tarashcha. "I cannot explain why Georgi's body, found on November 3, was hidden up to now from his relatives and friends. Why did they assure us that the discovered corpse was two years old? And finally, I do not understand why the body was in fact kidnapped", Prytula wrote.

Dzhyha lies about the corpse

Next day, November 16, angry members of parliament called interior minister Kravchenko to explain what had happened in Tarashcha. Kravchenko declined to come and instead sent his deputy, Mykola Dzhyha.

The journalists' discovery of the corpse should have been a major scandal for Kravchenko and the president, as they were concealing and attempting to destroy what the local police and coroner said was Gongadze's corpse. Instead, the event proved to be only a minor embarrassment as the speaker of parliament managed Dzhyha's appearance well and the deputy minister simply lied.

Dzhyha gave what must have been the shortest presentation a minister ever gave in parliament – only 20 seconds long. Dzhyha said that on November 3 a headless corpse had been discovered in Tarashcha, a murder inquiry had begun and that the identification of the corpse was taking place. "Today it cannot be asserted that this corpse is Gongadze's, there is no basis to say this."

The speaker then allowed only a few questions from the hall. Dzhyha was asked why he didn't think the corpse was Gongadze's. He answered that it was 174 to 177 cm in height – "very much less than Gongadze". It was also too old, and besides had "lived" through a winter or two, while Gongadze had disappeared only two months earlier. In other words the same misinformation carried by *Segodnya* newspaper on November 10, except that article said the corpse was in the ground for three years, instead of two.

Dzhyha had made up the lie about the corpse being old though there were many witnesses who saw a fresh corpse on discovery, including four officials – the local district prosecutor, investigator, police chief and coroner. Also, if the corpse was that old, how could the chief coroner of Ukraine, Shupyk, take away all the internal organs from the Tarashcha corpse, including the heart, lungs and stomach? This removal was witnessed by not only the local coroner but also by the prosecutor of the Kyiv region, Babenko.

A long queue of MPs lined up to ask Dzhyha questions. Prompted by a pro-presidential deputy, Dzhyha complained that the mass media was interfering in the inquiry – a reference to the visit by Gongadze's journalist friends, and the subsequent critical media reports. A deputy asked him whether the jewelry found on the corpse matched Gongadze's. Dzhyha said it was similar, but that this didn't mean it was identical, and that the relatives would only be allowed to view the jewelry after the corpse was identified. This odd answer got a few MPs cross and they demanded that the relatives and friends be shown the jewelry immediately and that Dzhyha should resign for his evasive and stupid answers. He tried to reassure parliament by saying that the autopsy results on the corpse would be available within a week. (A report was not available until January 10, 2001, when Potebenko presented it to parliament, and then it was different from Dzhyha's).

Fifteen minutes after Dzhyha began speaking, the speaker thanked him for coming to parliament and closed the session for lunch. Dzhyha had deceived parliament and the public, as he had previously with his misinformation about Gongadze being alive and sighted in Kyiv, Lviv and Moscow.

Next day, November 17, a minority of deputies in parliament demanded a debate on Dzhyha's assertion that the Tarashcha corpse was not Gongadze's. MP Serhiy Holovaty expressed his indignation at what Dzhyha had said: "I don't understand what is going on. But when I am told that the corpse lay for two weeks, and no one took responsibility for it, when I am told that the mother and wife are not allowed to identify it, that it is not necessary to show the items (the jewelry) to the mother and wife, that this is not allowed by law, well pardon me, what is this?" Holovaty accused the authorities of attempting to provoke parliament and political forces to dare confront the state security and police organs over the corpse.

However, other MPs came to the government's rescue. "There is not even a single fact that would convincingly say that the discovered corpse is Georgi Gongadze's," said Oleksandr Zinchenko, head of the parliamentary committee on questions of freedom of speech and information. Zinchenko was a member of the SDP(U), and de facto president of the private TV station – Inter – which had the biggest viewing audience in Ukraine.

On November 17, the day after Dzhyha spoke in parliament, the police and prosecutor's office raided Vorotyntsev's office and apartment in Tarashcha. They confiscated all his records, and not only those that referred to Gongadze's corpse. They also took his computer, keyboard, mouse and all his diskettes. His computer was returned with a virus that wiped out every file that was opened, until he had no records on any corpse.

To be sure Vorotyntsev stayed quiet, the prosecutor's office made him a witness in the murder inquiry, which meant he could be imprisoned if he spoke to the public on the subject.

As the authorities had confiscated all the evidence on the corpse and had it in their possession, Dzhyha was free to say whatever he wished about it. He even "cancelled" Vorotyntsev's autopsy report, because "We proved that the law was violated in the first coroner's examination".

President Kuchma joined the media counter-attack. "I don't know in whose interest it was to organize this 'scandal' [referring to the journalists' visit to Tarashcha], which took place yesterday. To say that the discovered body belongs to Gongadze means taking responsibility for what you say," the president lectured students studying to be civil servants at the Institute of International Affairs on November 17. But just as the president and the interior minister thought they had weathered the scandal, Moroz was planning to reveal evidence directly linking Kuchma to Gongadze's disappearance.

18

President accused

In mid-October, 2000, the presidential guard Mykola Melnychenko secretly approached Oleksandr Moroz with information that the president had ordered Gongadze's disappearance. They agreed to a plan where by Moroz would make public the recordings with the president ordering Gongadze's disappearance only after Melnychenko and his family left Ukraine. Both expected that parliament, after hearing the evidence, would vote for impeachment and then Melnychenko would return to testify and to a hero's welcome. It didn't turn out like that.

On October 23, Melnychenko handed in his resignation. On October 30, he applied for a foreign passport (every citizen has to have an internal passport and an optional foreign passport) for himself, his wife and daughter, and received it on November 2. It was surprising that his application didn't attract the notice of the State Security Service – the SBU. (Coincidentally, the day Melnychenko received his passport, the two farmers came across a hand sticking out of the ground near Tarashcha.)

After obtaining his foreign passport on November 3, Melnychenko hesitated to apply for a Czech visa until November 21. During this three-week period, he prepared for Moroz excerpts on Gongadze from his huge collection of recorded conversations – said to be about 1,000 hours of recordings in the president's office. He also produced on video for Moroz a statement on why he had recorded the president (this video would be shown to parliament on December 14, 2000). Both Moroz and Melnychenko must have personally feared for their safety if they were discovered. Their fear must have worsened on November 7, when Moroz learned that the local police and coroner had concluded that the headless corpse was Gongadze's. Melnychenko applied for a 90-day visa to the Czech Republic for himself and his family on November 21, and obtained it two days later. Again Ukraine's supposedly all-knowing secret police failed to notice.

Moroz went to Central Europe to set up a place to stay for Melnychenko and his family. He was in Budapest on November 24-25, where he told a Dutch journalist that he received recordings of President Kuchma ordering Gongadze's disappearance. He gave her a copy of a recording with fourteen excerpts selected by Melnychenko implicating Kuchma in the kidnapping of Gongadze. (The reporter, Corine de Vries of the Dutch newspaper *Volkskrant*, will place the recordings on the *Volkskrant* web site on November 28, the same day Moroz reveals them in parliament.)

On Sunday, November 26, Melnychenko and his family went to Kyiv's Boryspil airport to board a flight to Warsaw. As a further precaution to make sure that the 1,000 hours of recordings on some form of digital media – like digital recorder's memory cards, CD-Rom disks etc – got through Ukraine's customs, Moroz had obtained for Melnychenko a diplomatic passport as his adviser. This meant that customs and security staff did not search Melnychenko, as MPs and their assistants enjoy the same immunity from searches as diplomats when crossing international borders.

(Again the secret police failed to notice Moroz's request for a diplomatic passport for Melnychenko or his departure from Boryspil international. He must have been very lucky or he had help, as he recorded the president for a year, contacted one of the most spied on politicians, and applied for a foreign passport and Czech visa.)

Upon arriving in Warsaw, Melnychenko took a further precaution. Instead of continuing to Prague by air, he and his family took a bus to the Czech Republic.

With Melnychenko safely out of the way, Moroz selected the earliest day parliament was in session – Tuesday, November 28 – to make what would be a dramatic announcement. The dropping of this political bombshell coincided with the day parliament met to discuss the state of Ukraine's human rights record in the presence of the foreign diplomatic corps.

"President Leonid Kuchma ordered the disappearance of the journalist Georgi Gongadze" Moroz unexpectantly announced from the podium of parliament's assembly hall. As evidence, he said he had in his possession recordings of President Leonid Kuchma, the Interior Minister Yuriy Kravchenko and the head of the president's office, Volodymyr Lytvyn, conspiring to kidnap Georgi Gongadze. Moroz told the shocked MPs that an officer from the state security service had provided him with the recording, who was ready to testify to their authenticity. He called upon parliament to immediately begin impeachment proceedings, as this was the only way that such a matter could be properly investigated.

The president's supporters rose one by one to denounce Moroz. The president's representative in parliament, Roman Bezsmertnyi, called Moroz a provocateur. The SDP(U) member Oleksandr Zinchenko accused him of being a criminal.

The leaders of the majority – the right wing parties – signed a joint statement accusing Moroz of a publicity stunt to raise his political profile. Besides the leaders of the oligarch parties, it included the two heads of the divided Rukh party, Henadiy Udovenko and Yuriy Kostenko. It was surprising that they had put their names to the statement given that they were casting suspicion on Kuchma's subordinates for organizing the car accident that killed Rukh leader Vyacheslav Chornovil.

Neither did parliament's left wing respond favorably to the socialist leader's accusations. The Progressive Socialist leader Nataliya Vitrenko accused Moroz of attempting to divert attention away from his responsibility for the grenade-throwing incident against her and her supporters.

The communist party chief, Petro Symonenko, played down Moroz's revelation. He explained that he too had been offered the recordings but declined them, suggesting, that unlike Moroz, he could not be so easily fooled. The communist leader said that on November 11, people – who might have been state security service officers – had approached him with a tape containing the order to kidnap Gongadze. He said, he had refused because he had to regularly deal with frauds and allegations.

Melnychenko has denied that he ever approached Symonenko:

FT: It's been said that Moroz wasn't the only or even the first person you went to. For example, [Communist party leader Petro] Symonenko has said you also went to him.

M: It wouldn't be expedient to put in print now where, how, what, who - these are matters for a secret inquest. Categorically, I did not go to Symonenko, because I knew, Symonenko and Kuchma are one and the same.

(Source: Tom Warner, ft.com, Sept. 15, 2002)

Mistakes on Moroz's transcripts

Following his announcement in parliament, Moroz played an audio cassette to a press conference packed with journalists and MPs. They heard nine short excerpts purporting to be conversations the president had with his subordinates on kidnapping Gongadze and punishing other journalists. Immediately after Moroz's press conference, the transcripts of the audiocassette recordings appeared appropriately on the web site founded by Gongadze – pravda.com.ua.

An analysis of Moroz's transcripts shows they contained very serious mistakes. Melnychenko had presented the audio excerpts to Moroz poorly. He put together a recording with excerpts taken from original recordings without clearly indicating where the excerpt began and ended and what day it was from. Missing sentences in the excerpt were not indicated. The transcription was obviously very hurriedly and clumsily done.

Moroz's transcribers presented nine excerpts when they were fourteen. Moroz's fourth excerpt actually consisted of three excerpts recorded at different times. The first came from the president's conversation in July 2000, while the second and third excerpts came from a conversation in September 2000. Moroz's eighth excerpt was also wrong. It consisted of two separate conversations the president had with two different people and on different days.

Kuchma's discussions on Gongadze

In the light of the mistakes in Moroz's presentation on November 28, the evidence will be represented to show the responsibility by Kuchma, Kravchenko, Derkach and Lytvyn for the disappearance and murder of Gongadze. A total of 24 excerpts from the Melnychenko recordings have been found on Gongadze or relevant to him. They excerpts are presented in chronological order as far as possible, as some of them had been released by Melnychenko without dates.

The first of the 24 excerpts has been mistakenly presented as a discussion about Gongadze. It illustrated the kind of serious mistakes that transcribers could make, especially if they don't know the date of the recording. The excerpt contained the following words by the prosecutor general, Mykhaylo Potebenko – "[word indistinct] has gone missing". The president replied: "In Chechnya, the Chechens abducted him" and both are heard laughing. On January 26, 2001, *Ukrayinska Pravda* transcribed the indistinct word as Gongadze. But it did not refer to Gongadze, as the conversation took place on February 10, 2000 – seven months before his disappearance. It must have been about someone else.

The second excerpt from June 12, 2000, while not dealing with Gongadze directly, has great relevance to his case. It showed how the interior minister dealt with the president's critics. On June 12, the interior minister reported to the president how his undercover police unit – which had "no morals, no nothing" – kidnapped and beat Oleksiy Podolsky. This unit is the prime suspect in the kidnapping, murder and beheading of Gongadze.

The third excerpt also from June 12, is important because it contained the conversation that motivated the president to take some form of action against Gongadze. The state security chief, Derkach, told the president that Gongadze had to be punished for spearheading a media campaign against his son as well as the president in Ukraine and Russia on the behalf of the oligarch and MP Mykhaylo Brodsky. "The time for him [Gongadze] to mouth-off will come to an end. This fucker I will crush", Derkach told Kuchma.

The fourth excerpt, again from June 12, didn't appear in Moroz's collection of excerpts. "Behind that article in *Nezavisimaya Gazeta* stands Gongadze", the president told Vyacheslav Pikhovshek, the TV presenter of 1+1 Epicenter news program.

In the fifth excerpt, recorded on June 22, the state security chief told the president that his agents "were watching him [Gongadze] closely", and reported again that the oligarch and MP Brodsky was funding Gongadze.

The critically important sixth excerpt records the president on July 3 discussing what to do about Gongadze. After reading more articles from Gongadze's web site, Kuchma resolved to punish him. He told his office chief, Volodymyr Lytvyn, that "Chechens should kidnap him and ask for a ransom".

The seventh and eighth excerpts came from a conversation recorded on July 3 with the Interior Minister Yuriy Kravchenko. In the seventh excerpt, the president ordered him to silence Gongadze – "The Chechens should kidnap him and take him to Chechnya on his dick ... and demand a ransom!". Later in the same conversation – the eighth excerpt – Kuchma informed Kravchenko that Brodsky was providing Gongadze's finances – "... since the summer [he] has been financed by Brodsky".

The ninth and tenth excerpts are from the July 3 recording of the president's conversation with the state security service chief. In it, Derkach told the president what action he had taken against Gongadze and his staff – "At this time, [we are] listening to all matters in all his channels". Later in the conversation, the president returned to it to verify who was financing Gongadze – "Who gives the Georgian the money? This is the question." "I have already told you, this time Brodsky gave the money," replied Derkach. Neither of these two excerpts appeared in Moroz's presentation.

In the July 10 excerpt, Kuchma reminds Kravchenko the punishment that Gongadze should receive: "I'm telling you, drive him out, throw out, and give him to the Chechens and then a ransom". Kravchenko reassures him that he will have this job done because: "The team I have is combative and will do whatever you want".

In excerpt 12, August 30, the president confronts the interior minister for not taking care of Gongadze as instructed. Kravchenko again promises to have Gongadze kidnapped – "Gongadze will be sorted in two days".

Kravchenko failed to take out Gongadze, as excerpts 13 to 16, all recorded on September 11, testified.

In excerpt 13, Kuchma complained to an unidentified person (probably Lytvyn) that Kravchenko had failed to get rid of Gongadze – "What did he take care of … Not a dick connected. … I will tell him to do so quickly … there is a separate article on him [in *Ukrayinska Pravda*]".

In excerpt 14, the president confronted the interior minister for not getting rid of Gongadze – "Why are you silent about Gongadze?", while in excerpt 15, at the end of the same conversation, Kravchenko promised the president once again to take care of Gongadze – "I won't let him go".

In excerpt 16, the state security service chief, Derkach, told the president that Ihor Bakay had supplied information to the muck-raking journalist Oleh Yeltsov – "It was Bakay who got in touch with him".

Excerpt 17 comes from a conversation with Prime Minister Viktor Yushchenko on September 18, after he presented a long presentation on the state of the economy. In the conversation, Yushchenko complained to the president about allegations in the mass media that his American wife was a spy. The president made his infamous reply: "I don't take revenge; I keep silent and don't say anything to anyone …". What Yushchenko didn't know then was that the story about his wife being a spy was planted by Derkach on Kuchma's orders, according to Melnychenko.

In excerpt 18, probably from September 18 or 19 (Melnychenko didn't provide the date), the president and Derkach engaged in a shouting match over Andriy Derkach's role in the showing of a TV documentary, shown on September 15 and 16, linking a crime boss to the interior minister. "If they show Kisil on a state channel together with this fucking Kravchenko. They can just fucking show anyone!" the president shouted at Derkach senior.

Excerpt 19, probably from September 18 (Melnychenko didn't provide the date), had the president and Lytvyn discussing the Georgian Embassy's announcement on September 18, that it had received a telephone call accusing two of the president's closest allies – Volkov and Kravchenko – and the crime boss Kisil of organizing Gongadze's disappearance. The person who made this phone call may not have chosen the names randomly but in the knowledge that both Volkov and Kravchenko had been linked to Kisil in the media on the eve of Gongadze's disappearance.

In excerpt 20, probably from September 19, the president and the head of his office, Volodymyr Lytvyn, were heard commenting on a TV report of a press conference held on September 19 by Gongadze's wife Myroslava and the *Ukrayinska Pravda* editor Olena Prytula.

Excerpt 21, probably from September 20, is of special importance. It starts off with the MP Oleksandr Volkov asking Kuchma what happened to Gongadze which the president doesn't answer. The two then were joined by the state security chief Derkach who reported on the harassment of the journalist Oleh Yeltsov, who supposedly had fled Ukraine after being warned: "if you don't keep out of all kind of affairs, we will cut your head off".

Excerpts 22 and 23, are without dates but occur after Gongadze's disappearance. They contain Kuchma's telephone calls to Derkach complaining that he had failed to silence the opposition newspaper of his fierce enemy, the MP Hryhoriy Omelchenko. What Derkach said in response could not be heard, as Melnychenko's recorder only picked up what was said in the office.

In excerpt 22, Kuchma told Derkach off for not shutting down the Omelchenko's Kremenchuk newspaper Informbyuleten (Information Bulletin). He told Derkach to speak to deputy prime minister Yuliya Tymoshenko and tell her to stop financing the newspaper. "It was me who appointed you. So go and do it", Kuchma told Derkach. In excerpt 23, the president once again told Derkach off for failing to close down Omelchenko's newspaper.

Excerpt number 24, without a date, contained the president's rage against oppositional journalists: "Yes, including [Tetyana] Korobova,

Grani, Yeltsov. Just imagine, what kind of bitch that [roams] among newspapers [indistinct] … That Gongadze, the shit of an independent journalist, came and went" bellows Kuchma to the head of his office – Volodymyr Lytvyn.

Melnychenko has not produced nor has he explained why he has not made available any conversations between the president and the interior minister Kravchenko after Gongadze's disappearance. One expected Kravchenko to explain what happened to Gongadze. Is Melnychenko holding back this evidence for a trial? He told the national press club in Washington DC on August 14, 2001 that President Kuchma knew Gongadze had been killed within five days of his disappearance. The public expects from Melnychenko either the recordings or an adequate explanation why he has not made available the conversations with Kravchenko after Gongadze's disappearance.

Dec. 14, 2000 –Ivan Melnychenko in front of his house in Vasylivka holds a picture of his son Mykola with President Leonid Kuchma (UNIAN)

19

The response

Melnychenko's recordings that the president, his office chief, the interior minister, and the security service chief conspired in Gongadze's disappearance should had immediately instigated a major investigation. The recordings contained evidence of serious crimes. In comparison, President Nixon's Watergate affair was a storm in a teacup. This was not about breaking into a rival party's headquarters to steal documents; it was about the president organizing the kidnapping and forced deportation of a citizen, which turned into a grisly murder.

While the political elite was reeling from the shock of Moroz's revelation, the public at large heard little of substance about it, or what they heard was muffled by counter-accusations. The accusation made in parliament on November 28, 2000 was heard in full only on a single local Kyiv FM radio station, Radio Rox, the private station broadcasting parliamentary proceedings. Most of the mass media attacked Moroz for making the accusation. The national state channel (UT1), in the spirit of being the president's TV station, ignored the accusation and blasted Moroz. "The president of Ukraine considers that the methods used by Oleksandr Moroz are unacceptable and unforgivable. He reserves the right to take the necessary measures, including legal ones, to defend his honesty and character," it quoted Martynenko, his press secretary as saying. The head of the president's office, Lytvyn, denied the authenticity of the tapes and promised a libel action against Moroz. A state security service press officer called Moroz's accusation a provocation and a crime punishable by law, and accused him of attempting to divert attention from the trial of his grenade-throwing supporters. In contrast to the bellicose SBU press statement, the interior ministry modestly called for the prosecutor's office to take legal measures against Moroz.

The most watched national TV station Inter (UT-3), and the second most popular station, 1+1 (UT-2), relegated the story to short items in their news broadcasts. Both questioned the credibility of Moroz's accusations. The "commissar" whom the oligarch Volkov had installed at 1+1 to manage the news was clearly doing his job.

The prosecutor general, Mykhaylo Potebenko, attempted to show that he upheld the rule of law and was not just the president's lap-dog. On Thursday, November 30, he took statements from the three accused. He informed the media that the president, the interior minister and the head of the president's office had all described the accusations as lies. Hence the recordings were falsified, the chief prosecutor told the press.

As for the long delayed DNA test on the corpse, Potebenko said that it would be performed either on December 8 or 11. He said the delay in obtaining a blood sample was caused by the illness of Gongadze's mother. This brought a sharp reply from the mother, who retorted that no one had asked her for a sample. Potebenko apologized to the mother and blamed the Kyiv oblast prosecutor, Volodymyr Babenko, for the delay. (This was the same Babenko who told the Tarashcha coroner on November 8, 2000, to get rid of the corpse.)

Moroz's accusations and Melnychenko's transcripts were only published in small opposition newspapers like *Svoboda, Grani* and *Tovarysh*. Only the weekly quality newspaper, *Zerkalo Nedeli*, and its Ukrainian version, *Dzerkalo Tyzhnya*, provided an in-depth analysis of the affair, but refrained from publishing excerpts from the recordings. The news on Kuchma's son-in-law's ICTV aggressively defended the president and attacked the authenticity of the recordings. What was surprising was that ICTV's attack was led by the journalist Mykola Knyazhytsky, who was a victim of Kuchma's attempts to crush STB fin 1999 or not supporting his re-election.

Only on the internet could Moroz's accusations and Melnychenko's recordings and transcripts be heard and read in full. The web sites pravda.com.ua and radiosvoboda.com led the way. They provided hundreds of pages of transcripts from the recordings. The IPI collection of 45 hours of recordings was placed on the Harvard University

web site, wcfia.harvard.edu/melnychenko. Although less than two percent of Ukraine's population had access to the internet, hundreds of
thousands turned to pravda.com.ua for their information, by accessing
it from their workplaces.

The president first replied to Moroz's accusations on December 1,
in the Belarussian capital Minsk, where he was attending a
Commonwealth of Independent States (CIS) summit. At an
impromptu news conference, flanked by Georgian President Edward
Shevardnadze nodding in agreement, Kuchma accused an unnamed
foreign secret service of creating a "provocation". Journalists and politicians assumed that the president was referring to the Russian secret
service, given that Shevardnadze had made similar accusations against
it, and the Georgian leader was on good terms with its US equivalent
which was providing him with support.

It took Kuchma more than a week to formally respond to Moroz's
accusations. On December 6, 2000, Kuchma made an unscheduled
appearance on TV to make a statement to the nation. In it, he managed not to even mention Moroz's name, the accusations against him,
or the Melnychenko recordings. The gist of his statement was that "the
November 28th statement in parliament" was a secretly planned
provocation aimed at pushing Ukraine into chaos, anarchy and social
disorganization. These provocateurs were orchestrating "a dirty game",
using Ukraine's politicians "to show Ukraine to the world as an unciv-
ilized country, a wild and benighted society", he said. He accused
politicians of using the fate of Gongadze and the grief of his family
"for political speculation". He ended his short counter-blast by proclaiming himself a stout defender of free speech and the press. "I have
stood and continue to stand for freedom of speech, against any pressure on the mass media, for the possibility to express one's thoughts
freely and publicly … After all, you can judge for yourself. The publi-
cations that consider themselves an uncompromising opposition have
been continuously published".

As he spoke, his subordinates were busy repressing free speech and
the critical press. The state security agents were making sure that no
newspaper would print Moroz's revelations. Tax officials harassed the

few foreign media outlets in Ukraine that reported Moroz's accusa-tions, like the local private re-broadcasters of the Ukrainian services of the BBC and Radio Liberty, and the American owned English-lan-guage business magazine *The Eastern Economist*.

There was one journalist who had the information and the opportu-nity to counter some of the official misinformation pouring into the mass media. Vyacheslav Pikhovshek, the presenter of the weekly TV program Epicenter could have recalled how he witnessed the presiden-tial staff threatening Gongadze, Prytula and Sholokh in Washington DC because of their lobbying efforts against the president. He could have contradicted the police claim that Gongadze was seen at Eric's Bar the day after his disappearance. Finally, he could have given credi-bility to the Melnychenko recordings and undermined Kuchma's claim that they were a provocation and that he didn't know who Gongadze was, as he could verify a recording where the president discussed Gongadze with him.

Instead Pikhovshek contributed to the misinformation. On December 10, he dedicated a whole program to Moroz's accusations. However, Pikhovshek's sole aim was to discredit Moroz. To start with, he didn't bother to interview Moroz. Instead, he interviewed those who accused Moroz either of not being patriotic or of using falsified recordings. He had the head of the parliamentary committee investi-gating Gongadze's disappearance, the MP Oleksandr Lavrynovych, castigating Moroz for "tarnishing Ukraine's international image and reducing the public's trust in state authorities". The deputy chief of the presidential security service, Oleh Pysarenko, was filmed explaining how it would have been impossible for Melnychenko to record conver-sations in the president's office.

Pikhovshek denied initiating any conversations on Gongadze with the president. "I can say with 100 percent assurance that I never raised the question of Georgi Gongadze" when talking to the president, he told Radio Liberty's Ukrainian service on January 10, 2001. He was not telling the whole truth. It might be true that he didn't initiate a discussion on Gongadze, but the president did.

20
Kuchma threatens parliament

How do you investigate and put on trial the president of Ukraine? The constitution of Ukraine says that only the 450-strong parliament can investigate and try the president. The process can be initiated by a simple majority of 226 votes to create a special parliamentary committee with a prosecutor and an investigator. Its conclusions would be presented to parliament, which would then have to decide the president's guilt or innocence. A preliminary guilty verdict needs a two-thirds majority, or 300 MPs. The process then moves to the Constitutional Court which checks that parliament carried out the procedure correctly, and then the Supreme Court, which decides whether the charge against the president constitutes a crime. Finally, the president is impeached if at least three-quarters, or 338 MPs find him guilty.

The initial reaction in parliament to Moroz's accusation against the president was met with widespread rebuke or skepticism. The oligarch party leaders, along with the two Rukh parties, and led by the president's parliamentary representative, together issued a statement calling Moroz's revelation "sensational" and a "bloody provocation with the aim of increasing his popularity".

A number of right-wing leaders didn't sign this statement, including Viktor Pynzenyk of Reforms and Order (Myroslava Gongadze worked as their press spokesperson); the oligarch Petro Poroshenko and his new parliamentary Solidarity faction (he probably was the "Petrovych" who initially funded Gongadze's pravda.com.ua); and deputy prime minister Yuliya Tymoshenko of the Fatherland Party – what was left of Lazarenko's Hromada party.

Neither were the left-wing parties supportive of Moroz. Though the communist party did not sign the statement, its leader Petro Symonenko attempted to play down the impact of the scandal. He said that he too had been offered the recordings by security agents but declined them. He likened it to many other attempts to involve him and his party in "frauds and insinuations".

The Boryspil incident

The pro-Kuchma parliament speaker Ivan Plyushch was determined not to allocate parliamentary time to debate Moroz's accusations. He succeeded for about a week. On December 8, the day after the president went on TV to say the revelation was a conspiracy against the state, his subordinates created an incident that made a debate and impeachment possible. At Kyiv's Boryspil airport, customs officials stopped and searched three members of parliament's Gongadze committee – Serhiy Holovaty, Viktor Shyshkin and Oleksandr Zhyr. They were returning from the Czech Republic with a video containing an interview with the presidential guard Melnychenko.

As the MPs were going through customs, officials searched their belongings and seized the video and returned it damaged. The search and seizure was illegal as Ukrainian MPs have the same privileges as diplomats on Ukraine's borders, that is they are immune from customs checks. The ploy to destroy the video failed, as the MPs had taken the precaution of bringing a copy through another channel. The incident backfired, as a very large majority of parliament objected to the infringement of their privileges and demanded a debate on the incident, along with reports from the three MPs and the showing of the video.

Tuesday, December 12

In an attempt to appease MPs, Prosecutor General Mykhaylo Potebenko came to parliament to state that the search had been illegal and the guilty would be brought to justice. Potebenko appearance was a tactical error for the president. In his apology to parliament he rambled into the Gongadze case and opened a Pandora's box. He blamed the Health Ministry for the delay in completing the medical tests on the Tarashcha corpse. Previously he had blamed the Kyiv Oblast prosecutor for not arranging the blood sample from Gongadze's mother. Responding to the complaints that relatives had not been allowed to view the corpse, Potebenko explained that viewing was unnecessary, as it would upset them – it would be better to wait until the corpse had been positively identified by the DNA tests.

Potebenko then moved on to Moroz's accusations. He appealed to Moroz to trust his investigation and said he would guarantee the security of the person who had provided the recordings.

After Potebenko's address, the speaker attempted to return to the scheduled agenda. The majority of MPs wanted an emergency debate on the airport incident. A total of 307 MPs voted for the three MPs to tell them their version of the story. Only about 100 MPs from the hard-core presidential factions – NDP, Working Ukraine and Rebirth of Regions – voted against. Suddenly, expectations arose among the president's opponents that parliament might vote to investigate the president.

However on the first vote, it became clear that the issue which concerned the majority of the MPs was not the president's guilt in the murder of Gongadze, but their immunity from being searched by customs. A resolution to hold an emergency debate to investigate the president over Gongadze failed miserably. It received only 140 votes, far short of the 226 required.

After the three MPs illegally searched at the airport – Holovaty, Shyshkin and Zhyr – had given their accounts, the chief of customs, Yuriy Solovkov, took the podium. He attempted to persuade the MPs that his airport staff had not singled out the MPs, but were acting under instructions to search for contraband diamonds being smuggled into Ukraine. Solovkov's inept explanation caused an explosion of anger.

The speaker again attempted to get back to the planned agenda by calling for a vote to stop the discussion about the airport incident. Instead 281 MPs voted to view the video that the customs officials had attempted to destroy.

The video had the three MPs conducting an interview on December 7, in an undisclosed location in the Czech Republic with the former

153

Dec. 12, 2000 – Members of parliament watch an interview on video
with the presidential guard Mykola Melnychenko (UNIAN)

presidential guard. This was the first time that his identity had been made public.

"My name is Mykola Ivanovych Melnychenko. I am a retired officer of the Ukrainian Security Service. ... I was a senior security officer serving in the department of presidential guards," he began.

When asked in the video why he had recorded the president, Melnychenko explained that he began to record him after he witnessed the president "giving a criminal order".

After the showing of the video, the president's subordinates answered questions from the parliament's podium. Prosecutor General Potebenko was asked by a number of MPs to prosecute the president, while others questioned his credibility as an independent investigator. Moroz asked among other things, why Potebenko had not charged the president and the interior minister with plotting Gongadze's disappearance. Potebenko promised an impartial investigation but said that Melnychenko first needed to be interviewed because the recordings on their own did not constitute sufficient evidence to charge Kuchma with any crimes.

The state security chief, Derkach, denied that he or his agents had anything to do with the Boryspil incident. The MPs laughed at his reply and many called him a liar. He said he couldn't comment on what had happened at the airport until an investigation had been completed.

The interior minister, Kravchenko, received the worst mauling from the MPs. He said he had not received orders from the president to kidnap Gongadze. Despite being asked, he would not say whether it was his voice on the Moroz tapes. Instead, he replied that only an expert analysis could answer this question. So far no experts have taken up the challenge of comparing his voice or anyone of the other accused with the voices attributed to them on the recordings.

A parade of MPs continued to fire accusations at him. The "anti-mafia" MP Hryhoriy Omelchenko hurled a new charge against him. He alleged that Kravchenko had organized the car accident that killed the MP and Rukh leader Vyacheslav Chornovil in early 1999.

MPs called for a secret ballot to investigate the president, so that he couldn't take revenge on individual MPs. But the speaker wouldn't allow a vote to take place on this motion, arguing that parliament had voted against secret ballots, and that the procedure to change this rule would take weeks to implement.

The speaker resisted attempts to vote on a resolution to condemn the airport incident, arguing that voting on resolutions took place only on Thursdays and Fridays. Finally, he asked for a vote on who wanted to vote on resolutions that day. A constitutional majority of 303 said they wanted to vote immediately and in secret.

While the session broke for lunch, the president's spokesman in parliament, Roman Bezsmertnyi, met MPs informally and passed on a warning from President Kuchma that if parliament voted to investigate him, he would dissolve it and rule by emergency powers.

When parliament reassembled after lunch, the president's threat had the desired effect. The head of the Gongadze committee, Oleksandr Lavrynovych along with many MPs failed to reappear in the debating chamber. The speaker said that the committee's resolution on the airport incident could not be voted on if Lavrynovych was not there to present it.

As MPs protested, the speaker simply closed the session and left the chamber, leaving behind over 200 angry MPs. Without warning the lights went off, and the MPs found their way out in the darkness. The December 12 parliamentary session had come to an inglorious and humiliating end for the president's opponents, after such a promising beginning that the allegations against the president would be dealt by constitutional means.

December 13 – Kuchma threatens MPs

Next morning, Wednesday December 13, angry deputies rounded on the speaker over the switching off of the lights the previous evening and again demanded that voting take place in secret. The MP Valentyna Semenyuk told the speaker that if he didn't allow voting in secret, he would be personally responsible if any MP came to harm. (Ironically, on March 3, 2001, a policeman singled out Semenyuk at an anti-presidential demonstration and beat her unconscious.)

The speaker reminded the MPs that voting would not take place today, Wednesday, as it only took place on Thursdays and Fridays. As for who had switched off the lights in the chamber the previous evening, he said that an employee, thinking the session had come to an end, had switched off the lights and gone home! On the vexed question of secret voting, he again claimed that it required a long procedure. He added that it was also impossible for technical reasons, as the electronic vote counter would need major alterations.

As an MP presented a resolution to set aside the whole of Thursday to debate and vote on the airport incident, the speaker interrupted him. He announced that the president's representative, Bezsmertnyi, had an important announcement to make. Bezsmertnyi repeated what he was saying in private to MPs. He warned them that the president would introduce a state of emergency if they voted to initiate the impeachment process. "You will simply not be allowed to destabilize the situation in Ukraine; keep that in mind."

Moroz responded to the president's threat with another surprise for the MPs. He told them he had in his possession a statement made on video by Melnychenko on November 16, before he fled Ukraine, in which he named the organizer of the grenade-throwing at the presidential candidate MP Nataliya Vitrenko and her supporters.

Following these shocking announcements, the speaker then closed all further discussion on Gongadze, Melnychenko and the airport incident, parliament agreed to set aside Thursday to discuss these matters. The remainder of Wednesday were taken up with routine matters.

That evening the media failed to report the president's threat to parliament and clearly state Moroz's latest allegation. Instead it focused on denouncing Moroz and Melnychenko and denying any wrongdoing by the president. The president's press secretary Martynenko once again asserted – "The president never gave any kind of order to law and order bodies to take action against the journalist Gongadze or any other journalist". Prosecutor General Potebenko at an unscheduled press conference called Melnychenko a liar. He was referring to Melnychenko's statement made on the video that Moroz was planning

Dec. 12, 2000 – Interior Minister Yuriy Kravchenko in parliament
(UNIAN)

to show to parliament the next day. Moroz had given him a video copy of Melnychenko's statement, in which he also accused Potebenko of taking part in a conspiracy to blame Moroz and his election agent for the grenade attack on the MP Vitrenko and others.

Thursday, December 14

The Thursday session began with MPs voting overwhelmingly by 324 votes to hold an emergency debate that afternoon on the Gongadze affair. It seemed that the previous day's warning from the president's spokesman had backfired. The session began with a report by Lavrynovych, the head of the parliamentary committee investigating Gongadze's disappearance. His report simply listed the committee meetings held and the decisions taken since its last report to parliament on November 17. Opposition MPs lambasted Lavrynovych for not listing the problems of the investigation – the unanswered questions on who harassed Gongadze, the investigation of his disappearance, the attempts to cover up and destroy his corpse, the lack of progress on DNA and other tests on the corpse, and the refusal to allow relatives to identify the corpse and the jewelry found with it. Lavrynovych failed in his report to explain why he was absent from the December 12 evening session to present the committee's resolution for a vote.

The three invited officials – the interior minister, the state security chief, and the prosecutor general spoke in turn. "It is undeniably difficult for me to appear before you, as a priori, I have been found guilty of committing a serious criminal offense", said the interior minister Yuriy Kravchenko in his opening statement. "I officially state today, I didn't have such discussions with the president. I didn't obtain any (such) orders from the president and didn't give any to my subordinates." But when asked by the Rukh MP Vasyl Chervoniy to deny that it was his voice on the Melnychenko recording, Kravchenko refused, as he did during his appearance in parliament on December 12.

The interior minister claimed the identification of the corpse had been delayed because the local coroner had failed to follow the correct procedures, as the jewelry on the corpse appeared "a day or two later". As for the delay to the DNA tests, he said this was the prosecutor's responsibility. Finally he pointed out that his ministry had ceased to be involved in Gongadze's investigation following Moroz's November 28th statement accusing him of organizing the disappearance. The prosecutor's office would now head the investigation, using the state security service (Derkach's SBU) to conduct the investigations.

An MP asked why Gongadze's corpse was not kept in a safe place after its discovery? "There was nothing to suggest that it was Gongadze's corpse", Kravchenko answered. No one seemed to have asked why the corpse was not kept safely even if the corpse wasn't Gongadze's, as the headless corpse was a murder victim.

The critical MPs didn't seem to be aware of Tarashcha coroner's autopsy report, the conclusion of the local police, or the visit by the top officials to Tarashcha. Consequently they had not challenged Kravchenko on his misinformation or that put out by his deputy, Dzhyha, that the corpse was too old, too short and too long in the ground to be Gongadze's.

Following Kravchenko's appearance, parliament watched the video statement by Melnychenko on who was to blame for the grenade attack on the presidential candidate Vitrenko. Melnychenko had made this statement in Kyiv on November 17 before he fled Ukraine. In it, he accused Kuchma of organizing the grenade attack against Vitrenko and blaming it on Moroz. He also accused the prosecutor general, the interior minister, the head of state tax office, and the security service chief of taking part in a conspiracy to blame the grenade attack on Moroz.

Melnychenko also made additional allegations against the president, that he had taken millions of dollars from state coffers for his re-election, falsified the 1999 presidential elections and the 2000 referendum on parliament, and persecuted newspapers and individuals.

The allegations had the opposite effect to that hoped for by Moroz. The sweeping accusations against the president and his subordinates presented without any evidence made many MPs suspicious that Moroz was using them. MPs did not like Melnychenko's description of

Moroz as some kind of saint: "When analyzing the material, I decided on the most honest and decent person who could be trusted with it to stop the criminal activities of President Leonid Kuchma."

The prosecutor general, who spoke after the Melnychenko video statement, caught their mood: "When I saw that I also was a party to this affair (the grenade throwing conspiracy), then I have no doubt that they (Melnychenko recordings) have been falsified." He accused Moroz of using Melnychenko to interfere in the planned trial of his election agent, Serhiy Ivanchenko, for the grenade attack.

As for the reason for the delay in the DNA tests on the corpse, Potebenko again blamed the health minister. (Kravchenko had blamed Potebenko's office for the delay in the test results.) The prosecutor general announced that his deputy, Oleksiy Bahanets, would take charge of the investigation from the police (led by deputy interior minister Dzhyha) and would have under him the best investigators in Ukraine.

After a break, the evening session began with the state security chief Leonid Derkach at the podium. He spoke very combatively. He told the MPs that on December 7, his service had been asked by the prosecutor's office to provide the investigators for the Gongadze investigation. He questioned the authenticity of the Melnychenko recordings, claiming that it was technically impossible to record the president. And then he said that if Melnychenko had recorded the president, it was illegal, suggesting that Kuchma or himself couldn't be prosecuted for whatever was said on the recordings.

In reply to a barrage of criticism about what he had just said, Derkach answered that any highly qualified expert could create recordings like Melnychenko's. He added that the state security service had never under his command carried out an illegal order and only worked according to the laws and constitution. This brought jeers and laughter from many MPs.

The special day on Gongadze ended without a resolution being proposed to begin the process of impeachment. The president's opponents knew there were not enough votes for this kind of resolution. Instead they showed there disunity by proposing three different resolutions calling upon the president to dismiss his subordinates.

The president's representative in parliament, Bezsmertnyi, added to the confusion by accusing Moroz's supporters in Tarashcha of having moved the corpse after it was discovered. What did he mean by this, he never explained.

All three resolutions proposed by the opposition failed to receive a simple majority of 226 votes. As the speaker announced that the special session had come to an end, pandemonium broke out, as the president's opponents demanded another vote on one of the three resolutions. The speaker shouted above the noise that it wasn't necessary, as he had correctly put it to the vote. But four MPs demanded a recount because their votes on it had not been recorded. They accused the staff controlling the parliament's electronic counting system of sabotage. After more argument, the speaker finally allowed another vote on the resolution. It passed with 235 votes. Only the president's representative Bezsmertnyi voted against it. The rest either didn't vote or had left the chamber.

The resolution that passed was the one backed by Moroz and presented by his fellow socialist Valentyn Zybov. It recommended that the president dismiss the interior minister and called upon the prosecutor general to report to parliament on the Gongadze investigation.

In retrospect this resolution was meaningless, and the debate was the defining moment in the investigation of the Gongadze case. Parliament did not vote to investigate the president. It avoided its responsibility to initiate a serious investigation of the president's responsibility for Gongadze's murder.

After this vote, events would work in Kuchma's favor. Soon the communist party would move behind the president in return for the dismissal of the "pro-western" prime minister Viktor Yushchenko. The president had successfully frightened parliament with the threat of dictatorship if it dared to investigate him. Kuchma had called the MPs' bluff and they would not risk calling his. Now parliament had joined the president in covering up a murder.

21

The first demonstration

Dec. 18, 2000 – Tents with protesters on Independence Square in Kyiv
(Photo Vasyl Artyushenko / Irex-ProMedia)

On December 15, 2000, the day after the special session in parliament failed to begin the process of impeachment, Kuchma's more radical opponents turned to street demonstrations in a bid to force him to step down. The protest was led by young Socialist Party members headed by the editor of the radical *Grani* newspaper, Yuriy Lyutsenko, and by a group from the right led by the former MP and head of the Republic Research Institute, Volodymyr Chemerys. The demonstrators put up tents and settled down to a very visible protest in the the capital's center – Independence Square.

The tent protesters were soon joined by an unlikely ally for the socialists – the nationalist paramilitary group UNA-UNSD

(Ukrainian National Assembly - Ukrainian National Self-Defense) headed by Andriy Shkil. The paramilitary group had a personal reason to express solidarity, as Gongadze had made a film – Shadows of the War – about their ARGO battalion fighting on the side of Georgia against Abkhazia in 1993. Other right-wing paramilitary groups soon joined the protesters, including the Shield of the Fatherland, led by the former leader of UNA-UNSD, Dmytro Korchynsky, and the Stepan Bandera Trident Brigade (a group created by Ukraine's state security service, according to a relative of the pre-war nationalist leader Stepan Bandera).

Lyutsenko said the socialists for their part welcomed the paramilitaries for practical reasons. He said they were needed to protect the tent protest from physical attacks. But the inclusion of these paramilitaries in the protests would haunt the political opposition. Their presence among the protesters would give President Kuchma the opportunity to label all the tent city protesters "national socialists" and "Ukrainian style fascists". Ultimately, the violent actions of these

April 9, 2001 – The paramilitary group UNA-UNSD participate in a demonstration (Photo by Vasyl Artyushenko /Irex-ProMedia)

groups would disgrace the opposition.

The protesters received support both from the socialist party and from right-wing parties – among them the two Rukh factions and Reforms-and-Order. Support from the Rukh led by Henadiy Udovenko was weaker than from the Yuriy Kostenko led group. Udovenko's group was irrevocably split. Some of its MPs, like Oleksandr Lavrynovych, the head of the parliament's committee to investigate the disappearance of Gongadze, supported the president, while others, like Taras Chornovil, the son of Rukh's famous leader, led some of the street demonstrations.

The public reaction in Kyiv to the tent protesters could best be described as indifferent. At most ten thousand people out of the capital's three million people attended the first demonstration on Sunday, December 17. The Kyiv demonstration did not have the size or impact of the protests taking place at this time in Manila, Jakarta, and Belgrade, which succeeded in toppling their respective totalitarian presidents. Kyiv's residents did not even come close to the citizens of Prague, who repeatedly came out in 50,000-strong rallies in solidarity with TV journalists on strike against an autocratic management.

Desperate to make an impact, the tent protesters on December 19 threatened to begin a hunger strike if President Kuchma did not meet them within twenty-four hours to discuss their demands. With this threat, the protesters were hoping to emulate the success of the student hunger strike in Kyiv in 1991, which forced Soviet Ukraine's prime minister Vitaliy Masol to resign. At first, the threat seemed to have worked, as Kuchma saw the delegation the next day.

The meeting with the president almost ended just as it began, Lyutsenko recalled. Kuchma had opened the meeting by telling the delegation that if their action had taken place in the West, it would had been met with water cannons. In response to the president's comment, the delegation stood up to leave. The deputy head of the presidential office, Oleh Domin, stepped in and persuaded them to stay. The protesters demanded that the president remove the "armed" ministers – the interior minister Kravchenko and state security chief Derkach. Kuchma answered that he would ask the cabinet of ministers to make this decision. He also agreed to their demand for an impartial international investigation of Gongadze's disappearance and the Melnychenko recordings. In addition, he promised they would get access to Ukraine's state TV to make their views known to the public. Two days later, on December 22, the protesters, feeling that they had made their point, decided to close the tent protest action. Kuchma did not honor any of these promises.

In interviews Kuchma often contradicted what he had said previously. On December 17, Kuchma appeared on the state UT-1's flagship news program 7-Days, to express his innocence. He recalled Gongadze as a journalist. "You see, a picture of participants in 'Epicenter' [on UT-2] which I took part during the presidential campaign has recently been published. As usual, a memorial picture was taken at the end of the program. Gongadze stood almost next to me. I recall that he participated in my other news conferences. For me, he was no different from the journalists who are critical of actions taken by the authorities and myself all the time."

If on 7-Days Kuchma said he knew Gongadze as a critical journalist, he said the opposite two weeks later. "Firstly, I did not know this journalist", he told Radio Liberty's Russian service on December 30. Kuchma went on to say that very few people, except for media specialists, even knew of Gongadze's existence. He repeated the assertion first made in Minsk on December 1, that the Melnychenko recordings were a provocation by plotters, backed by an outside power and that Moroz was being used as their "megaphone". However, again he failed to identify the plotters or the outside power.

Kuchma did not deny he might have been recorded in his office, or that he swore, as the recordings testified. Instead he accused Melnychenko of espionage and doctoring the recordings. In his rhetorical style, he asked why a re-elected president would bother with a journalist hardly anyone had heard of. "I am not mad" and it was "simply immoral" to accuse him of such things, Kuchma said.

He said he wanted a transparent investigation of Gongadze's dis-

Oct. 17, 1999 – President Leonid
Kuchma with Georgi Gongadze
and other journalists
after the Epicenter interview.

appearance with the involvement of international experts. He assured his listeners that the Gongadze investigation was under his "firm supervision".

On December 30, while President Kuchma was being interviewed on Radio Liberty's Russian service, Mykola Melnychenko was giving a telephone interview on Radio Liberty's Ukrainian service. This was his first public interview. He admitted that in recording the president, he had received help from other people. Also, he suggested that he did not have any recordings of the president discussing how Gongadze was killed, but didn't explain what recordings he had after Gongadze's disappearance.

He illustrated the level of the president's corruption by alleging that Kuchma had accepted Scythian gold jewelry – a national treasure – worth five million dollars from a businessman from the town of Zhytomyr. Melnychenko refused to name the businessman. (It was probably Ihor Bakay, the oil and gas trader and then head of Ukraine's state oil and gas conglomerate, Naftohaz. The three-thousand-year-old jewelry had probably been found on Bakay's private estate – an area of 11,000 hectares south of Kyiv, called Trakhtemyriv, which contains many ancient sites. He privatized this former hunting estate for the Soviet elite under the pretense of creating a national park.)

In response to the tent protests in Kyiv and elsewhere by the president's opponents, on January 10, 2001, the regional governors orchestrated mass rallies across the country in support of the president. On a working day, the authorities ushered the employed population and students to the city centers to demonstrate, just like in the Soviet days. By far the biggest demonstration took place in Kharkiv, where up to 100,000 took part. Significantly, no such rallies took place in the capital, where the population probably would not have cooperated.

An attempt on January 11 to organize a counter-demonstration in Kharkiv was met with police violence. They demolished the protesters' tents and beat unconscious the local socialist leader Bilohryshchenko.

Feb. 18, 2001 – Lesya Gongadze at a rally in protest at her son's disappearance, and Yuriy Lyutsenko (Photo UNIAN)

168

22

Potebenko's cover-up

On January 10, 2001, Prosecutor General Mykhaylo Potebenko presented to parliament his report on the Gongadze investigation, as he had been asked by parliament on December 14. In a rather long-winded report, Potebenko made three main points: President Kuchma was not responsible for Gongadze's disappearance, Melnychenko's recordings were counterfeit and Gongadze was alive and in hiding. His report went also over the Tarashcha corpse exhumation and autopsy; Gongadze's "image"; the Russian DNA results; the sightings of Gongadze; the tests on the Melnychenko's recordings, and the denials by officials accused, including the president.

Jan. 10, 2001 – Prosecutor General Mykhaylo Potebenko
and *Ukrayinska Pravda* editor Olena Prytula
at an impromptu press conference in parliament
(Photo by Vasyl Artyushenko / Irex-ProMedia)

Tarashcha corpse

The prosecutor general began his report by criticizing the exhumation of the Tarashcha corpse. He said that on November 3, 2000, "an investigator from the prosecutor's office accompanied by the district prosecutor, coroner and police" found no jewelry during the unearthing of the body. But that the local coroner find a white metal ring and bracelet on the corpse's right hand after the corpse was brought to the local morgue. The next day, the investigator went to the burial site and found a white metal necklace with half a pendant. It was not clear from his report who Potebenko was blaming for not checking the body and burial place for the jewelry on discovery. By law, the local prosecutor should had been responsible for the exhumation. (Almost two years later, on August 29, 2002, the Tarashcha district prosecutor, Serhiy Obozov, was arrested on the orders of the new prosecutor general, Svyatoslav Piskun. He was charged with adding the jewelry to the corpse after the exhumation. The investigator was also arrested but the charges have not been specified.)

Potebenko stated that soil tests on the jewelry against the soil of the discovery place showed they were different. This suggested that the corpse had been buried in another place and then transferred to the Tarashcha woods. Potebenko did not say where the other place might have been.

As for the jewelry found, he did not tell parliament that three days after the discovery, the police investigator, Hryhoriy Harbuz had contacted Myroslava Gongadze and Olena Prytula and learned from them that the jewelry found was identical to Gongadze's.

From the exhumation, the prosecutor general skipped the local coroner's autopsy and police reports and the visit by the Kyiv officials, and went on to the visit of the four journalists to Tarashcha on November 15. He admonished the local coroner, Ihor Vorotyntsev, and supporters of the local MP, Oleksandr Moroz, for helping Gongadze's friends to view the corpse. Furthermore, he reprimanded the coroner for X-raying the right hand, and for giving Prytula a death certificate in the name of Gongadze. He further castigated the coroner for giving the journalists a piece of tissue left behind after the police had secretly removed the body. But he didn't comment on the legality of the police stealing the corpse from Tarashcha morgue.

Instead of Vorotyntsev's autopsy, he presented the report by Ukraine's chief coroner, Yuriy Shupyk. He didn't give the date when this autopsy was carried out. The results of the chief coroner's autopsy was that the corpse belonged to a male aged 30-40 (Gongadze was 31) years-old; 177-184 cm tall (Gongadze was about 193 cm); with shrapnel wounds in many places on the bone structure (Gongadze had 26 shrapnel wounds, including on his right hand); who had been dead 60 to 90 days (it was at least 63 days after Gongadze disappeared, as Shupyk's autopsy was carried after November 15, when the police siezed the corpse and brought it to Kyiv).

Potebenko didn't mention that Shupyk's autopsy contradicted totally what the deputy interior minister, Dzhyha, had told parliament on November 16 of the previous year. Dzhyha had said the corpse was 174 to 177 cm in height, a much older man, and in the ground a winter or two.

The prosecutor general also failed to mention Vorotyntsev's autopsy. The Tarashcha coroner's autopsy differed from Shupyk's mainly on the question of height. The local coroner had measured the headless body as 162 cm in height (with a head it would have been over 190 cm).

The critical fact missing from Potebenko's report was that his Kyiv Oblast prosecutor, Babenko, and Ukraine's chief coroner, Shupyk went to Tarashcha five days after the corpse was discovered. He didn't tell parliament that Shupyk had taken the corpse's internal organs and the food found in the stomach and then ordered the local coroner to bury the body. Why would Potebenko want to conceal this information?

He also didn't explain why a pristine corpse – obviously a murder victim – was not safeguarded and allowed to rot. He didn't mention President Kuchma's assertion made on CBS 60 minutes that "law enforcement bodies originally thought it was a homeless person and didn't pay any attention to the body at all".

Instead of criticizing officials, like himself, for abandoning the corpse in Tarashcha, Potebenko attacked those who saved it for future investigations and DNA tests which determined that the corpse was Gongadze's. He singled out Olena Prytula and Koba Alaniya, for going to Tarashcha, for not cooperating with his investigation and for refusing to be interviewed. He quoted a telephone conversation – which was obviously recorded by the police or security services – in which Prytula told Vorotyntsev not to cooperate with the investigation.

He failed to explain how a fresh corpse exhumed on November 3 was a pile of bones on December 17, when viewed by Gongadze's wife. Why wasn't a headless corpse – a murder victim – immediately taken to the Kyiv morgue to be refrigerated and kept securely? Why was an order given to dispose of the corpse?

The prosecutor general did not even mention the November 17 police raid on the Tarashcha coroner's home and workplace, or the confiscation of his autopsy report. He also failed to say that his office had forced Vorotyntsev to admit himself to a hospital so he would not attend the meeting of the parliamentary committee investigating Gongadze's disappearance on January 9, the day before Potebenko's appearance in parliament. Obviously, Vorotyntsev's presence in Kyiv would have contradicted Potebenko's report to parliament.

Furthermore, to keep Vorotyntsev silent, Potebenko made him a witness in the Gongadze case, thus forbidding him to speak to the public about the case. (The prosecutor general's office has now silenced three of the four people officially present at the exhumation – the local coroner, prosecutor, and investigator, leaving the local police chief untouched, at least for now.)

Potebenko, as if he was a defense lawyer for Kuchma, attempted to rubbish Gongadze as too unimportant a journalist for the president to be interested in. He began with an "image" and "psychological" analysis of Gongadze as a journalist by the political scientist Mykhaylo Pohrebynsky, the director of his Kyiv Center of Political Research and Conflict Studies. If the intention was obtain an independent opinion, then the wrong person was selected, as Pohrebynsky's image is that of an apologist for Kuchma.

Pohrebynsky analyzed Gongadze's journalism as having "the deficiencies associated with all Ukrainian journalists of writing in support of some political power and evaluating events from the viewpoint of that political power". Precisely the criticism that is made of Pohrebynsky.

Potebenko also quoted the national security and defense secretary, Yevhen Marchuk, as saying that Gongadze's journalism did not pose any danger to politicians. The chief prosecutor probably quoted Marchuk in order to counter the view that his dislike of an article caused the benefactor "Petrovych" to withdraw financial support from pravda.com.ua.

The prosecutor also said that the president had no motive to get rid of Gongadze because other journalists wrote articles that were more critical. This statement clearly showed that the Potebenko was not acting as Ukraine's chief prosecutor, but as Kuchma's chief defender.

Potebenko presented the long-awaited DNA test results, which were carried out in Moscow because Ukraine did not have the necessary equipment. The test, he said, had been carried out between December 12, 2000, and January 5, 2001 at the Russian Federation Health Ministry by Dr Pavel Ivanov.

The prosecutor general said that the test of the corpse's DNA when compared with that of Gongadze's mother concluded there was a 99.6 percent chance that the corpse was Gongadze's. This probability, Potebenko said, was not enough to say with certainty that the corpse was Gongadze's, as there was possibility the corpse was the son of four other mothers (four out of 1,000 mothers or 0.4 per cent).

This small uncertainty gave Potebenko the opportunity to argue that Gongadze was still alive, based on evidence that had huge uncertainties. He listed a number of witnesses who claimed they saw Gongadze after his disappearance. "Two employees of a organization that Gongadze visited often" saw him the day after he disappeared, said Potebenko. "They declared, and then confirmed from a photograph that on September 17, between eight and nine in the evening, they saw Gongadze."

This so-called "organization" was Eric's Bar in Kyiv's city center. Potebenko purposely avoided mentioning that two journalists –

Vyacheslav Pikhovshek and Katya Gorchinskaya – who knew Gongadze well and were at Eric's at the time, did not see him there.

As to the authenticity of the excerpts of recordings presented by Moroz to parliament, Potebenko said that experts had found them to be fakes. He said the Kyiv Scientific-Research Institute of Court Experts had tested the recordings and found that the excerpts used by Moroz were not originals but copies. The institute found that the recordings had been manipulated, with deletions and additions of "phrases, words, fragments of words, and sounds". Because of these manipulations and the low quality of the recordings, the experts said they could not compare the voices on the recordings with voice samples of the accused – Kuchma, Kravchenko, Lytvyn and Derkach.

This was a surprising thing to say, as the voices of these individuals are clearly heard on some of the recordings involving Gongadze. As for the manipulations, it was obvious that Moroz's collection were carefully selected excerpts, like a collection of quotations. What needed to be tested were not the excerpts presented by Moroz but the recordings which the excerpts were taken from. From the five known tests on the recordings, only Potebenko's tests concluded that additions were made to the recordings. Potebenko didn't provide any laboratory reports for these conclusion, like which words were added or deleted.

The tragicomedy was that he had interviewed the accused – the president, the interior minister, head of president's office, the head of the tax office and the state security service chief – and they all had had denied any wrongdoing. This was an unconvincing attempt by Potebenko to show his impartiality. He only forgot to interview himself, as on one of the recordings the head of the tax office, Azarov, told Kuchma that he was corrupt and protecting the prosecutor of Dnipropetrovsk who was involved in large-scale protection racket.

Melnychenko could not have recorded from under the sofa, as tests by experts with a recorder placed under the sofa showed, Potebenko told parliament. In addition, he reported the head and deputy head of the president's guard service as stating that it would have been impossible for Melnychenko to make recordings as the president's office was regularly checked for listening devices.

(Later this statement was contradicted by one of Potebenko's deputies, Oleksiy Bahanets who was put in charge of the Gongadze case. He told Rostislav Khotyn of the BBC Ukrainian service on February 9, 2001, that Melnychenko had recorded in the president's office. Also, Bahanets' was asked by the interviewer Tom Mangold in the BBC TV documentary "Killing the Story" the following question: "If an independent analysis of the tapes establishes that the conversations took place which amounted to a criminal conspiracy, will you take action? "Even if the recordings were made inside the president's office, this was an illegal act which means that they cannot be used to charge an individual with a criminal act", answered Bahanets with stupid righteousness.)

Potebenko tried to undermine Gongadze's letter to him complaining of being followed and threatened. He cited Kyiv's deputy police chief, Petro Opanasenko, as saying that he could not confirm Gongadze's claims. Opanasenko had also denied that Interior Minister Yuriy Kravchenko had put pressure on him not to investigate Gongadze's complaint.

The prosecutor general rubbished the testimony of Radio Continent director Serhiy Sholokh about the police officer – Oleksiy Bahrov or Badrov – who had told him that Gongadze and Alaniya participated in a gangland style execution of Chechens in Odesa. Potebenko said no such police officer could be found.

In conclusion, Potebenko said that the Melnychenko recordings used by Moroz could not be used as evidence as they were fabrications, and concluded that the accused had nothing to answer for as Gongadze was alive and in hiding.

Potebenko had left out of his report any mention of the Podolsky and Yelyashkevych incidents. It he wanted to test the recordings by comparing them with actual events, he did not have to look much further than these two events.

The exposure of Potebenko's cover-up

Moroz responded to Potebenko's report with the icy remark "it confirms that the prosecution is doing everything to hide the real reasons for the disappearance of Georgi Gongadze". Another presidential opponent, Oleksandr Yelyashkevych, said he was shocked by Potebenko's attack on Georgi's friends for attempting to discover what had happened to him.

In contrast, the head of parliament's Gongadze committee – soon to become the justice minister – Oleksandr Lavrynovych, described the prosecutor's presentation "as an unprecedented example of making public a massive amount of information which is part of the investigation". This, he said, showed "how responsible are the people who are working on this case".

The communist leader's response carried weight because his party, with a quarter of the MPs in parliament, could had, with the president's opponents, voted for Potebenko's dismissal. Petro Symonenko said he welcomed Potebenko's report as well-balanced and professional.

However, Potebenko's main thesis in his report that Gongadze was alive and on the run was soon demolished by Pavel Ivanov of the Russian Health Ministry, the person who was carrying out the DNA tests for Potebenko. On February 17, in an interview with the Russian TV company, NTV, scheduled for broadcast on February 22, Ivanov said his second DNA test had shown a 99.9 percent certainty that bones tested belonged to Gongadze. He added that the Ukrainian authorities had taken no interest in this news, but he didn't say when he had informed Potebenko of his findings.

Potebenko was keeping this news a secret, as on February 22 parliament was scheduled to vote on a resolution calling for his dismissal. Thanks to the support from the communists, the resolution failed misarably.

On the evening of February 22, the NTV program with Ivanov was broadcast. It news had the potential to cause a great scandal. But nothing happened as the mass media simply ignored it. The next day, at a press conference, the deputy prosecutor general, Bahanets, said that he was not excited about the 99.9 percent result, as the corpse could be that of Gongadze's brother, his mother's brother or a relative. Many journalists thought that this was a very stupid remark, which it clearly was. However, what they didn't realize was that Bahanets was making a sick joke aimed at Gongadze's mother. He had suggested the Tarashcha corpse might belong to her other twin son who was stolen from a Tbilisi hospital 31 years earlier.

Finally on February 26, 2001, the prosecutor's office declared that the pile of bones in their possession was Georgi Gongadze's. This was weeks after they were told about the results, more than three months after the Tarashcha corpse was discovered and the local police and coroner thought it was Gongadze's. Despite the official decision, there will be another attempt to claim that Gongadze was alive.

To save face, the day after the second Russian test became public, President Kuchma announced that another DNA test would be carried out, this time by the FBI. Their agents, along with William C. Rodriguez III, Chief Deputy Medical Examiner of Special Investigations at the US Armed Forces Institute of Pathology, came to Kyiv on March 6 and April 26, to conduct their tests.

They began by assembling the bones into a skeleton, and found they belonged to one individual. After comparing the bones to the X-ray pictures provided by Gongadze's mother, they found them to be the same, as were the injuries received on the bones from shrapnel he received in the war in Abkhazia.

DNA spot checks on the various parts of the skeleton showed that it was from the same person. The comparison of the skeleton's DNA to that of Gongadze's mother showed that both were the same. In addition, the DNA of Gongadze's twin girls showed that the skeleton was the remains of their father (see the statement from the pathologist Rodriguez in Appendix 2).

The FBI tests left no doubt that the bones held by Ukraine's authorities belonged to Georgi Gongadze. Once again the authorities had been shown to be incompetent in their cover-up.

Just as there was some clarity on Gongadze's disappearance, another DNA test concluded that the Tarashcha corpse was not Gongadze's. This conclusion came from one of the president's strongest critics, the MP and secretary of the parliamentary committee investigating

Gongadze's disappearance, Serhiy Holovaty.

On March 20, 2001, he presented a DNA test result by the German laboratory Genedia that showed that corpse discovered in Tarashcha was not Gongadze's. The laboratory had compared the DNA of tissue given to Holovaty with Gongadze's mother's blood, and a drop of dry blood on Gongadze's medical card.

Genedia had tested tissue taken by Gongadze's friends from the Tarashcha morgue on November 15. The Tarashcha coroner had given Lavrenti Malazoni tissue left after he severed the corpse's hand to X-ray it for shrapnel. In Kyiv, Malazoni gave it to Olena Prytula who kept it for over a month in her freezer. She handed it over on December 26 to Dr Valeriy Ivasyuk, the medical expert for the parliament's committee, who gave it to Holovaty to take to Germany for the DNA test.

There might be a number of explanations why the German test showed a negative result. The tissue could have become cross-contaminated as it was not professionally stored. It could even have been exchanged, when it was kept either by Malazoni or Prytula. For example, it was known that Prytula was keeping the tissue in her freezer.

There is the possibility that the Tarashcha corpse was not Gongadze's. But this raises the question where did the bones come from for the Russian and American tests, which definitively belonged to Gongadze.

Both Holovaty and Ivasyuk have called for another DNA test on the tissue and the bones, which the government has steadfastly refused. It transpired that another test could be made on the original tissue, as Ivasyuk had kept a section of it. Whatever the truth of the German test – and it is the weakest of the three DNA tests – the Russian and American DNA tests showed that Gongadze was dead. If, the German test proves that the tissue doesn't belong to Gongadze, then there will be two murders to solve – Gongadze's and that of the headless corpse in Tarashcha.

23

Attacks on the opposition

President Kuchma reacted to the charges made against him by Moroz and Melnychenko by accusing the opposition of wanting to take political power by undemocratic and violent means. To reinforce this image of his opponents, his subordinates designed events to create in the public's mind the image of the opposition as anarchic, violent, unpatriotic and corrupt. While some subordinates were using propaganda, others resorted to one of the more traditional methods of dealing with the president's opponents – violence.

On January 26, 2001, a Zil – a heavy Soviet-style limousine – intentionally attempted to smash into a car driven by the director of Radio Continent, Serhiy Sholokh – who was a close professional colleague of Gongadze's. He managed to avoid a serious collusion. The event was similar to the October 1999 attempt on his life. This latest attempt was followed by an an anonymous telephone on January 30. The caller warned him he was receiving "the final Chinese warning", unless he stopped the critical broadcasts on his radio station. It then was succeeded by a series of threats and harassments against him and his family. Sholokh wrote a complaint to Prosecutor General Potebenko, but, like Gongadze, didn't receive a reply.

But, unlike the previous "accident", he discovered who was behind it. On February 10, he learned through that it was Police Col-General Edward Vadimovych Fere, the administrator of the national office of the interior ministry. His informer told him what Fere had said: "We had warned this Jew Sholokh, but he isn't listening. He was friends with that Georgian – we will put him through the Georgian variation, but this time, quietly without any publicity".

Sholokh remarked that it was odd for Fere to make this anti-Semitic remark against him, as he wasn't Jewish but that Fere probably was.

On February 12, Sholokh delivered to the state security service a letter protesting about Fere's threats. To his surprise, its new chief, Volodymyr Radchenko (Leonid Derkach had been dismissed on February 10) called him in on the same day to discuss the complaint. What action Radchenko took was not known, but following the meeting the death threats ceased. But Fere and the others who took part in this attempt on Sholokh's life haven't been brought to justice.

Other criminal accusations have been made against Fere. He has been accused – along with other senior officials of the interior ministry, including Police Lieutenant-General Yuriy Dagayev, who become President Kuchma's senior security adviser – by an American-Ukrainian businessman Borys Mostovyi of extorting over $700,000 from him, in the form of cars, holidays, furnishings and apartments. In return for the bribes, they promised Mostovyi a big state contract that never materialized (Petro Lyutyi, "Corruption in Kuchma's administration and Interior Ministry", pravda.com.ua, Feb. 18, 2002).

The extortions occurred before 1999, when Dagayev headed the interior ministry's notoriously corrupt traffic police – the State Auto-Inspection Office (DAI or Derzhavna Avto-Inspektsiya). Ukraine's public perceives DAI as the most corrupt government institution in the country.

In 1999, Kuchma appointed Dagayev director of the state office for presidential affairs. What this office does is a topic for speculation. "We have come across information concerning the activities of the president's close entourage, in particular, the then minister of interior affairs Kravchenko, Yuriy Dagayev, Fere and other persons from the president's inner circle," said the head of parliament's Gongadze committee, Oleksandr Zhyr in March of 2002. The suspicion is that this trio have been the organizers of numerous special operations against Kuchma's opponents, involving beatings, car accidents, kidnappings, assassinations, and grenade-throwing, as well as provocations against demonstrators.

The February 6 police provocation

On January 30, 2001, the opposition began a second wave of protests. A new tent camp was set up on the capital's main thoroughfare, Khreshchatyk. The nearby Independence Square, where the previous tent city had stood, was now fenced off for a major rebuilding project to mark the 10th anniversary of Ukraine's statehood on August 24.

To mark the opening of a new parliamentary session on February 6, opponents organized a "Ukraine without Kuchma" rally in Kyiv's city center. The interior ministry took advantage of the occasion to carry out a provocation with the aim of discrediting the opposition as creators of mob violence and chaos. The president would follow with a statement to the nation, signed also by the prime minister and speaker of parliament, calling the opposition Ukrainian Nazis.

As five thousand demonstrators were away from Khreshchatyk, first marching to the parliament building and then to the president's office, the police staged an attack on the tent city. At about 3 pm, about 300 "anarchists" appeared to confront the few protesters left behind with the tents. Peculiarly for "anarchists", who pride themselves on individuality, they held identical black flags and wore identical arm and head bands with the word Anarchist printed on them. From among these uniformed anarchists emerged about 30 young thugs who knocked down the tents and beat up anyone who got in their way.

This spectacle was watched by dozens of plain-clothes policemen standing alongside the many passers-by on Khreshchatyk. The uniformed policemen, who were so noticeable minutes before, had conveniently disappeared for the duration of the anarchist attack.

The young thugs left, after violently beating a number of protesters, leaving the "anarchists" – mostly impoverished polytechnic students rented by the police at 30 hryvnya (about $6) each – not knowing what to do. As if on cue, appeared the Stepan Bandera Trident brigade, allegedly sponsored by the state security service, to confront their "leftwing" adversaries. The "anarchists" fled in panic to the nearby Ivan Franko Square where they had come from. In the square, riot police sat in parked cars looking indifferently at the panic stricken students, who returned their identical flags, arm and head bands, and went back to their student hostels. All this was witnessed by two American journalists who interviewed a few of the "anarchists".

The mass media abetted this disgraceful provocation, which was intended to turn the tide of public opinion against the president's opponents. State and private TV and radio stations and newspapers lashed out at the opposition for bringing anarchy to the streets of the capital. Newspapers showed pictures of fighting between "anarchists" and right wing paramilitaries. The headline of the newspaper *Kievskie Vedomosti* on February 7 screamed "A bloody match over Ukraine" and asked if this wasn't the beginning of civil war, "like the fighting between nationalists and Bolsheviks in 1917-18". Top interior ministry officials told the press how the police sustained injuries in heroic attempts to halt the violence.

There was more fighting that day. Later in the day, a minor skirmish took place between UNA-UNSD, and the Left Solidarity and All-Ukrainian Union of Workers. Shield of the Fatherland attacked a camera crew from the TV channel Inter.

At five o'clock in the evening, as the opposition rally began on Khreshchatyk, the Bandera Trident brigade reportedly roughed-up a group of communist party demonstrators. This attack gave the communist leader Petro Symonenko the excuse he needed to break with the president's opponents and join the president's side – at least until the next parliamentary elections. February 6 was a bad day for the opposition, as the fights and propaganda badly tarnished its image among the general public.

Tymoshenko arrested

While violence was used against his opponents, Kuchma's most significant successes against his opponents were political. He and his advisers found a ways to discredit his opponents before the public and put them on the defensive. In some ways it was easy. The opposition lacked organization, leadership, cohesion, and the strategy to become a

Feb. 6, 2001 – "Anarchists" attacking tent city protesters in Kyiv
(Photo by Dmytro Havrysh / UNIAN)

formidable political force to challenge Kuchma. In the first instance, its disunity was not surprising as it consisted of various competing ideological groups. It had right wingers like the anti-communist Rukh MPs, and former communists like the socialists led by Moroz. For a time it even included the communists. These ideological divisions favored Kuchma as he could play one side against the other. At first it seemed that President Kuchma made a political mistake when he had the deputy prime minister, Yuliya Tymoshenko, dismissed. It gave rise to the possibility that at last the disunited opposition could have a leader in common.

On January 5, 2001, after almost a year of threatening Tymoshenko, the prosecutor general's office charged her with two crimes – illegally importing natural gas in 1996 and falsifying financial documents. On January 19, Prime Minister Yushchenko, fearing maybe for his own job, dismissed his favorite ally in the cabinet.

Tymoshenko wasted no time in joining and leading the opposition. On February 9, she launched the Forum for National Salvation – a political umbrella for the president's opponents across the political spectrum. It set itself the target of mobilizing public opinion to force Kuchma out of office with demonstrations. These acts ensured that within days the president would take his revenge on her.

Tymoshenko had the potential to lead a bunch of disunited groups. She had political stature, guts, organizational capabilities and even looks. But above all she had the money to launch a large-scale propaganda campaign to bring Kuchma down.

The problem with Tymoshenko was that she was a poacher turned gamekeeper. She, too, was an oligarch, becoming rich and powerful through corruption. Tymoshenko was vulnerable to the same charges the opposition hurled against the president and his stable of oligarchs. She had accumulated millions of dollars from illegal energy trading under the political "roof" of the once powerful Pavlo Lazarenko, who was waiting in an American jail for his trial.

Yushchenko explained why he selected her as his deputy in December 1999. "Fight fire with fire", she had "repented" for her sins as an oligarch and was ready "to serve Ukraine honestly and sincerely" (*Ukrayina Moloda*, January 26, 2000). As deputy prime minister, Tymoshenko did bring law and order to the energy sector. By the end of 2000, she had drastically cut the "free energy" supplies to some of the most powerful oligarchs, causing them financial pain. The Social-Democratic Party oligarch Hryhoriy Surkis was said to have received a few hundred million less from the seven oblast electricity distributors he owned. The president's favorite oligarch, Oleksandr Volkov, had to buy state produced oil and gas at auctions, instead of receiving it at special discounts. She claimed her new regime contributed 3 billion hryvnya, or about $600 million, to the state treasury in 2000, not a small amount for the cash starved Ukrainian budget. This did not win favor with the president, who depended on keeping his stable of oligarchs happy, and if Melnychenko was to be believed, on their contributions to his private overseas accounts which now total over two billion dollars.

The president, in his sadistic political style, began preparing a crim-inal case against Tymoshenko soon after he had approved her appoint-ment as deputy prime minister. On February 10, 2000, according to a Melnychenko recording, the head of the tax office, Mykola Azarov, reported to the president that her banker, Borys Feldman, the chair-man of the Slovyansky bank, had refused to provide evidence against Tymoshenko as well as Lazarenko. Kuchma responded by ordering Feldman's arrest. On March 13, 2000, the tax police arrested Feldman as well as most of the bank's management and seized the bank's records, causing panic among customers. In this way Ukraine's most profitable bank was destroyed, putting many of its depositors out of pocket. The bank's elimination took place because the president pun-ished Feldman for not cooperating against Tymoshenko.

In prison, Feldman continued to refuse to cooperate. On May 24, Azarov complained to Kuchma that Feldman "during interrogations he keeps absolute silence. They won't give evidence against Yuliya ... ." In reply, Kuchma suggested that he be "placed among criminals ..." to make him talk. These actions by Kuchma say a lot about the arbitrary rule of law in Ukraine.

Feldman would pay a heavy price for his silence. On April 19, 2002, a Luhansk city court sentenced the 44 year-old banker to nine years imprisonment, confiscation of all his property and forbade him to work in banking for three years after his release. To add insult to injury, the judge ruled that Feldman could not make a final statement to the court because it might be political.

In the May 24 conversation, Azarov presented Kuchma with spying reports including on government officials in other ministries. He showed him a report on a meeting between interior minister Kravchenko's master spy, Kholondovych, and a representative of Feldman's. Azarov asked the president not to tell Kravchenko that his spies were spying on his head of surveillance.

It has been suggested that there was an ulterior motive behind Azarov's desire to have Feldman arrested. It would, as it did, destroy Slovyansky Bank – up to then the most profitable Ukrainian bank.

The head of the tax office, as a leading member of the financially powerful Donetsk clan, wanted to take over Slovyansky Bank's share of the Makiyivka metallurgy plant, one of the largest steel plants in Europe, located in Donetsk region.

Azarov's tax police also spied on leading officials of the prosecutor general's office. He reported at length on the corrupt activities of the Dnipropetrovsk prosecutor, Volodymyr Shuba. He accused him of taking bribes, up to $80,000 per month, from alcohol producers in return for covering up their tax avoidance schemes.

He also accused Shuba along with officials in the prosecutor general's office in Kyiv of having taken $200,000 for dropping a case against a ship caught at the beginning of May 1999 carrying 2,800 tonnes of untaxed metal. Azarov told Kuchma that the reason Shuba was able to get away with his criminal activities was that he had "some informal and very serious relations with [the prosecutor general]Mykhaylo Oleksiyovych Potebenko". Here Azarov was accusing Kuchma's top law official of participating in corruption.

Azarov wasn't shy of promoting himself to Kuchma. He claimed on May 24 that the increase in the state revenue was due not to the efforts of prime minister Yushchenko and his deputy Tymoshenko, but to him. This elicited a strange response from Kuchma. He ordered Azarov to prepare a criminal case against Tymoshenko, and said:

[Kuchma] Yuliya must be destroyed.

[Azarov] We are working on Yuliya. I have issued an order, she is not such a fool, she –

[Kuchma] We need a criminal case against her and to put her ass in prison.

(*Grani*, May 24, 2001)

Though Kuchma spied on all his ministers, he took a great interest in reports on Tymoshenko. On June 12, his spy chief, Leonid Derkach, presented him with telephone and mobile phone intercepts showing her close relationship with the president's noted critic, his chief accuser of corruption, Hryhoriy Omelchenko. Kuchma enjoyed putting pressure on Tymoshenko. He had her husband, Oleksandr, arrested on August 18, 2000, supposedly for tax avoidance, while she was deputy prime minister. He had the police interview her sixteen year-old daughter. Later the charges against her husband were dropped, and he was released.

The street fights on February 6 gave Kuchma the excuse to go on the offensive. On February 13, he had Yuliya Tymoshenko arrested and incarcerated in Kyiv's Lukyanivska prison. On the same day, Kuchma issued an extraordinary declaration also signed by the prime minister and speaker of parliament. It condemned the opposition as Ukrainian style fascists. The simultaneous arrest of its most dynamic leader, the declaration and the propaganda barrage caused confusion and disarray in the ranks of the opposition. The right-wingers in the opposition were at a loss, as they had looked to Yushchenko as their leader and Kuchma's replacement.

The declaration could serve as a textbook example of how to turn opponents' accusations against them. "Dirty techniques are not rare in the current world, which is characterized by tough methods of political struggle. But even against such a background, the current events in Ukraine stand out by their cynicism and disrespect for moral norms: discrediting state officials, politicians and political forces, blackmailing the state organs and manipulation of public opinion", the statement said.

The statement labeled the opposition – which included over 100 MPs across the political spectrum – as Nazis. "It is enough to simply take a closer look at their symbols and slogans, the attributes they use in the theatrical political shows in order to see that we are facing a Ukrainian kind of National Socialism."

It also accused the opposition of being used by unnamed plotters engaged in "a psychological war" against Ukraine. "Ukraine and the world will eventually know the names of those who ordered, masterminded and carried out – the moving forces – of this provocation."

As for Gongadze, the statement attacked the opposition for not being interested in what actually happened to him but only in political power – "instigating an atmosphere of hysteria and psychosis, hoping to put out of balance the legitimate state institutions and to get to power at any cost".

It accused it of attempting to create civil war by instigating "street elements", using "blatant provocations ... to deepen the split in society and push the authorities to the use of force", and to "create a real threat to the national security of the state ... We should not forget the lessons of history. You will recall how fascism started". The statement ended by warning the opposition that the state would use force to stop "anarchy, arbitrary action and unlawfulness".

Kuchma, by getting Yushchenko's and Plyushch's signatures under the declaration, and having Tymoshenko arrested at the same time, had politically outmaneuvered his opponents, not for the first and last time. But why did Plyushch sign it? He told reporters that he had signed it without even reading it. Thought he meant it as a joke, he was willing to do or sign anything the president placed before him. As for Yushchenko, he said he had signed it because he was the president's prime minister. What this meant wasn't clear. He would have done much better if he had resigned. Kuchma showed him the door only a few weeks later, when parliament forced him out of office.

The right-wing opposition was stunned by Yushchenko's actions. The Rukh MP and deputy leader of the Forum for National Salvation, Taras Chornovil called them "shameful". He predicted that Yushchenko had "no chance to lead the national-democratic movement". (A year later, Taras Chornovil joined Yushchenko in a coalition for the March 2002 parliamentary elections, and after the elections, Yushchenko and Symonenko joined Tymoshenko and Moroz in a coalition against Kuchma.)

With the opposition in disarray, prosecutor general Potebenko, as mentioned before, survived a no-confidence motion in parliament on February 22 for his investigation into Gongadze's disappearance. This was despite the fact that the Russian Health Ministry had confirmed that the Tarashcha corpse was Gongadze's. Potebenko survived the exposure of his cover-up that Gongadze was alive and on the run – thanks to an ineffective opposition, a controlled mass media, and the communist party which came out against his dismissal.

24

The March 9 debacle

While imprisoning opponents and calling them Nazis at home, President Kuchma presented his better side in an interview published in London's *Financial Times* on February 10, 2001. "About Gongadze. I can swear on the bible or on the constitution that I never made such an order to destroy a human being. This is simply absurd. Maybe the name Gongadze came up in conversations, I don't remember. But I give you my honest word, I did not even know this journalist."

The Melnychenko recordings had been faked using "some kind of super-apparatus", the president told the *FT* correspondent Charles Clover. Asked which secret service had faked the recordings, Kuchma denied he had ever accused a foreign secret service. "I completely reject the idea that this was done on the level of states, that it was the Americans or the Russians. Though one cannot rule out some sort of civil institutions from these countries are at work." What foreign "civil institutions" Kuchma had in mind, he did not say. On December 1, 2000, Kuchma, speaking in Belarus at a summit of CIS presidents, had accused a foreign secret service of creating the recordings.

On February 27, 2001 the *FT* published a letter from Kuchma in which he again declared his innocence. He portrayed himself as doing everything possible to solve the Gongadze case – citing as examples his invitations to the Russian Health Ministry and the FBI to conduct DNA tests. He also said he was cooperating with the Paris based Reporters Sans Frontieres (RSF). He mentioned that he had recently replaced the head of the state security service, Leonid Derkach, suggesting that he got rid of him for not solving the Gongadze case.

His letter emphasized his belief in democracy and a free press. "Above all, I want to reiterate emphatically my commitment to a free and open democracy in Ukraine and to protecting freedom and safety of the press, which is an essential element to any democracy."

Kuchma's often-repeated assertion about "democracy and free press" stands in sharp contrast to a report by RSF only a few weeks earlier. On January 22, it produced a damning report on his government, called "Ukraine: Mutilation of the truth". "RSF denounces the serious shortcomings in the way in which the Ukrainian judicial authorities have conducted the inquiry into the murder of Georgi Gongadze. The organization considers, in particular, that the state prosecutor of Ukraine has conducted his investigations with the sole aim of clearing the name of the political authorities from any responsibility in this affair."

In the *FT* letter, Kuchma added a new spin on whether he knew Gongadze before his disappearance. "I was not acquainted with Mr. Gongadze but was certainly aware of the articles he wrote criticizing my policies", he said. In the earlier *FT* interview he had said he discovered who Gongadze after he had disappeared.

In his letter, Kuchma made the very questionable claim that: "From the very start, I publicly called for forensic analysis of the remains and investigation of the circumstances of Mr Gongadze's disappearance. This includes utilizing foreign experts and special services in order to find the truth."

Everything in Kuchma's letter was an offense to the facts. At first his subordinates attempted to bury the corpse They delayed the DNA test as long as possible, and then didn't report the Russian DNA test when it concluded that the corpse was Gongadze's.

The day after President Kuchma's letter, the *FT* published a letter from a close observer of Ukraine – the BBC journalist Stephen Dalziel. He brought up the uncomfortable fact that the Ukrainian authorities had taken repressive actions against the Tarashcha coroner Ihor Vorotyntsev for concluding the corpse was Gongadze's.

It was left to one of the world's great financial speculators and philanthropists to clearly state how the West should respond to Kuchma. In a letter to the *FT* on March 2, George Soros did not mince his words: "The west must take a clear position, denouncing Mr Kuchma's behavior and actions. There is no way for the international community to continue to do business with Mr Kuchma until an impartial investigation [into Gongadze's murder] has been completed and those responsible are held to account. The population needs to know that the west stands with them, opposing any attempt by Mr Kuchma to evade responsibility and, ultimately, the law."

The president continued proclaiming his innocence in a whirlwind of interviews. On February 19, he appeared on Russia's RTR TV channel to state his willingness to swear on the Bible and the constitution that he did not give orders to destroy Gongadze. On February 21, he took questions from telephone callers organized by the newspaper *Fakty* (the largest newspaper in Ukraine, owned by his son-in-law Viktor Pinchuk), and made similar statements.

He took his case to an international audience and attacked the opposition as a reactionary force. On February 23, he told CNN that the opposition was "half-fascist" and "anti-Semitic". (This was a bit rich coming from someone who could be heard repeatedly on the Melnychenko recordings making anti-Semitic remarks, whether against the oligarchs Brodsky or Surkis, or bankers like Feldman or oppositional MPs like Oleksandr Yelyashkevych. Probably the only surprise was that he was not heard making anti-Semitic remarks against his son-in-law, Viktor Pinchuk.)

Along with the tent city protest in the center of the capital, the opposition staged colorful but ineffectual mock trials of President Kuchma across Ukraine. At the February 25th rally in Kyiv, five thousand people watched as a "national tribunal" found Kuchma guilty and sentenced him to a "Soviet special psychiatric hospital for examination" – the type of hospital that Soviet dissidents used to be incarcerated in.

These mock trials could not compete with the president's exposure in the mass media. For example, on the same day as the Kyiv mock trial, ICTV (Viktor Pinchuk's TV station) had the president fielding questions from the public across Ukraine via a satellite connection, in which Kuchma again accused the opposition of being financed by "dirty money" and of being Nazi.

Action against the tent city

On Thursday, March 1, the authorities suddenly closed down the month-long tent protest camp along the capital's Khreshchatyk street – what had became known as "The Kuchma-Free Zone". At 9 am, at the height of the rush hour, the police blocked all the traffic. About 400 police, led by court officials holding an eviction notice, expelled the more than 100 campers from the tent city on the pavement. Behind the police came sanitation workers and garbage trucks sweeping the pavement and removing the tents, belongings and assorted placards. The police arrested 44 protesters who resisted, among them 25 UNA-UNSD paramilitaries. Within twenty minutes all traces of the tent city protest had disappeared. Forty-five minutes after the police action began, traffic resumed along Khreshchatyk.

In the face of armed state power, all that "Ukraine without Kuchma" and the "Forum for National Salvation" could do was to issue statements. It seemed that even popular support had evaporated. Only about 50 people appeared later in the day on Khreshchatyk to protest against the police action, heavily outnumbered by plain-clothes police.

The president's totalitarian side reappeared again on March 6. He threatened to sack any government official or civil servant who supported his opponents. "I invite every state servant, starting with ministers, who take communion, sympathize – not to speak of act – with opposition formations, in the course of a week, to decide: either they resign from their jobs in state organs, or publicly dissociate themselves from anti-state formations," Kuchma told a conference of central government and local officials. This was the Kuchma heard on the Melnychenko recordings calling for the punishment of all officials who did not support him.

The pro-Kuchma media speculated that the threat against unfaithful politicians was aimed at Prime Minister Yushchenko. His office rejected this suggestion. Yushchenko's press secretary, Nataliya Zarudna, said that the prime minister and his cabinet were not involved in politics. This was somewhat of an understatement.

Yushchenko was making contradictory statements on the Gongadze affair. On February 13, he had co-signed President Kuchma's statement calling his opponents Nazis, and not protested at the arrest of his former deputy, Tymoshenko. On the other hand, in interviews he did not back the president or the opposition, and instead took a centrist view. On February 26, he told Radio Liberty's Russian Service that the tent protesters were in the streets "because they want answers, which is quite reasonable, what has happened, why is there such a history with a journalist, and other questions that demand answers which are not forthcoming"…"These people asked questions, and I think the problem is not in the people who ask them, but who allowed these questions to appear, why do these questions surface in society."

Yushchenko also told Radio Liberty that it wasn't necessary to arrest his former deputy prime minister, Yuliya Tymoshenko, and praised her good work in the cabinet. In contrast, President Kuchma told the conference of central government and local officials on March 6, that her reforms in the energy sector were "cosmetic", "demagogic" and "useless".

Another example of Yushchenko's divergence with the president was over the Melnychenko recordings. On February 28, Austrian TV recorded him as saying that foreign agencies were not involved in the recordings. He would not commit himself on whether the recordings were genuine or not. In his opinion, it was not possible to investigate the recordings because Ukraine did not have the mechanisms to deal with such a crisis. He again came out in defense of Yuliya Tymoshenko. He accused unspecified people in Ukraine of treating gas, oil, and electricity as a "free resource", and said they were now complaining about him and his cabinet. Yushchenko came perilously close to denouncing Kuchma for imprisoning his former deputy and to saying the recordings might be genuine.

Yushchenko foreign interviews were designed to show that he was his own man. Maybe the media speculations were right that he wasn't loyal to Kuchma. However, Yushchenko would not resign as prime minister, and would instead be pushed out.

March 9, 2001 - President Kuchma flanked by prime minister Yushchenko
and deputy speaker Medvedchuk at Shevchenko park (UNIAN)

The March 9 demonstration

On March 9, 2001, a demonstration took place that finished the
opposition as a political entity – at least until the March 2002 parliamentary elections. It was a re-run of the February 9, 2001 street
brawls, except on a much greater scale, and followed by an even more
virulent media attack.

The opposition decided to use an annual event to confront
Kuchma. Every year, on March 9, the president along with the country's top officials marks the birth in 1814 of Ukraine's most famous
bard, Taras Shevchenko. The revolutionary poet is an unusual figure in
Ukraine as both the left and right claim him as their own.

Opposition MPs decided they would not allow the "politically
soiled" president to lay flowers at the Shevchenko statue located at the
park bearing his name in central Kyiv. Normally, the annual
Shevchenko wreath-laying ceremony by the president goes unnoticed.

Demonstrators began gathered at the Taras Shevchenko park in the early hours to prevent a presidential tribute from taking place. Before the official 9 am ceremony, a few thousand strong police force cleared the park of protesters. Present on the occasion were the Interior Minister Yuriy Kravchenko along with the Kyiv police chief Yuriy Smirnov.

After the park was cleared, a cordon of uniformed police with shields and batons encircled it, while hundreds of plain clothes police filled it as spectators for the official ceremony. An attempt by opposition MPs to exercise their legal right to enter any place in Ukraine was met with violence. A policeman hit the socialist deputy Valentyna Semenyuk so hard that she required hospitalization for skull injuries. A Reuters' cameraman caught the moment of the attack on her with the Kyiv police chief Smirnov standing not far from the incident.

At 8:30 am, while crowds of demonstrators attempted to break through the police cordon, the president, accompanied by Prime Minister Yushchenko and the deputy speaker, Viktor Medvedchuk, as well as many other leading politicians and personalities, laid flowers at the Shevchenko monument. After a brief ceremony the president left

March 9, 2001 – Demonstrators attempt to break through police lines at Shevchenko park in Kyiv (Photo by Dmytro Havrych / UNIAN)

March 9, 2001 – Demonstrators march towards the president's office
(Photo by Oleksandra Synytsi / UNIAN)

the park, as large-scale fighting erupted between a crowd led by UNA-UNSD and the police. After making a few dozen arrests, the police also left the park. Demonstrators led by the MP and coordinator of the Forum of National Salvation, Taras Chornovil, rushed to the monument to remove the flowers placed by the president. The state TV cameras would later show how the son of the famous nationalist leader Chornovil had "desecrated and vandalized" Shevchenko by picking up bouquets of flowers (left by the president) and throwing them away.

The opposition spent the next few hours holding a rally in the park with speakers of every political persuasion addressing the crowd, while a large crowd marched to Kyiv's central police station, surrounded it and successfully forced the police to free those arrested in the morning scuffles. Among the demonstrators there was a noticeable presence of a few thousand young angry males looking for a fight with the police if the occasion presented itself, as it soon would.

After one o'clock as many as 15,000 demonstrators marched towards the president's office, where six rows of helmeted police stood, shields and batons at the ready, backed up by interior ministry troops. Taras Chornovil recalled that at 3 pm, he was in the first column that approached the metal fences the police had placed in front of them. He said that along with other MPs, he stood between the police and the demonstrators to prevent any confrontation. After the front row of demonstrators had shouted their slogans and were about to move off, about fifteen unknown individuals suddenly appeared and began pulling down the metal fences and attacking the police. In the chaos it was not possible to identify these unknown individuals, but it would not be surprising if the police had created another provocation as they did on February 6. But the paramilitaries also did joined the violent attack on the police cordon. Attempts by the leaders of "Ukraine without Kuchma" – Volodymyr Chemerys and Yuriy Lyutsenko – to stop the fighting proved useless.

For the pro-Kuchma mass media the violent scenes captured by TV cameras proved to be even better propaganda to attack the opposition with than the February 9 "anarchist" incident. For weeks afterwards, TV stations relentlessly played back images of demonstrators violently

March 9, 2001 – Demonstrators attack the police
guarding the president's office (Photo Oleksandra Synytsi / UNIAN)

attacking the police with everything they could find, including metal railings, bricks and iron bars.

After the police had pushed the demonstrators back from the president's office, the police went on the rampage against groups of demonstrators across the city. At about 6 pm, the MPs Taras Chornovil and Taras Stetskiv received calls on their mobile telephones that police were violently attacking demonstrators at the main railway station. On arrival, they found that the police had indiscriminately beaten about 300 people and herded them onto buses and police vans. Their intervention freed some of those arrested on the spot. The others were taken to police cells, and most were freed after paying fines.

While the police were attacking and arresting demonstrators at the station, police commando units trashed the headquarters of UNA-UNSD and the nearby offices of the anti-presidential Conservative Republican Party. The attack on the UNA-UNSD office left the blood of the employees spattered on the walls, according to its spokesman.

Altogether, the police imprisoned 205 people, most of whom the courts released, while 50 (mostly UNA-UNSD members) were charged with serious crimes, according to the deputy interior minister, Dzhyha. On March 14, he also told parliament that 63 interior ministry personnel had required medical attention, of whom 36 had been hospitalized – 18 with head injuries. Dzhyha did not provide any figures for the number needing hospitalization from the opposition. For example, the MP Semenyuk, the head of "Ukraine without Kuchma" Chemerys, and the UNA-UNSD leader Shkil, required hospitalization for head wounds. Semenyuk's attack was recorded by a Reuter's film crew with many witnesses, yet no legal action was taken against the

March 9, 2001 – Police arrest UNA-UNSD paramilitaries in Kyiv
(Photo by Viktor Pobedynsky / UNIAN)

policemen involved.

Now the opposition found themselves the accused in parliament. Dzhyha showed parliament a film clip with supporters of the opposition attacking the police in front of the president's office. He described the demonstrators as violent, anarchic and traitorous, bent on attacking the legal authorities.

He failed to show any film of the events at the station, claiming that the arrests there were legal, as they were based on photographs and videos taken at the brawl between demonstrators and police. The victims complained that they were university students – mostly from Lviv University – who at the time of the brawl were attending a conference of student oppositionists.

Dzhyha's righteous presentation was dented when an opposition MP asked him about the February 6 demonstration. "The so-called anarchists, tens of people, who were videoed [breaking up the tent protest on Khreshchatyk]. Did you find them? Tell us who they are", asked Oleksandr Yelyashkevych. Dzhyha, not expecting this question, said that the investigation into their identity was continuing. The truth was that the police knew exactly who the "anarchists" were, as they had organized them. As in the previous November when he told parliament untruths about the headless corpse found in Tarashcha, Dzhyha was caught telling them again.

After Dzhyha spoke, the new state security service chief, Volodymyr Radchenko, addressed parliament. As in some classical "hard cop – soft cop" scenario, Radchenko appeared as the good guy. He said that the March 9 event was being thoroughly investigated and appealed to the opposition to refrain from future actions that could cause similar disturbances. He avoided Dzhyha's provocative language and promised that the state security service would not be a political instrument for either side and that he would serve the interests of the state faithfully and legally. He said the state security service was available for a constructive dialogue with all interested parties to avoid future trouble and called for political fighting to take place within the law. He reminded the MPs that Ukraine, unlike many former Soviet republics, had avoided civil war and that this should continue to be the case.

However, in the details he revealed his good-cop limitations. When a deputy asked him if knew whether the fight between the demonstrators and police had been started by police provocateurs, the country's top spy said he had no evidence for this, but welcomed it from those who had.

Another deputy asked him how it had been possible to make the arrests at the railway station on the basis of photographs and videos of those fighting with the police in front of the president's office, when most of those arrested had been attending an opposition student rally at the time. The courts would decide the guilt or innocence of those charged, retorted Radchenko, who also had nothing to say about the indiscriminate beatings by the police at the station.

Kuchma's supporters in parliament poured scorn on the opposition for organizing the demonstration. The "official opposition", the communists, joined the chorus of condemnation. The communist leader Symonenko said that the clash was a replay of the method used by the ultra-right to bring down Soviet power in 1989-90 and it "represented the interests of certain oligarch groups". A statement from the communist leadership of Crimea, led by the Crimean autonomous parliament speaker Leonid Grach, described the event as an attempt by "ultra-right nationalists and oligarchs in the interest of international capital to destabilize the political situation and take power". These statements by the communists must have been music to Kuchma's ears.

The only boost the opposition received was that on Good Friday, April 13, the United States immigration authorities granted political asylum to Mykola Melnychenko and his family and to Gongadze's wife, Myroslava, and the twin daughters. This decision embarrassed and rattled the president, as it undermined his attempt to present himself to the world as innocent of Gongadze's murder. It would be the first step in an increasing spiral of tension between Ukraine and USA. The subsequent revelation that Kuchma secretly approved the sale of military radar to Iraq would cause his relationship with the Bush administration to reach breaking point.

The knock-out blow?

The right-wing of the opposition received a symbolic knock out blow on April 19. The president's supporters had called for a vote of no confidence in Prime Minister Yushchenko. The two Rukh parties and Reform-and-Order organized a nationwide petition signed by 3.6 million people calling for him to remain in office. On April 17, they stacked boxes of petitions around Yushchenko as he stood on the podium in parliament defending himself. Two days later, an overwhelming majority, 283 MPs, representing the oligarch parties along with communists and socialists, voted against Yushchenko. Only 65 voted for him – the two Rukh parties and Reform-and-Order. Ironically, the political outcome of the Gongadze and Melnychenko affairs was the ouster not of Kuchma but of Yushchenko, and the imprisonment of Tymoshenko.

May 29, 200 – Oleksandr Volkov celebrates the vote to approve Anatoliy Kinakh as the new prime minister
(Photo by Vasyl Artyushenko / Irex-ProMedia)

25

Gongadze killed by gangsters?

After seven months of maintaining that Gongadze was alive, the prosecutor general's office announced that they had found his killers. Now that the Russian DNA test, announced on Russian TV on February 22, 2001, had confirmed that Gongadze was dead, the authorities had to come up with an explanation for the murder that did not involve the president.

On March 3, the deputy general prosecutor, Oleksiy Bahanets, revealed that two gangsters, one nicknamed Cyclops (Tsyklop), had killed Gongadze. His office had information from a prisoner that the two suspects "drove a journalist, Georgian by nationality, to the woods where they demanded some kind of debts", and then killed him. He said he did not rule out the possibility that the two killers were also dead, as they had disappeared on November 5, 2000.

Bahanets said the information had come from a prisoner whose name he would not disclose, except to say that his nickname was Grandfather and that he was of Caucasian origin.

Then two weeks later, on March 19, the authorities appeared to backtrack. Bahanets' office informed the press that a witness had seen Gongadze in the Czech Republic in February 2001. This unconfirmed sighting was released despite the supposed discovery of the killers and the Russian DNA test on February 22 showing almost 100 percent probability that the bones tested were Gongadze's. This misinformation was probably released to coincide with a fax sent by the state security service to mass media outlets in Ukraine purporting to show that Gongadze and Melnychenko had applied together for visas to the Czech Republic in November 2000.

This dubious Czech sighting soon faded away completely, while the two-killer story grew in prominence. On April 4, there seemed to be a major breakthrough. The police announced that they had found the corpses of the two missing killers. On April 18, the former head of Kyiv's police and now the new interior minister, Yuriy Smirnov, announced that the Gongadze investigation should be closed as the killers had been identified and their corpses found. (Kravchenko had resigned and would soon be appointed governor of Kherson Oblast, one of 26 governors through whom Kuchma rules Ukraine directly).

Smirnov rebuked the prosecutor general's office for not naming the killers and not closing the Gongadze investigation. "The investigation has reached a dead end because it was in someone's interest to prolong it", said Smirnov. "If everyone wanted to get out of this dead end, in my opinion, we would have been out of it long ago. I think that it is convenient for someone not to come out of it, because it is interesting, and in this dead end it is possible to seriously make things up."

But on May 4, there was a bit of backpedaling. Smirnov's deputy, Mykola Dzhyha, qualified his boss's assertion that the Gongadze investigation should be closed. He said that if the investigation continued to develop in this direction, Gongadze's murder would soon be solved, and it would be clear that it had nothing to do with politics.

The "purely" criminal explanation for Gongadze's killing took center stage after the May 8 announcement by the FBI that its tests categorically proved that the corpse held by the authorities was Gongadze's. From this day, no official would ever again say that he had been seen alive.

On May 14, President Kuchma came down firmly on the side of his interior minister in the two-dead-killers story. Gongadze's killers had been identified and the case would soon be closed, the president told Russian ORT TV.

When asked if there might be another solution to Gongadze's murder, Kuchma replied: "I cannot rule anything out." He then ruled out himself and his subordinates. "Gongadze was not known as an opponent of the government", said the president. Was this another slip of the tongue? Did Kuchma mean to say that if he was an opponent then he could have killed him?

The day after the president's TV appearance, the interior minister announced that the Gongadze case was closed. Smirnov named Gongadze's killers as Cyclops (Tsyklop), who he called a "criminal boss", and Sailor (Matros) his subordinate. The country's leading policeman re-emphasized the "purely" criminal motive for the murder – simply a "spontaneous" robbery that ended in murder. "Regrettably", he added, the killers were also dead, murdered by a rival gang, who had been arrested.

He revealed new evidence that linked the two dead killers to Gongadze's murder. A map marking the spot where Gongadze was buried was found on one of the two suspects, he said.

It turned out that this was not a map, but a cross placed between a forked line on the back of a small holy picture. Smirnov had interpreted this cross as indicating the place that Gongadze was buried.

The interior minister failed to say why his explanation for the murder – killed during a spontaneous robbery – was more authoritative than the prosecutor general's – killed for "some kind of debts". Both explanations seemed highly suspicious, not least because both the killers and the informant were dead, and there were no other witnesses who could verify that Cyclops and Sailor had murdered Gongadze. Also a cross on the back of a holy picture might be just that, a Christian cross. Neither of the competing official versions explained why the corpse was buried in Tarashcha, the constituency of Moroz, some 140 km away from where Gongadze disappeared.

But the prosecutor general's office was not pleased with the interior minister's announcement and usurpation of its investigation. It declared that the interior minister had no right to speak on it, and added that shortly the deputy prosecutor, Bahanets – who was in charge of the Gongadze case – would return from his holiday and present the official view.

On May 16, instead of Bahanets, the prosecutor's office presented to the press the investigator Oleh Vasylenko. He said the investigation was not complete and repeated that the motive behind the killing was to recover debts, and not, as Smirnov had said, robbery.

Coincidentally, on the same day as Vasylenko's press conference in Kyiv, Smirnov's deputy, Dzhyha gave the first details on how and when

April 13, 2001 – Deputy Interior Minister Mykola Dzhyha reports
to parliament on the violence at the April 9 demonstration in Kyiv
(Photo Vasyl Artyushenko / Irex-ProMedia)

Gongadze was murdered. Speaking in the Georgian capital Tbilisi, to
the 30th European regional conference of Interpol, he said that two
drug addicts had killed Gongadze on the day of his disappearance during a spontaneous robbery. He claimed that after giving Gongadze a
lift in their car, they attempted to rob him and murdered him when he
resisted. He further added that they had initially buried him near Kyiv
and then reburied him near Tarashcha.

Just in case some of the Interpol delegates had heard that President

Kuchma was a suspect, Dzhyha emphasized that the crime was not political but motivated only by robbery, and that only these two gangsters were responsible for Gongadze's murder.

On May 25, the interior minister and the prosecutor general came to parliament to explain their respective versions of why Gongadze was murdered. They sadly didn't mention Dzhyha's version. But their previously aired views were upstaged by an article in the Kyiv newspaper *Segodnya*. The article, by the paper's crime correspondent, Oleksandr Korchynsky, undermined the official version of who killed Gongadze. He wrote that on the day of Gongadze's disappearance Cyclops was a guest at Sailor's wedding, and that this could be backed up by a video, guests, and Sailor's bride.

Following *Segodnya's* revelation, what would Smirnov and Potebenko tell parliament? Surprisingly, no one in parliament referred to Korchynsky's revelation published on the same day. Another example how ineffective the opposition was.

Smirnov's presentation to parliament suggested that he must have been informed of the potentially embarrassing article in *Segodnya*. He did not repeat the assertion that the Gongadze murder inquiry had to be closed because the killers had been found. Instead, he told parliament there were a number of suspects who could have killed Gongadze. In addition to Sailor and Cyclops, he reeled off other possible killers – a suspect being held in Kyiv for the killing of ten people; a gangster imprisoned in Dnipropetrovsk; and Chechens who wanted to prevent Gongadze from publishing articles about illegal arms purchases in Ukraine.

Unexpectedly, Smirnov shifted from reporting on Gongadze's killers to arrests made in the city of Ternopil on May 9, 2001. The arrests took place following an attack on a communist party rally to mark the Soviet victory in World War Two, in which a communist member of parliament was hurt. Smirnov's news – as intended – delighted the communist faction in parliament and infuriated the Rukh MPs from Ternopil. The consequence of the diversion was that the MPs spent half of the parliamentary time set aside for the Gongadze affair discussing the merits or crimes of Stalinism.

The socialist MP Ivan Bokiy took advantage of the interior minister's concern about MPs by asking why he had not reported on the policeman's attack on the MP Valentyna Semenyuk, which took place during the demonstration in Kyiv's Shevchenko Park on March 9. Bokiy also reminded Smirnov, then as Kyiv's police chief, that he had been standing very close to the spot where the attack took place. The interior minister answered that his department had prepared a case, but the Kyiv prosecutor, Yuriy Haysynsky, had repeatedly refused to bring it to trial.

Another MP asked Smirnov if he had any results from the investigation into the car and license plate number that Gongadze had reported in his July 14, 2000 letter to the prosecutor's office. The interior minister replied that the license plate had been stolen from the police, and an investigation was continuing into whether the car belonged to the interior ministry (previously the police claimed that the license plate was made-up). He promised a report to parliament on this matter in the future. (This promised report never materialized.)

Potebenko provided the official version on the two persons suspected of killing Gongadze, but avoided saying whether the motive was robbery or debt collection. He also added a third person to the story, who also had died subsequently.

> It was discovered in the course of investigations that two inhabitants of Kiev, members of an organized criminal group, citizens D and H, who disappeared in early November 2000, were possibly involved in the murder of Gongadze. The investigation learned that these persons had been killed and by the joint efforts of the prosecutor general's office and the police, the burial place of their bodies was found. It also found those suspected of their murder. How these people were involved in the murder of Gongadze is currently being checked.

> Now this version deserves attention because a sketch of the place where the Tarashcha corpse laid was found in the clothing of one of them. The sketch exactly matches [the place where Gongadze was buried]. In addition, in G and D's car and in their spare wheel soil was found which was the same as the soil on Gongadze's body.

There is information from two witnesses about the circumstances of Gongadze's murder from somebody who witnessed it. Unfortunately, the person who witnessed the murder is dead. Therefore, it is too early to talk categorically about closing the investigation. On the other hand, it is certainly the most probable scenario, which deserves attention and is near completion.

(Source: Parliamentary records, May 25, 2001)

The prosecutor general did not reveal the names of the two suspects. However, the local Kyiv police identified "D" as Ihor Dubrovsky, or known as Cyclops, because he was partially blind in one eye, and "H" as Pavlo Hulyuvatyi or Sailor. Both had worked at the Troyeshchena market in Kyiv's Vatutynsky district, and were members of the gang who ran the market.

Apparently the gang had excluded Dubrovsky and Hulyuvatyi from the market for frequent drinking and other unsocial behavior. On November 5, 2000, Hulyuvatyi and Dubrovsky came back to the market drunk and bent on having a fight. The market gang, armed with steel pipes and knives, attacked them. After beating up and knifing them, they locked the bleeding Hulyuvatyi and Dubrovsky into storage containers, where they died during the night. Next day, the gang buried their victims in the garden of cottage in the village of Khalepya, south of Kyiv. The police had arrested the gang, and on April 4, 2001, its leader, also called "D" by the police, showed them where the bodies were buried.

As for *Segodnya's* claim that the two killers were at a wedding, and hence could not have kidnapped Gongadze, it took Potebenko's office over a month to respond. On June 16, in an interview with *Segodnya*, Bahanets explained that he knew all along that Sailor was at his wedding, but that Cyclops was not. He said that Sailor's role in the affair was limited to helping Cyclops bury the body in the woods near Tarashcha. Earlier, Bahanets, Kuchma, Smirnov, Dzhyha, Potebenko, and Vasylenko, had all said that two gangsters killed Gongadze, and had said or implied that the other person was Sailor.

On the first anniversary of Gongadze's disappearance, Bahanets appeared on Russian TV. He named Gongadze's killer as Cyclops who was aided by Sailor. He also said they had been killed in turn by other gangsters, and produced their photographs.

The prosecutor and police said they were in possession of their corpses. It turned out that this story created by people in authority was not true. Hulyuvatyi or Sailor was alive.

On December 13, 2001, documented information was presented to parliament's committee on Gongadze that Hulyuvatyi was living in Dnipropetrovsk. The St. Petersburg journalists' investigating group, AZhR, provided the evidence. The whereabouts of Cyclops were unknown.

Again, as after the revelation that Cyclops was at Sailor's wedding on the day of Gongadze's disappearance, it took a month for the prosecutor general's office to respond. On January 25, 2002, Bahanets announced that Cyclops and Sailor were no longer suspects. However, he couldn't say any more on the case due to the secrecy of the investigation.

There was no response to what was a major deception in the Gongadze case by three leading officials – President Kuchma, Interior Minister Smirnov, and Prosecutor General Potebenko and their respective deputies, Bahanets and Dzhyha. The Kuchma controlled mass media didn't bother with this embarrassing news. The disorganized opposition had nothing to say. The story that Sailor and Cyclops killed Gongadze had come to a dead end. No one officially would mention it again.

26
Russians accuse editor

March 2001 – The site where the Tarashcha corpse
was discovered on November 2, 2000.

Though a group of Russian journalists had sunk the official version
that two gangsters killed Gongadze, most of what they published on
the incident proved to be inaccurate and tendentious. The St.
Petersburg Agency of Journalistic Investigations, known by their
Russian acronym AZhR (Agentstva zhurnalistskikh rassledovanii),
ignored the evidence of President Kuchma's involvement, and that of
his top officials. They primarily focused on showing that the editor of
Gongadze's internet publication, Olena Prytula, participated in a conspiracy to kidnap and murder Gongadze.

211

AZhR was the first body to conduct an unofficial investigation of the disappearance of Gongadze. The popular Russian crime writer Andre Konstantinov heads and owns the agency which normally limits its crime investigations to St. Petersburg (fontanka.ru). However, soon after Gongadze's disappearance, the American-funded Irex-Promedia – an American NGO specializing in providing educational support to journalists in Ukraine – invited AZhR to Kyiv to teach Ukrainian journalists investigative journalism. They lectured their Kyiv counterparts to sort out fact from fiction, not to engage in political speculations, not to feed on each other for information, but to interview sources and carry out original investigations.

While in Ukraine, the Russian journalists took the opportunity to investigate Gongadze's disappearance and produced a report on it. Konstantin Shmelev wrote an article which appeared on their website in November 2000. The first part appeared on November 11, 2000, before it became known that Gongadze's corpse had been found. The last part was placed on November 20 – after Gongadze's friends had rediscovered the corpse on November 15, but before Moroz revealed the recordings implicating the president on November 28.

Shmelev's articles began by making fun of how Ukrainian journalists depended on the police instead of doing their own investigating. It mocked Olena Prytula's inclusion in the police investigation team, claiming that her chief contribution to the investigation was to direct the police to where Gongadze was being held after supposedly having learned of his whereabouts at a séance.

Shmelev accused Prytula of being part of a conspiracy to get rid of Gongadze. She had behaved, he said, as if she had been following a "PLAN" (his capitalization). He questioned her motive for raising the alarm so quickly after Gongadze's disappearance, suggesting that she knew what had happened to him. Why did she raise the alarm within two hours of his disappearance, while Gongadze's wife took his short absence in her stride? He mocked her story that just before he had left her apartment, Gongadze had gone out and returned with cat food, because the only store that could have sold it did not have a record of the sale.

Shmelev sweepingly dismissed Gongadze's internet newspaper – pravda.com.ua as a quality publication: "Most of the political articles in *Ukrayinska Pravda* are built on guesses and emotions, and not on concrete facts. From the point of view of formal logic, there can only be one conclusion – the neutralization of Georgi Gongadze, as a political figure, makes no sense. On September 16, 2000, no one had any serious interest in the little-known *Ukrayinska Pravda* and the scandalous-harmless Georgi Gongadze".

After trashing the supposedly politically meaningless Gongadze and his worthless publication, Shmelev went on to weave a story about how multi-million dollar oligarchs had fought to control it. He gathered speculations to show that Prytula was an agent of Hryhoriy Surkis, and that she wanted to keep away from the publication and Gongadze other oligarchs like Yevhen Marchuk and Oleksandr Volkov. It was her fault that Gongadze lost Marchuk's financial support and then Volkov's, Shmelev said, because she purposely published articles attacking them. Prytula's goal, Shmelev wrote, was to have Gongadze's internet publication work exclusively for Surkis. He identified her supposed controller – the Surkis journalist, Lavrenti Malazoni. "Olena Prytula acted as a classical agent of influence in the interest of Hryhoriy Surkis," wrote the St. Petersburg "sleuth" and instructor on investigative journalism.

Fact and fiction become indistinguishable in Shmelev's account of the discovery of the headless corpse in Tarashcha on November 2, 2000. He falsely claimed that it was discovered with a head, and then reburied temporarily for the night whereupon animals "ripped it off". He also erroneously alleged that the "corpse had been in a hermetically sealed container" so it could be readily transported.

Worse still, the supposedly professional investigator failed to interview any of four local officials present at the exhumation. He seemed not to be aware of the local coroner's autopsy report, nor the visit by the two officials from Kyiv, who ordered the corpse to be buried. Nor did he mention the false information issued through a newspaper, claiming the corpse wasn't Gongadze's because it was too long in the ground and the wrong height.

Instead, Shmelev included Vorotyntsev as part of the conspiracy. He claimed that the coroner planted the jewelry on the corpse to make it look like Gongadze's. He repeated the rumor that the corpse had been treated with chemicals by the killers to speed decomposition (this story was planted by the authorities to forestall questions about why a corpse found in pristine condition had decomposed by November 15 when seen by Gongadze's friends).

In Shmelev's account there was no explanation of why the deputy interior minister Dzhyha claimed the corpse was not Gongadze's. His aim was to show Prytula and Malazoni as agents of Surkis, begging the question of which oligarch the St. Petersburg journalists were working for.

Another journalist working alongside AZhR, Oleksiy Nezhyvyi, published a similar report, "The foggy Gongadze affair", in the Crimean newspaper *Krymskoe Vremya* (The Crimean Times), on December 12, 2000.

Nezhyvyi's article was like Shmelev's, except in two respects. He mentioned that two of Gongadze's professional acquaintances, Katya Gorchinskaya and Vyacheslav Pikhovshek, were at Eric's Bar and had not seen Gongadze the day after his disappearance, as alleged by the police witnesses. Nezhyvyi dismissed Moroz's revelations that the president was responsible for Gongadze's disappearance by saying that it would have been impossible to record the president.

However, on what happened in Tarashcha, Nezhyvyi presented the same disinformation as Shmelev. This included the fabricated story that animals ripped off the head, and that the local coroner planted the jewelry on the body. He also concluded, like Shmelev, that Prytula was somehow involved or knew why Gongadze disappeared.

After Smelev's report, the St. Petersburg journalists made new allegations against Prytula and Malazoni. At first sight they seemed credible, but on closer scrutiny most of their evidence disintegrates into misunderstandings.

On March 26, 2001, at a hurriedly called press conference in Kyiv, Andre Konstantinov, AZhR's director – flanked by his investigators, and their new sponsor, the former Prime Minister Valeriy

Pustovoytenko – announced major revelations on the Gongadze case: (1) Gongadze had known about the recordings; (2) Melnychenko had been in touch with Moroz before Gongadze's disappearance; and (3) Prytula and Malazoni, along with Moroz's subordinates, had conspired in the disappearance of Gongadze.

Pustovoytenko, sitting next to Konstantinov, signaled he was there to take credit for sponsoring supposedly

March 26, 2001 – Valeriy Pustovoytenko and Andre Konstantinov

these major revelations. Answering journalists questions' about the financing of AZhR's investigation, Pustovoytenko admitted that he and his NDP were financing it, but only modestly and limiting it to their expenses in Kyiv. He also sheepishly confessed he had the complete set of Konstantinov's crime novels.

The real reason the press conference was called hurriedly was to steal the thunder of NDP's rival party, Working Ukraine, who on March 23 had announced that it had hired the American Kroll detective agency to investigate who killed Gongadze. The National Democrats, like Working Ukraine, had opposed in parliament a constitutionally-based investigation of the president. Instead both of them opted for sponsoring investigations which had as their purpose to either show the president's innocence or blame the Gongadze incident on someone else.

Konstantinov attempted to be diplomatic about his accusations against Prytula. "The behavior of Olena Prytula on the evening of Georgi Gongadze's disappearance may not be criminal. We think her response was strange. We have been trying to ask her questions in the last few days about the telephone calls, but she does not want to talk to us on this theme or any other. She simply puts down the receiver and does not answer. We simply wanted to ask her these straightforward questions".

In the first instance, AZhR's accusations seemed very credible. They included logs of telephone calls made before and after Gongadze's disappearance which seemed to show that Tarashcha served as the hub of a conspiracy involving Prytula, Melnychenko, Malazoni, and someone in the Czech Republic. The implication was that they killed Gongadze, planted his body in Tarashcha, and organize Melnychenko's escape to the Czech Republic.

The Russian journalists said that, according to telephone records, Prytula had received a call from Tarashcha to her home on August 28, before Gongadze's disappearance, and a call from Tarashcha to her office on October 4. The unknown person in Tarashcha had also made telephone calls to the Czech Republic on August 27, November 23 and November 24.

The implication was that these calls to the Czech Republic were to arrange Melnychenko's departure, as he had obtained his Czech visa on November 23, and left Ukraine on November 26. The journalists emphasized that after Melnychenko left Ukraine, no more telephone calls were made from Tarashcha to the Czech Republic.

In addition, they accused another participant in this affair (Malazoni) of having made and received numerous telephone calls from mobile telephone numbers, often one digit apart on September 4 and September 16. The St Petersburg journalists made the point that these telephone calls had all the hallmarks of a classic conspiracy where a mobile telephone was used once and then thrown away so that it could not be traced.

The first question from the Kyiv journalists to the investigators was where did they obtain the private telephone records? The Russians replied that it was their professional secret. Eyes turned to the former prime minister, who with a sheepish smile, said that the only help he gave was financial. It would not be surprising if the the state security service or the police, who have access to telephone records, had given them this information.

Investigations proved that these allegations were mostly mistaken. The August 28 telephone call from Tarashcha to Prytula's apartment came from a caller who dialed the wrong number. This was the view of the American Kroll detective agency, who also were given these private telephone records. The American sleuths concluded that a Tarashcha caller was trying to get through to the central food market in Kyiv, whose telephone number was only one digit different to Prytula's.

Kroll could find no explanation for the two telephone calls from Tarashcha to the *Ukrayinska Pravda* office – on October 4 at 10:49 am and on October 31 at 3:57 pm. The last call was made just before the discovery of Gongadze's corpse. Both calls were made from a telephone in the Tarashcha engine factory. Prytula told Kroll that she had no knowledge of these telephone calls, and they have yet to be explained.

However, the St. Petersburg investigators' claim that telephone records showed that Malazoni was involved in a conspiracy proved to be comical. They said that telephone calls one digit apart were made to him on September 2 and September 16. This charge proved to be a fantasy.

The Kyiv journalist Oleksiy Stepura obtained a copy of Malazoni's telephone record used by the St. Petersburg journalists. The mysterious telephone numbers that differed by one digit turned out to be at the work place of his girlfriend. All the Russian sleuths had to do was to ring these numbers and find that they all belonged to the 1+1 TV station where Lyudmyla Dobrovolska worked as a TV news presenter. All calls in or out are automatically routed to a free telephone line – which are all one digit apart.

As for the telephone calls from Tarashcha to Czech Republic, on August 27, November 23 and November 24, they need to be investigated, as do the two telephone calls from Tarashcha to *Ukrayinska Pravda* office on October 4 and 31.

The aim of AZhR's investigation was to show that Moroz had organized both the Melnychenko recordings and Gongadze's murder with the help of Prytula. The evidence of telephone calls presented by AZhR failed to make the charges stick.

What AZhR failed to do was to even consider the possibility that President Kuchma was involved in Gongadze's disappearance as presented on the Melnychenko recordings. If they had considered such a possibility, the likes of Pustovoytenko would not had financially sponsored them.

On June 18, 2001, AZhR published its final report, entitled "The death of Georgi Gongadze was convenient for many". It did not add anything substantially new to what it had said before. It concluded that the president was innocent and the killing was carried out by an unknown "third force", which included Prytula, Moroz and Melnychenko.

The St. Petersburg journalists, for the most part, did the opposite of what they preached to Ukrainian journalists. They indiscriminately mixed facts with fiction, and failed to interview many of those involved. AZhR's investigation into Gongadze's disappearance and murder would have merit if it was labeled as fiction.

March 2001 – The author JV Koshiw at the site where the Tarashcha corpse was discovered

27

American gloss

Two investigations by Americans declared President Leonid Kuchma innocent of Gongadze's disappearance. They both claimed that the recordings were fabricated. Because they presented themselves as impartial, professional and American, their findings had a much greater impact on public opinion than the official story about the two dead killers, or the insinuations about Gongadze's close colleague.

The investigations were different. The Kroll risk consulting company of New York City supposedly carried out a police type of investigation, while the former *Financial Times* correspondent based in Kyiv made a TV documentary.

The Kroll agency did not hide its financial sponsor, Working Ukraine – a parliamentary group that supports the president. Its two chief benefactors have been the president's son-in-law, Viktor Pinchuk, and the then state security chief's son, Andriy Derkach. Working Ukraine would not reveal how much money it paid Kroll, but it certainly was in the hundreds of thousands of dollars.

In contrast, the *FT* journalist had refused to reveal who gave the money to make his documentary. But, judging only by who promoted the documentary in Ukraine, the money probably came from the same source as Kroll's.

President Kuchma was the first to announce that a private, foreign and supposedly impartial investigation would take place into what he called the "so-called tape scandal" and Gongadze's disappearance. He told Polish journalists on March 6, 2000, that foreign detectives would be hired to carry out the work and that they would work independently of Ukraine's prosecutor general's office and other investigative bodies. From what he said, it might have been assumed that the government was about to hire impartial investigators.

On March 23, 2001, the head of Working Ukraine, Serhiy Tyhypko, told a press conference that his party had hired Kroll to investigate the disappearance of Gongadze. He added that President Kuchma had agreed to this investigation, and that its conclusions would have legal validity, as Ukrainian officials would work alongside the Kroll detectives.

Kroll's president, Michael Cherkasky, also present at the press confernce, said the investigative team would be led by himself and Robert J. Viteretti. Their report and conclusions would only be given to Working Ukraine. Tyhypko reassured the worried journalists that there would be no cover-up, and that the report would be made public whatever its conclusions.

What was abhorrent about Working Ukraine's invitation to Kroll was that the party had opposed an investigation of the president as set out by Ukraine's constitution, and that Kuchma had threatened parliament with a state of emergency if it dared to investigate him. Now they were passing the responsibility to a private foreign company, whose conclusions would have no legal consequences – despite Tyhypko's and Kuchma's assurances. Cynics predicted that the only purpose of this investigation would be as a public relations exercise to find the president innocent.

On the first anniversary of Gongadze's disappearance, Working Ukraine released Kroll's report in three languages – English, Russian and Ukrainian. The first surprise was that Kroll had not, as Working Ukraine had promised, focused on who killed Gongadze. Instead, it claimed that President Kuchma was innocence. In other words, it did what it was paid to do by its customer.

Kroll avoided investigating the evidence against the president heard on the recordings. It did not investigate "the eagles" – the plainclothes secret police unit who have been suspected of kidnapping and killing Gongadze, as well as kidnapping and beating up the legal-rights activist Oleksiy Podolsky. It failed to investigate Kuchma's order to hit the MP Oleksandr Yelyashkevych. It didn't investigate the official cover-up launched after Gongadze's disappearance and intensified after the discovery of his corpse. It failed to look into the fabricated story that the Tarashcha corpse was too old and short to be Gongadze's, or why it was not properly preserved. Kroll didn't discover why Ukraine's authorities kept secret the Russian DNA test that concluded the Tarashcha corpse was Gongadze's. It didn't look into the officially produced myth that Gongadze was alive and seen by eyewitnesses in Kyiv, Lviv, Moscow and Prague. It didn't investigate the two killers officially accused of killing Gongadze.

The heart of Kroll's investigation was "proving" that the Melnychenko recordings were faked and that he was of questionable character. It hired an electronics expert to conduct a series of tests. It didn't identify this British expert, except to describe him as "a senior forensic audio consultant".

The expert's primary test was on one of Melnychenko's recordings, which Kroll did not identify. The expert said he pulled down a recording from an internet site, which the report also did not identify (from the report's appendix, one can see that the internet site was "The Temporary Home for the Melnychenko Tapes Project" situated at Harvard University). As for which file was downloaded, this was also not stated. It seems that the expert downloaded a file of excerpts and not a copy of file containing an original recordings. He also seems to have no idea what actually was being said on the recording tested.

Kroll's expert said he found gaps on the file he tested, which he concluded were caused either by downloading from the internet, or were "due to selective editing of the material". "There are a number of short gaps in the recording, including 15 separate sections of speech. One gap in particular, occurring at 10.21, is noteworthy, as it has a very short burst of audio in the middle of it. The speech between the males continues before and after each gap", reported the consultant.

The expert could have answered his own question – whether the gaps were caused by the downloading from the internet – by purchasing the recording from Vienna's International Press Institute (IPI), instead of downloading it from the Harvard site.

Kroll's expert had no idea whether he was testing. If the file was a collection of 15 excerpts, then it would not be surprising that there were gaps between them, and within an excerpt. Despite the consultant's ignorance about what he was testing, the Kroll report concluded that the recording was "selectively edited".

The second test involved the expert making a recording in the president's office and comparing it to the Melnychenko recording. It concluded that the acoustic environment of both recordings was similar, so it was possible Melnychenko had "recorded somewhere in the President's office". (This was the opposite conclusion of the prosecutor general's tests as stated in his January 10, 2001 report, which Kroll did not mention.)

In the third test, the expert placed his recorder under the sofa and discovered that "significant interference" came from the walk-through metal detector situated on the opposite side of the wall behind the sofa. As this interference did not appear on the Melnychenko recording he had tested, the expert concluded that the recorder wasn't placed under the president's sofa. This led Kroll to charge Melnychenko with not telling the truth, and hence to conclude that he was not to be trusted.

It turned out that the expert was wrong about the lack of noise on Melnychenko's recordings. If he had used the same recorder as Melnychenko – a Toshiba SX1, instead of his Sony TCD 8 DAT, he would have discovered that the metal detector noise didn't affect the Toshiba while it did affect the Sony. There was no excuse for the expert not to have used a Toshiba, as it was clear from the recordings what instrument Melnychenko had used.

The Toshiba's ability to protect against the noise of the metal-detector was checked by the *Financial Times* correspondent in Ukraine, Tom Warner. In an interview with Melnychenko on August 17, 2002, he discussed the tests conducted by Kroll:

> *FT*: And the recorder was really hidden under the sofa? That's obviously hard to believe. Kroll Associates, the private investigators, wrote in their report that it would be impossible to record under the president's sofa, because of interference from a nearby metal detector.

> M: It's obvious to anyone who has read that report that Kroll were acting in the role of Kuchma's lawyer. When Kroll's specialists conducted

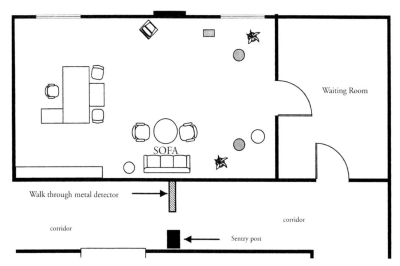

The sofa in President Kuchma's office
(Source: Kroll report)

their tests in Kuchma's office, they didn't use the Toshiba, they used some other machine that had no protection from interference. The Toshiba is protected (points to the Toshiba's case).

FT: Actually I've placed my Toshiba next to metal detectors around Kiev and it records without any problems. I think the interference Kroll heard may be because they used a magnetic tape recorder.

M: You could be right. There were many mistakes in Kroll's report. They also wrote that the recordings were edited. But they didn't even try to obtain the original recordings. They hired some so-called expert, who they don't name, who listened to some files downloaded from the internet.

Further evidence of Kroll's questionable investigation can be seen in its claim that the recordings were not dated. "Most of the taped conversations that have been made public are not dated in any obvious way". Consequently, Kroll said, it was difficult to "evaluate the authenticity of the tapes and evaluate the context in which comments, if any, were made about Gongadze". This was not true. If Kroll had spent $150 – surely a tiny sum compared to the few hundred thousand dollars it received for the investigation – to buy a collection of recordings from Vienna's IPI, it would have found dates in the file names in the copies of the original recordings.

Kroll's conclusion that Kuchma was innocent because the recordings were faked has no credibility. Its investigation was an American gloss on an already heavily soiled cover-up. It is just as well that Kroll didn't name its British expert, as his anonymity protects him from ridicule.

A TV promotion for Kuchma

The second American gloss also had a British tinge. The former *Financial Times* correspondent in Ukraine, Charles Clover, made what was purportedly an American TV documentary called PR (public relations) on the Gongadze affair. It attempted to argue that the Gongadze and Melnychenko affairs were being used by the American government to replace the innocent and elected president, Leonid Kuchma, with the incompetent, if not corrupt prime minister, Viktor Yushchenko.

PR was used to influence the March 31, 2002 parliamentary elections. It was broadcast three times on the eve of the election – on March 17 and 18 on Kuchma's son-in-law's national TV station, ICTV, and on March 27, on the 1+1 channel, which Kuchma's favorite oligarch, Oleksandr Volkov, controls through a "news commissar".

Two themes dominated the documentary. The first was that the American government and their sponsored non-governmental organizations (NGOs) took advantage of the political crisis to push for the replacement of Kuchma with Yushchenko. It claimed that this conspiracy failed when parliament voted the prime minister out of office, as he was no longer able to automatically replace the president if Kuchma left in disgrace.

The second theme was that President Kuchma was innocent of ordering Gongadze's disappearance and that the same plotters were behind both the Gongadze and Melnychenko affairs. Clover's strongest argument, like Kroll's, was the attempt to show that the Melnychenko recordings were fabricated. As evidence, he offered one excerpt used by Moroz to accuse the president. He showed that it was stitched together from two conversations held on different days, one in May and the other in September.

However, this was nothing of the kind. What Clover proved was that he, like Moroz, didn't know where the September excerpt stopped and the May excerpt began. If Clover had shown manipulation on a copy of a original recording, and not on selected excerpts, then he would have had proof for his argument.

After claiming that Kuchma was a victim of manipulated recordings, Clover presented two arch conspiracy theorists to explain who was behind the fabrication of the recordings and Gongadze's murder. The first, Oleksiy Stepura, said: "I believe that the people who made the recordings were the same people who killed Georgi Gongadze". Stepura didn't say in the documentary who these "people" were, nor was he asked.

The second conspirator presented was Andre Konstantinov, whose organization of investigating journalists, AZhR, had pointed at Gongadze's editor, Olena Prytula, as taking part in his disappearance. Konstantinov also believed that "a third force" was behind the murder with the aim of ousting Kuchma out of office in which Melnychenko "unknowingly" took part. He also was not asked who this "third force" was.

Clover also presented Lavrenti Malazoni, who claimed Olena Prytula got him involved in a conspiracy organized by the socialist leader Moroz. What Clover didn't mention was that Konstantinov's investigators had accused Malazoni of conspiring with Prytula on the behalf of the oligarch Surkis against other oligarchs and Kuchma.

Malazoni, on his part, missed the whole point of the significance of his going to Tarashcha. If he and the other three journalists hadn't "discovered" the corpse, there probably would not have been a corpse to carry out DNA tests on, and we might had never known if Gongadze was dead or alive as the officials had claimed.

In the documentary, Clover also interviewed the head of Kroll –

Jules Kroll. The chief sleuth provided a novel reason for President Kuchma's innocence. "Not every president requests an independent organization to come to investigate". One also could also say the converse – not every accused selects who will investigate him.

Most of the documentary purported to show that the American government was orchestrating events in order to replace Kuchma with Yushchenko. The US Embassy in Kyiv, using Radio Liberty, NGOs, and demonstrations, allegedly attempted to push an elected president out of office.

PR used film clips that suggested CIA agents were directing the March 9, 2001 demonstration. However, it failed to say that the film clips were made by Ukraine's state security service, and that the "agents" were the third secretary of the US embassy, Louis Krizhok, and his bodyguards – locally hired Ukrainians.

The US Ambassador to Ukraine, Carlos Pascual was shown at a press conference on March 16, 2001, announcing $750,000 worth of grants to be given to media projects in Ukraine. To highlight the purpose of these grants the documentary focused on Volodymyr Cheremysh's Republican Institute, which had received grants in the past, and saying that it was one of the main instigators of demonstrations against Kuchma. PR seemed to be following the script of the TV documentary made by Kuchma's subordinates – repeatedly shown after the March 9, 2001 demonstration – claiming that the American ambassador was directing the opposition.

The PR documentary could not resist repeating the allegation made by the Russian and Ukrainian press that Yushchenko's American wife was or had been an American secret agent. Clover had made this allegation in a *Financial Times* article published on April 18, 2001, which Yushchenko's wife, Kateryna Chumachenko, denied in a letter to the *FT* on April 24, 2001. But he continued to make the same claim in the film without offering any evidence of substance. The former presidential guard Mykola Melnychenko stated that President Kuchma ordered the security chief, Derkach, to provide a Ukrainian newspaper with the false information that Yushchenko's wife was a CIA agent (a sworn statement made in New York on August 27, 2002).

The documentary suggested that the NGO sponsored by George Soros took part in this plot to replace Kuchma. In the interview in PR, Soros said he had distributed over $100 million in grants through his NGO – the Renaissance Foundation in Ukraine. He also told Clover that he wanted Yushchenko to replace Kuchma. Soros had also called openly in a letter to the *FT* on February 3, 2001, for the president to step aside and allow an independent investigation to take place on the allegations made against him. As he had said this on camera and in a letter to the *FT*, where is the plot claimed by Clover?

The documentary also showed the US government sponsored Radio Liberty agitating for Yushchenko and against Kuchma through local radio stations across Ukraine. Clover gave President Kuchma the last word on the subject: "Radio Liberty for 17 hours every day broadcasts filth that they would not even have used during Soviet times". At the same time, Clover avoided mentioning Kuchma's grip over the Ukrainian mass media which had earned him the notorious award of one of the world's worst enemies of the press. As a long-serving *FT* correspondent in Ukraine, Clover could not have been unaware of this, as well as the cover-ups staged by officials on the Gongadze case, which he didn't mention in his film.

The documentary gave Kuchma the opportunity to say that once Yushchenko was removed as prime minister on April 26, 2002, the protests against the president stopped. "No premier Yushchenko, no president Yushchenko. Why bother to waste any more money. The next day everything quieted down", the smiling Kuchma said. Never mind that this factually was untrue, the demonstrations had already stopped after the March 9 debacle, weeks before Yushchenko was kicked out of office in late April.

In case anyone had failed to understand why the documentary was made, this was clearly stated at the end. "In the March 31 parliamentary elections, all those supporting the cassette scandal are now supporting Yushchenko," the documentary PR said. Appearing on the eve of the parliamentary elections, PR was calling for a vote against Yushchenko and his political coalition, and a vote for the president's side.

The secrecy around the funding of the documentary raises numerous ethical questions. Was the documentary made to order? Who paid for it? Was it the president's son-in-law, Victor Pinchuk?

Clover has directed all questions dealing with money to Peter Powell, the producer, and Paula Scott, a board member of the company making the film, East European Media Research Project – a mysterious company which doesn't seem to be registered anywhere except the off-shore Virgin Islands. Scott replied that the documentary cost $200,000, but she would not disclose the source of the money, or who owned the off-shore company sponsoring the film. (See the article on the attempt to discover who paid for PR: Maryna Melnyk, "All the truth about the film 'PR'", pravda.com.ua, March 27, 2002.)

The source of the funding of PR is a matter of public concern. A journalist has been found beheaded. Recordings have appeared implicating the president in his disappearance. An official cover-up has descended on the affair. The people making a documentary film backing the official view and refusing to provide the source of their funding is totally unacceptable.

Dec. 22, 1999 – President Leonid Kuchma congratulates
Viktor Yushchenko on receiving parliament's approval as prime minister
(Photo by Vasyl Artyushenko / Irex-ProMedia)

28

Justice for Gongadze

The results of the March 31, 2002 elections dashed the hope that the new parliament would put President Kuchma on trial. The president's men won the majority of the seats and selected the speaker. This could mean that until the next parliamentary elections there will be no constitutional means to oust Kuchma, as only parliament can investigate and try a president.

But how did Kuchma's supporters manage to gain control of parliament following the revelations by the Melnychenko recordings about the crimes committed by the president and his subordinates? The answer lies in how parliament was elected. Half of the 450 MPs were elected on party-bloc lists, and the other half in constituencies. The voters were asked to cast two votes – one for a constituency MP and the other for a political party or bloc. Parties or blocs receiving four percent or more of the national vote would receive a proportion of 225 seats.

A respectable 70 percent (27 million out of the 38 million) of the voters turned out to vote. Even more wanted to vote, estimated up to ten percent, but were thwarted by long queues at polling stations. This was seen by the president's opponents as a way of lowering the vote for the opposition.

Only six parties and political blocs from the dozens that took part passed the four percent hurdle to share the 225 seats. Those who became the opposition in the new parliament obtained 76 percent of these seats: Yushchenko's Our Ukraine bloc (31 percent), the Communist Party (26 percent), Tymoshenko's bloc (10 percent) and the Socialist Party (9 percent). The president's side got only 24 percent: Lytvyn's For United Ukraine bloc (16 percent), and Medvedchuk's SDP(U) (8 percent). The outcome of this political bloc vote reflected the views gathered in opinion polls prior to the election. The election results in the 225 constituencies, however, gave the president's supporters – most of whom had misleadingly stood as independents – 80 percent of the seats. This gave the president's side the slimmest of majorities, one seat more than the opposition. But it was enough to elect the speaker and control parliament.

On May 28, the president's side elected as speaker Volodymyr Lytvyn, the former head of the president's office and an accessory to Gongadze's kidnapping. This helped to guarantee that Kuchma would not be put on trial by this parliament.

But Kuchma had to pay a high political price to obtain this guarantee. In return for 31 SD(U)P votes, Kuchma gave their leader, Viktor Medvedchuk, a very important post – the head of the president's office, Lytvyn's previous job. This will provide Medvedchuk the opportunities to expand the influence of his oligarch group and tighten its grip on the mass media.

Elected to the new parliament were many of the major figures involved in the Gongadze affair. Besides Lytvyn, it included Mykhaylo Potebenko, the former prosecutor general, who entered as a communist MP, but soon defected to the president's bloc. The former state security chief, Leonid Derkach, as well as his son Andriy, were elected in constituencies, as was Oleksandr Volkov.

Yushchenko's and Tymoshenko's blocs, and the communist and socialist parties reacted angrily to Kuchma's side taking over parliament. The communist leader Petro Symonenko was especially bitter. The election had seen his party's parliamentary strength plummet by half – from 117 to 66, and, within weeks, three of his MPs defected to the president's side. The communists had come second in the party-bloc vote with 20 percent, but had received only 3 percent of the constituency seats (7 MPs elected out of 225). Symonenko felt personally betrayed by Kuchma as he had shielded him from being impeached in the previous parliament.

Almost all the 51 constituency seats lost by the communists were taken by candidates sponsored by the Donetsk oligarchs, who appeared in parliament as a new and powerful force under the group-

Feb. 13, 2000 – Viktor Yushchenko in Nizhyn, Chernihiv Oblast,
campaigning during for the March 2002 parliamentary elections
(Photo UNIAN)

ing called the Party of Regions. Soon they would flex their political muscles and have one of its members become prime minister of Ukraine.

Like the communist leader, the former prime minister, Viktor Yushchenko, also was angry. He felt that his Our Ukraine bloc, which ended with a total of 110 seats, should had received a lot more votes both in the block vote and the constituencies. Our Ukraine came first in the bloc vote with 25 percent, but second in the constituencies where it received 20 percent of the seats. A post-election survey of voters found that the majority (58.6%) agreed with the statement that "Yushchenko won, but the president's men fixed the outcome in their favor".

The blatant denial of a constituency seat to his bloc's candidate, Oleksandr Zhyr, the head of parliament's Gongadze committee, transformed Yushchenko from a conservative to a militant. The election in Zhyr's Nikopol constituency was cancelled because of widespread fraud on behalf of the president's candidate, Viktor Drachevsky. But just two days before the repeat elections on July 14, a court removed Zhyr's right to participate. The legal grounds for the decision were very novel. The court ruled that because twenty MPs, including Yushchenko, had campaigned in the constituency on Zhyr's behalf, he was disqualified as MPs were state officials who were forbidden to campaign on behalf of candidates.

Yushchenko reacted with uncharacteristic vehemence. The former prime minister, who in February 2001 had signed a statement, along with Kuchma and the parliament speaker, calling demonstrators "Ukrainian Nazis", now called on Kuchma to resign immediately or be ousted by demonstrations. Prior to the election, he had said that even Kuchma's impeachment was not on his agenda in the next parliament.

In the third week of July 2002, in reaction to what they saw as the fixing of the elections, the leaders of four blocs or parties – Moroz, Symonenko, Tymoshenko and Yushchenko – signed an agreement to force Kuchma to resign. They selected Monday, September 16, 2002, the second anniversary of Gongadze's disappearance, as the day to hold rallies across Ukraine to force Kuchma out. As this was a working day, a huge turnout would have been akin to a nationwide strike.

The event, though successful, failed to bring down Kuchma. At the rally in European Square in central Kyiv, the conservative and former banker Yushchenko, the radical oligarch Tymoshenko, the socialist Moroz and the communist Symonenko stood together facing a crowd estimated to be 50,000. Though the turnout was impressive, it was not the success they had hoped for, as most of the working population stayed at their jobs.

Nevertheless it was a momentous historical moment; the political right and left shared the same platform, and their supporters the same square. For the first time in Ukraine's history, the communist and socialist red flags flew alongside the nationalist blue-yellow ones.

The four leaders issued a common statement that read like a revolutionary manifesto. It blamed Kuchma for the economic ills of Ukraine, accused him of becoming president illegally, called him a criminal and demanded his immediate resignation.

The authorities censored the event on TV. As demonstrations took place across the country, Ukraine's six national TV channels went blank due to "unscheduled repairs". In the evening their news bulletins downplayed the protests, focusing on the traffic problems they caused, and played up President Kuchma's visit to Strasbourg for a conference of heads of states aspiring to join the European Union.

An attempt to recreate the tent city by a few hundred protesters in the center of Kyiv was dispersed by an unprecedentedly large police force. The heavy-handed police action outraged the opposition.

The frustration at being denied access to the mass media boiled over on September 23, when Moroz, Symonenko, Tymoshenko and their supporters, with a large group of reporters following, forced their way into the broadcasting studio of UT1, the national state channel which the president's office directly controls. In response, UT1 decided not broadcast the evening news bulletin. Instead the TV screen carried a statement saying that the broadcast had been cancelled because Moroz, Symonenko and Tymoshenko were occupying the studio.

On September 24, there was another desperate if not theatrical attempt to oust Kuchma by attempting to occupy his office. Two dozen opposition MPs, including Moroz, Symonenko and Tymoshenko, but not Yushchenko, walked into the building housing the president's office. After a drawn-out confrontation with the guards, many of the MPs declared a hunger strike and settled down for the night in the foyer of the building. Next morning they demanded to see Kuchma, who agreed to see four of their representatives – Symonenko, Tymoshenko, Moroz and the MP Yuriy Orobets (representing Yushchenko).

Predictably enough, Kuchma told the delegates that he would not resign but stay in office until he completed his term in 2004. Afterwards the delegation and the rest of the MPs left the building promising to continue their struggle.

On September 28, Kuchma addressed the nation on TV with a scornful statement about the opposition. It was a masterly speech, broadcast on all the major TV channels. It accused the opposition of lawbreaking, irresponsibility, and intransigence.

The uncompromising opposition demands that I resign. I categorically state I will not do this because I have been elected by the people as head of state and everything that is taking place in the country is my responsibility.

Most of his speech accused opposition MPs of trying to take power by force. He cited as examples the occupation of the UT1 news broadcasting studio on September 23 and the presidential office building the next day. He mocked the opposition for uniting under one banner those who always opposed each other: "communists and nationalists, radicals and moderates, fighters against corruption and those accused of corruption".

He attempted to divide the leaders from their supporters:

Citizens of Ukraine, the September 16 and 24 rallies showed that there will be no coup in our country. Tens of thousands of citizens came to the meetings, expressed their dissatisfaction, but, unlike the MPs, did not provoke any fights, and not a single serious incident.

Kuchma ended his statement to the nation by promising that he would "never" break the law, but neither would he allow his opponents to do so.

His speech was just another propaganda blast by Kuchma which his opponents would not be allowed to answer on TV. Though they received 75 percent of the popular vote, and with every opinion poll before and after the March 2002 elections endorsing this, they were powerless to change the status quo. Their access to the mass media was blocked. They didn't have a majority in parliament. Neither could they mobilize enough demonstrators to push Kuchma out of office.

The situation took an ominous turn for the opposition on November 21, 2002, when Kuchma appointed a new prime minister, Viktor Yanukovych, who many viewed as a regional enforcer for Kuchma. As governor from 1997 of Ukraine's most populated and industrialized region, the Donetsk Oblast, Yanukovych has ruled it with an iron fist and has dealt summarily with the president's opponents.

An excerpt from the Melnychenko recordings illustrates his brutal character. On March 30, 2000, Kuchma had telephoned Yanukovych to sort out a judge in a court case in which the lawyer Serhiy Salov – who was Moroz's election agent in Donetsk during the 1999 presidential elections – was being tried for "spreading misinformation about the president".

> [Kuchma] Since December [1999]. Your court has been twisting it and returned the case which said: "this must be viewed not as spreading [misinformation], but as an offense against the president". Your judges are rif-raff. I am now obliged to come and testify! That's why you should take this fucking judge, hang him by the balls, let him hang for one night.
>
> [Yanukovych] I understand. We will look into it.
>
> [Kuchma] Judges altogether, fuckers...
>
> [Yanukovych] They are scum. The judge is not reliable. It is necessary to replace him.
>
> Source: IP, ZL3003.wav, March 30, 2000)

Salov was under arrest from October 30, 1999. In July 2000, Judge A. Tupytsky sentenced Salov to five years imprisonment, including two years in a labor camp, and fined 170,000 Hr (then about $50,000). A higher court squashed Salov's sentence in response to the European court of human rights taking up his case.

Also the Donetsk Oblast governor Yanukovych had his own "Gongadze" case. On July 3, 2001, persons unknown beat unconsciously Ihor Aleksandrov, a Moroz supporter and the general-director of the TV station TOR in the city of Slovyansk, Donestsk Oblast. Alexandrov never came out of the coma and died three days later. The murder incident remains unsolved.

On November 22, parliament approved Yanukovych as prime minister with 234 votes. Among those voting were nineteen MPs who were elected with the opposition – ten from Yushchenko's bloc, five from Tymoshenko's, and two each from the socialist and communist parties. This vote suggested that the opposition was getting weaker.

Kuchma and the oligarchs might have selected Yanukovych because he could be counted on to be tough with an opposition that has vowed to remove Kuchma by street demonstrations. Assisting Yanukovych as deputy prime minister and finance minister will be the fellow Party of Regions' member, Mykola Azarov. On the Melnychenko recordings Azarov, then head of the tax office, came across as a sinister manipulator who spied on his fellow ministers for Kuchma. Worse still if Kuchma was to resign, then according to the constitution, the prime minister, Yanukovych, would take his place until parliament decided when the next election would take place.

The stark political reality is that Kuchma will not be tried for any of the crimes he is accused of. The parliament will not investigate him. As the political situation looks today, Kuchma will stay in power until his term of office expires in October 2004.

As there will be no trial, Kuchma will not brought to account for his involvement – just in the period of twelve months – in the murder of Gongadze, the beatings given to Podolsky and Yelyashkevych, the imprisoning of Feldman and Tymoshenko, the throwing of grenades at Vitrenko and others, the fixing of elections and a referendum, the stealing of millions from the national treasury, the censoring of the media and the hounding of journalists.

The opposition, united for the moment, made the right decision to force immediate presidential elections by calling the population to street demonstrations. But the reality is that the opposition, ranging from communists to conservatives, will not remain united as its leaders are too opportunistic and different ideologically. Moreover, the population is too cowed to stand up to a strong police state.

Whatever happens next, the murder of Gongadze and the Melnychenko recordings have raised the consciousness of millions of people about Kuchma and his entourage of oligarchs. The recordings exposed him as an orchestrator of crimes. His attempt to convince the population that a foreign intelligence service murdered Gongadze and created the recordings to undermine Ukraine will, hopefully, not convince many people.

Postscript
NATO humiliates Kuchma

Antonov-124, one of the largest cargo planes in the world.
A popular plane to transport military weapons around the world
as it can fly 5,000 km with a load of 120 tonnes without refueling

The arrests of arms merchants by the Italian authorities in 2000 and 2001 blew the lid off an international criminal activity in which President's Kuchma's government had been participating in. Since the collapse of the USSR, Ukraine, along with most former Soviet states and East European satellites, had been unloading its stockpiles of weapons in violation of UN arms embargoes. But the issue became a major international scandal for Ukraine only after the revelation that Kuchma gave permission to break the UN embargo on the supply of military equipment to Iraq. But more important, he crossed the interests of the US government on the eve of its preparations for a possible war against the regime of Saddam Hussein. As a consequence, he was not invited to the NATO summit in Prague, but when he did arrive, he was duely humiliated.

Following independence in 1991, Ukraine's elite had discovered that it could make huge sums of money by selling the massive stocks of weapons left behind by the Soviet armed forces. In one documented example, the then Ukrainian President Leonid Kravchuk authorized the sale of $4 million worth of arms to Dmytro Streshynsky. The consignment included "6 million rounds of ammunition, 12 thousand artillery shells, 300 machine guns, and other arms". However, the then state security chief, Yevhen Marchuk, warned Kravchuk in a letter dated February 12, 1993, about the corruption it was causing among officials, as for example Streshynsky's paid $200,000 in bribes to officials in the Defense Ministry. He also warned the president of the "severe" international consequences if the violation of UN sanctions became public. He suggested that Kravchuk retrieve the documents showing his approval for Streshynsky's activities, because they could "compromise you personally as well as the Ukrainian state", and added "this information could find its way into the mass media".

Ukraine's elite had managed to keep this illegal weapon's trade away from public view by controlling the mass media. An attempt to publicize it provoked a violent response. A parliamentary investigation in 1998 estimated that tens of billions of dollars of state-owned arms had been sold abroad and the proceeds pocketed by officials. Details of this investigation appeared in the "We" periodical in its June 1998 issue. (Chapter 9 presented the case of the "We" member, Oles Podolsky, who was kidnapped and beaten by plain clothes policemen for distributing the publication in June, 2000.) In response to the article, an assailant on July 29, 1998 pumped three bullets into the legs of the editor Serhiy Odarych and told him to stop involving himself in the matter or "next time we'll kill you".

The arrest of the arms merchant Leonid Minin revealed the direct involvement of the Ukraine's official weapons' exporter – Ukrspetseksport (Ukrainian-special-exports). It also unveiled the sponsoring of this trade by the Ukrainian oligarchs, Andriy Derkach – the son of the former state security chief Leonid Derkach, and Vadim Rabinovich.

The August 4, 2000 arrest of Minin – Odesa born and with Israeli and German citizenships – was like something out of a seedy movie. He was arrested while naked and taking cocaine with four prostitutes at the Europe Hotel in Cinisello Balsomo, outside Milan, Italy. In his hotel suite, the police found half a million dollars worth of diamonds, $150,000 in cash, and 1,500 pages of documents about his trade.

The documents showed how Minin's operations had broken the UN arms embargoes on the sale of weapons to Liberia and Sierra Leone. The embaroes had been imposed on account of the atrocities committed against civilians. For example, in January 1999, the Revolutionary United Front in its attack on Sierra Leone's capital, Freetown, had hacked off the hands and feet of thousands of civilians. Documents found on Minin traced the weapons used by the Revolutionary Front as coming from Ukraine.

Minin had purchased the arms from Ukrspetseksport and sold them onto President Charles Taylor, the despotic ruler of Liberia, who passed them on to the Sierra Leone's Revolutionary Front. The Front had paid for the arms mainly in diamonds mined by slave labor.

UN investigators documented two of Minin's sales to Taylor. In March 1999, he provided weapons to the Front via Liberia from Burkina Faso, which wasn't on the UN embargo list. The delivery was made by an Antonov-124 from Kyiv and then reloaded onto a smaller plane. On this occasion, Ukrspetseksport provided 715 boxes of guns and cartridges, as well as anti-tank weapons, surface-to-air missiles, and rocket propelled grenades and their launchers.

In 2000, Minin again sold arms to Liberia destined for the Front. He hired the Moscow resident Valeriy Chernyi of Aviatrend to organize the delivery of three consignments from Ukrspetseksport. The first consignment consisted of 113 tons of 7.62 mm caliber cartridges, or five million bullets. An Antonov-124, with Ukrainian registration number UR82008, was chartered from Kyiv's Antonov design bureau to deliver the load.

On July 24, 2000, the Antonov flew from Hostomel (located north of Kyiv), to Abidjan, Ivory Coast, which wasn't on the UN embargo list. The local military unloaded the cargo, took its share, and the rest was flown in batches by a smaller plane, an Ilyushin-118 (Moldovan registration number ER-ICJ), to Monrovia, the capital of Liberia. The remaining shipments – AK47s, hand held rocket launchers and other weapons – were cancelled as following Minin's arrest.

Minin had paid a million dollars to Chernyi, according to the receipts found during his arrest. He paid Aviatrend $850,000 to its Alpha Bank account in Nicosia, Cyprus, and the rest to its Chase Manhattan Bank account in New York. This illustrated how easy it was to launder dirty money, even in the United States.

The Kuchma connection

In 2001, the Italian police had taken into custody a group of arms traders, who like Minin, had been enjoying the comforts of Italy. They were arrested on suspicion of selling weapons to Croatia in violation of UN embargoes. Among them was the former Soviet citizen – now British – Aleksandr Zhukov, who was arrested at his villa in Sardinia. His arrest became an issue when the former guard Mykola Melnychenko announced that he had recordings of President Kuchma with Zhukov discussing the trading of weapons. He also said that the money made from the weapons trade went into the private accounts of officials, including Kuchma, and that some it was used to bribe American politicians. ("Killing the story, BBC documentary).

In 2002, an Italian court announced that Zhukov and an assorted group of Europeans would be tried for attempting to sell arms to Croatia in contravention of UN Security Council resolutions. The arms weighed 13,000 tonnes and included AK47 assault rifles, ammunition, guided missiles and grenades. It was the largest haul of illegal arms in peace-time Europe. Though they had been seized in 1994 by NATO forces in the Adriatic Sea from a ship loaded in Ukraine, it took seven years to accumulate enough evidence to charge the accused. Apparently much of the evidence about arms smuggling came to light during the preparation of the case against the former ruler of Yugoslavia, Slobodan Milosevic.

One of those arrested was, Dmytro Streshynsky, who turned state evidence and received a reduced sentence. On April 3, 2002, a court sentenced him to one year and 11 months imprisonment as well as a fine. The trial of the others was scheduled for late 2002. At his trial Streshynsky implicated the then state security chief, Marchuk, as his sponsor. Marchuk, now secretary of the national security and defense council, vehemently denied the charge.

Streshynsky's accusation provided the opportunity, for the Ukrainian mass media outlets owned by the son of the former state security chief, Andriy Derkach, to call for Marchuk's sacking from the national security and defense council. Marchuk responded by accusing the younger Derkach of taking revenge on him for stopping his tax avoidance schemes which, according to Marchuk, had cost the state nearly a billion dollars in lost revenues. Marchuk blocked an attempt by Derkach to broadcast Streshynsky's accusations in a TV documentary in the Pohlyad slot on UT-1, presented by Yuriy Nesterenko.

Meanwhile, Minin at his trial in June 2002 had accused Andriy Derkach and his business partner Vadim Rabinovich of sponsoring his operations in West Africa. Rabinovich denied the charge while Derkach wasn't available for comment, according to Tom Warner in the *FT* on October 21, 2002. Rabinovich said his visit to Liberia in February 1999, along with a retired Ukrainian general and an arms expert, was related to his interest in iron-ore mining and not weapons.

Selling to Saddam

While the Kroll detectives and the former Financial Times correspondent Charles Clover dismissed the Melnychenko recordings as fabrications, the US government was taking them very seriously. From the day Melnychenko arrived in New York as a political refugee in April 2001, the US Justice Department had demanded that he hand over all his recordings. He has been threatened with imprisonment for not complying with the orders. In his defense, he states that not all the recordings can be released as some contain Ukraine's state secrets, like names of its foreign agents.

Melnychenko had provided US officials with an original recording, dated July 10, 2000, in which, in contravention of UN security council resolutions, President Kuchma gave permission to the Ukrspetseksport director Valeriy Malyev to sell a Kolchuga anti-aircraft radar system to Iraq for $100 million. The state security service chief, Leonid Derkach, was assigned the task of ensuring that the shipment was delivered to Iraq in secret.

[Malyev] We have been approached by Iraq through our Jordanian intermediary. They want to buy four Kolchuga stations and are offering 100 million dollars up front.

[Kuchma] What is Kolchuga?

[Malyev] Kolchuga is a passive radar station manufactured by Topaz. Each system consists of four pieces.

[Kuchma] Can you sell it without the Jordanian?

[Malyev] Well, Leonid Danylovych, I suggest Leonid Vasylevych (Derkach, then state security service chief) looks at the export structure to Iraq. Our KrAZ (Kremenchuk Avto Zavod) company ships its products in crates. We can use the crates marked by KrAZ. In other words, Kolchuga should be shipped to Iraq in KrAZ crates. Then we will send people with forged passports who will install the system.

[Kuchma] Just watch that the Jordanian keeps his mouth shut ... it will have to be checked that they do not detect it.

[Malyev] Who is going to detect it? We do not sell much to them. I mean to Jordan.

[Kuchma] Okay. Go ahead.

[Malyev] Thank you.

(Source: Center for Public Integrity – www.publicintegrity.org)

Some Ukrainian officials have not denied the recording's authenticity. Instead they have argued that the Kolchuga was not actually exported to Iraq. "This was a private conversation which did not result in any decisions", the director general of Topaz, Yuriy Ryabkin, told parliament's newspaper *Holos Ukrayiny* on April 19, 2002. He claimed that this military radar system had only been exported to Ethiopia and an order was being processed for China.

The release of the discussion on Kolchuga may have caused Malyev's death. A month before the March 30, 2002 parliamentary elections, the then head of the parliament's Gongadze committee, Oleksandr Zhyr, released the recording of Kuchma's conversation with Malyev. According to Zhyr, Kuchma discovered on March 3 that the committee would soon release the recording. Three days later, at 10 am, on the road from Poltava to Kyiv, the Audi driven by the 63 year-old Malyev smashed head-on into a Kamaz, a large heavy-duty truck, killing him. The police suggested that Malyev might have fallen asleep at the wheel. His passenger, Serhiy Krasiyev, said it occurred so quickly that he had no idea what happened.

After the FBI tested the Kuchma-Malyev recording and found it to be authentic, Ukraine's relations with the US government began to break down. A passive radar like the Kolchuga doesn't emit signals, and hence could threaten American and British pilots over Iraq.

On September 24, 2002, State Department spokesman Richard Boucher charged President Kuchma with approving the sale of military equipment that violated US and international law. As a consequence, he announced that the American government had ordered the suspension of $54 million in aid to Ukraine. If the radar system's presence in Iraq was verified, all aid would be suspended as required by US law.

In response, Kuchma invited American and British government experts to Ukraine to investigate whether a Kolchuga system was exported to Iraq. The thirteen-strong-group of experts carried out their inspection in the second half of October 2002, and issued a highly critical seventeen point report accusing the Ukrainian government of lack of transparency.

Kuchma's office rebutted the inspectors' report, and set conditions for future relations with USA and UK. On November 13, at a press conference, the new head of the president's office, Viktor Medvedchuk, blasted the report. He did not accept the FBI's verdict that the recorded discussion between Kuchma and Malyev was authentic, maintaining that Ukrainian experts had proved this recording to be fabricated. He did acknowledge that Malyev was in Kuchma's office on July 10, 2000, the day of the recording. He also confirmed that Malyev had discussions with the "Jordanian" middleman for the Iraqis, but said these talks were unofficial and were broken off following the intervention of Ukraine's state security service.

As to the inspectors' conclusion, that Ukraine was not transparent about whether a Kolchuga system was delivered to Iraq through a third party, Medvedchuk dismissed this as speculation. He accused the inspectors of not having any evidence that a delivery was made, and said it wasn't up to Ukraine to prove its innocence. He claimed that the government had given the experts all the information they could without endangering national security or relations with other countries that had purchased the radar, like China.

He then listed two conditions on which further relations with US and NATO countries would depend. They had to drop their accusation that Ukraine had sold the military radar to Iraq. As for the inspectors, they would be allowed in "only if they recognize our national interests and Ukraine as a sovereign state".

Medvedchuk concluded the press conference by musing that the Kolchuga affair, the disappearance of Gongadze and "the spying by Melnychenko", were perhaps part of a chain of events created by western intelligence services to discredit President Kuchma and Ukraine, and he hoped he was mistaken.

What Medvedchuk illustrated was his and Kuchma's arrogance of power. They were treating the Western governments with the same contempt for evidence as they showed towards their own citizens.

American Ambassador Carlos Pascual responded to a Ukrainian newspaper claim that the FBI test did not prove the authenticity of the Kuchma-Malyev discussion on the clandestine selling of the Kolchuga to Iraq.

> Experts at the FBI's Electronic Research Facility conducted a laboratory analysis of the original recording and the original recording device provided by Mykola Melnychenko. The recording was reviewed numerous times using a range of technical and audio techniques that together can determine if a digital recording has been manipulated or distorted. The experts' findings are that the recording is genuine, has not been altered, and contains a discussion between

President Kuchma and Mr. Malyev. The technical experts performing the analysis detected no breaks in the recording, found no manipulation of the digital files, and detected no unusual sounds that would have been present if the recording had been tampered with. In the course of the analysis, experts from three United States Government departments confirmed that the recording includes the voice of President Kuchma. They indicated that it would be implausible that a conversation such as the one examined could be fabricated, even with highly sophisticated electronic equipment. In short, there is no need from a technical standpoint for further analysis.

(Source: Letter from Ambassador Carlos Pascual to the newspaper 2000, Nov. 22, 2002)

The western governments responded by not inviting Kuchma to the NATO summit in Prague, November 20-22, 2002. NATO would use the occasion to invite seven additional east european states into its military alliance. Ukraine, though not scheduled for admission, its head was to be invited on account of Ukraine's special treaty with NATO. But Kuchma decided he would be coming to attend the summit. In response a State Department spokesman told Reuters on November

July 25, 2001 – US security adviser Condoleezza Rice and US ambassador to Ukraine, Carlos Pascual, at a press conference in Kyiv
(Photo by Viktor Pobedynsky / UNIAN)

18, that "the United States has no plans for any high-level meeting with Kuchma in Prague", while a NATO spokesman said it would be "'very unwise' for Kuchma to go to Prague".

At first it looked like Kuchma wouldn't come to Prague. On November 20, the opening of the NATO summit, Kuchma extended his state visit to China. On that day, NATO issued its Prague Summit Declaration, in which it invited seven countries to join NATO, including Bulgaria, Estonia, Latvia, Lithuania, Romania and Slovakia and Slovenia. Point 9 of its declaration scolded Ukraine. It said that if Ukraine wanted to join NATO it would have "to implement all the reforms necessary, including as regards enforcement of export controls". An oblique criticism of its violations of UN resolutions and sale of the Kolchuga to Iraq. It also said that "Continued progress in deepening and enhancing our relationship requires an unequivocal Ukrainian commitment to the values of the Euro-Atlantic community". In other words, Ukraine wasn't a democratic state.

On the second day of the summit, Kuchma flew into Prague in the late afternoon, to the surprise of the other heads of states. He crashed into a dinner given by the Czech president, Vaclav Havel. On the third and last day of the summit, Kuchma insisted on joining the heads of states in conference. The NATO Secretary-General Lord Robertson agreed but changed the alphabetical seating arrangements from English to French so that Ukraine, or Kuchma, would not sit next to Tony Blair, United Kingdom, and George Bush, United States. In French, Ukraine appeared in the end, after Turkey, where Kuchma sat. News of this reseating arrangement in which 48 heads of states searching for their seats flashed around the world.

The strong man of Ukraine was humiliated by his equals. He had set himself up for this embarrassment, as he misjudged his ability to fool everyone all the time. Will this affront cause Kuchma to create a backlash against the West, or will it speed his demise? Time will only tell.

Appendix 1
The BEK-TEK tests

On Feb. 7, 2002, Bruce Koenig of the American BEK-TEK Corp, a former FBI agent and an internationally recognized expert in audio and video recordings, tested five excerpts recorded from the president's July 3, 2000 discussions on Gongadze. Koenig reported that he received clones of two original recordings, and was asked to test five designated areas on them, which he called specimen Q1. Below are the conclusions of his tests, followed by the transcripts of the five excerpts tested.

Conclusions of the BEK-TEK Tests
of the July 3, 2000 excerpts on Gongadze

1. The specimen Q1 recordings are consistent with being clone recordings, and there are no indications of alterations or edits to the audio data in the five designated areas in the two .DMR files. Based on the flow of the speech in the five designated portions, no phraseology or sentence structure was pieced together by using individual phonemes, words or abort phrases.

If, as noted below, someone did attempt to digitally edit separate sounds together, the edits themselves might be inaudible, but the flow of the speech would be artificial, reflecting that the individual sounds came from separate sources. The recorded information in the five designated portions, and in D840100.2.DMR are generally consistent with the same environment, microphone, and recording system.

2. If any of the information in the designated specimen Q1 recordings has been altered or deleted in a such a manner that it cannot now be scientifically detected, then the following would have been required;

a. Access to all of the original and direct data copies of the specimen Ql recordings in existence, in their native .DMR format; not having all of the digital copies would allow a quick aural review of any unedited copy, that would clearly show the content changes in the edited version;

b. Access to the specific software, which allows for playback of the recordings in their native format;

c. Access to and implementation of software which allows for editing the digital data contained in the native format of the audio recordings;

d. Manipulation of the digital data by an individual, or group of individuals, that possess extensive product knowledge of the proprietary .DMR file format. This knowledge would include file, block, and header structure, the location and identification of the data within the file, and the effects that editing the data will have on the resulting recording when. it is played back; and

e. Access to other recorded information with identical room acoustics, background sounds, talkers, noise, and so forth.

3. However, it is the opinion of BEK TEK that the five designated portions. within the two specimen Q1 files, are continuous and unaltered, based on the above listed analyses. Though the existence of any digital manipulation is highly improbable, if it did occur, without now being obvious, then the most probable scenario would be a loss of data, and not additions or editing of content.

(Source: pravda.com.ua, Feb. 16, 2002)

Appendix 2
Excerpts tested by BEK-TEK

Below are the transcripts of the five excerpts tested by Koenig of BEK-TEK. The first three had been released to the public by the MP Moroz on Nov. 28, 2000. All five are found on the IPI collection of Melnychenko recordings from July 3, 2000.

Excerpt 1

"The Chechens should kidnap him and ask for ransom!"

[Kuchma] (speaking through an intercom to Volodymyr Lytvyn, the head of the president's office) Hello

[Lytvyn] Hello

[Kuchma] Give me the same about 'Ukrayinska Pravda', and you come in, we will decide what to do with him. He has gone too far.

[Lytvyn] I need to begin a [court] case

[Kuchma] What?

[Lytvyn] Start a case? ...

[Kuchma] Good

[Lytvyn] The case – we will make in duplicates

[Kuchma] No, I don't need a case.

[Kuchma] (According to Melnychenko, Lytvyn comes to Kuchma's office) 'Ukrayinska Pravda', well is simply too much - the scum, fucker, Georgian, Georgian

[Lytvyn] Gongadze?

[Kuchma] Gongadze. Well, who is financing him?

[Lytvyn] Well, he actively works with [socialist MP Oleksandr] Moroz, with Grani [a newspaper sponsored by Moroz's Socialist Party]. On Saturday I saw .... with [socialist MP Volodymyr] Makeyenko.

[Kuchma] Maybe take him to court, let the lawyers take it to court. This goes to the prosecutor, right?

[Lytvyn] In my opinion, let loose [the Interior Minister] Kravchenko to use alternative methods, and also [Horbanyeyev? or Komanyeyev?] and Kholondovych [Kholondovych heads the Interior Ministry department for logistic control or office for police surveillance and special operations].

[Kuchma] Simply shit – is there any limit, after all, son-of-a-bitch –

[Lytvyn] He should now within two ...

[Kuchma] Deport him – the scum – to Georgia and throw him there on his dick! Take him to Georgia and drop him there.

Lytvyn: I had a discussion ...

[Kuchma] Let the Chechens kidnap him and ransom!

(Source: Melnychenko files from the International Press Institute in Vienna (IPI) GO307p2.dmr, 0:07:38-0:10:45, July 3, 2000. The translation used the following transcriptions: Moroz 1; Oleksiy Stepura, "Te, chego ne sdelal Melnichenko (What Melnychenko didn't do,"), cripo.com.ua; and a transcription given under oath by Mykola Melnychenko to the head of parliament's Gongadze committee, August 27, 2002)

Excerpt 2

"the Chechens must kidnap and take him to Chechnya on his dick ... and demand a ransom."

[Kuchma] So that I don't forget, there's a Gongadze

[Kravchenko] I have heard such a name.

[Kuchma] Well, the scum is the limit

[Kravchenko] Gongadze, he has run through us before

[Kuchma] Find him. Understand this, he writes all the time in some "Ukrainian Truth" [Ukrayinska Pravda, pravda.com.ua], he pushes it in the Internet, understand. Find out who is financing him?

[Kravchenko] Yes

[Kuchma] Who finances him exactly?

[Kravchenko] Danilevych, I have ...

[Kuchma] But the main thing, he has to be, I say, not I, but Volodya [Lytvyn] says, Chechens must kidnap and take him to Chechnya on his dick ... and ask for a ransom.

[Kravchenko] Yes, I will do it. Danilevych, I understand this is an order, or shall we say not an order. ... I tell you ... They are such terrific people (laughing) ... , never failing, and don't tell anyone.

[Kuchma] Just drive him to Georgia, that's all.

[Kravchenko] So that, firstly, shall we issue an instruction, or no instructions, on that head of the [police] district department - well, you remember, in the Chernihiv Oblast, who said: "Let the president pay you".

[Kuchma] Yes-yes-yes

[Kravchenko] They've already released his deputy-head and began a criminal case

[Kuchma] Yes.

[Kravchenko] 165 that is for official service violations, and 185-a [also a criminal statute]. So I think this week we'll show him.

[Kuchma] Yes-yes. Let's.

[Kravchenko] We'll show who should say what.

(Source: IPI, G0307p2.dm, 0:49:00-0:51:00, July 3, 2000. Translated from transcriptions: Ibid.)

Excerpt 3

"On Gongadze … from the summer, he has been financed by Brodsky"

[Kuchma] On Gongadze apart from working together with Moroz, he writes for Moroz in his "Grani", that from the summer has been financed by Brodsky.

[Kravchenko] Well, that is a animal if ever there was one. I wouldn't be surprised if they had ties with the Socialists. … Well, we will discover everything about him. I think this is

[Kuchma] But Brodsky is [parliament's deputy speaker Viktor] Medvedchuk and [oligarch and owner of Dynamo soccer club, Hryhoriy] Surkis. First of all, Surkis.

[Kravchenko] That there is a connection between them is …

[Kuchma] No, if they are friends …

[Kravchenko] 100 percent!

[Kuchma] I remember that game around (the newspaper) *Kievskiye Vedomosti*. [Surkis bought the newspaper in 1999 from Brodsky after Kuchma's government had closed it down].

[Kravchenko] …

[Kuchma] Surkis, yes, this fucker, Jew,

[Kravchenko] …

[Kuchma] Just now I've read a few of their conversations

[Kravchenko] – They used to have a method which they still use. They create a problem, later they go to the person as if to help them, and then it turns out that the person becomes dependent on them. And this is the way it is here. They make a big spectacle; maybe they will play this on the national level … And, this may be such an action.

(Source: IPI, G0307p2.dmr, 1:04:30-1:05:53, July 3, 2000. Translated from transcriptions: Ibid.)

Excerpt 4

"monitoring all [Gongadze's] communications"

[Derkach] Leonid Danilevych

[Kuchma] (Timely?) (pause, several seconds of silence followed by incomprehensible conversation)

[Derkach] I.

[Kuchma] I, I have read it all!

[Derkach] You mean you read it all?

[Kuchma] *Ukrayinska Pravda* [pravda.com.ua]

[Derkach] A-ha! Yes, that bitch.

[Kuchma] What are we doing then?

[Derkach] We're all over him, monitoring all [Gongadze's] communications, checking out all [his] Kyiv contacts. ... He's already slunk over to Moroz.

[Kuchma] Aha! So he's cooperating with Moroz now, is he!

[Derkach] We will do some business! We hear him on all channels at the present time. We will turn all his connections in Kiev inside out. And that is that.

[Kuchma] [The press?]

[Derkach] And now he has crawled to that one, to [MP Oleksandr] Moroz

[Kuchma] Well, it's obvious that he is cooperating with Moroz there!

[Derkach] Overall, all of these are worthless people. And (Nikonov?) there (?) (pause)

[Kuchma] And where do they print?

[Derkach] "Grani?" [oppositional newspaper]

[Kuchma] Yes!

[Derkach] There, in Volyn [Oblast], read further there. We have already thrown them out of Volyn [Oblast]. And they are searching for a place now. And they also put out all their stuff through the internet. (Source: IPI, GO307p2, 1:52:38-1:54:57, July 3, 2000. Translated from the transcription: Radio Liberty 9 and Stepura, "Te, chego ne sdelal Melnichenko (What Melnychenko didn't do,").

Excerpt 5

"Who gives the Georgian the money?"

[Kuchma] ...And that "Ukrainian ..." [*Ukrayinska Pravda*, Pravda.com.ua], that same ... What about Brodsky, Brodsky? I am interested to know for sure that Brodsky is connected with them. You told me ...

[Derkach] Brodsky ... we watch.

[Kuchma] With what purpose? For that Georgian fucker? Who gives the Georgian the money? This is the question.

[Derkach] I have already told you, this time Brodsky gave the money.

[Kuchma] OK.

(Source: IPI, G0307p3.dmr, 0:23:44-0:24:12, July 3, 2000. Translated from transcription: Stepura, Ibid.)

Appendix 3
The FBI tests

Below is the statement from the pathologist used by the FBI to conduct tests to determine whether the bones held by the Ukrainian authorities belong to Georgi Gongadze.

Department of Defense
Armed Forces Institute of Pathology
Washington, DC 20306-6000

Positive Identification of Georgi Gongadze

On March 6th and April 26th , 2001 I conducted a forensic examination of the badly decomposed remains, which were reported to have been recovered on November 2, 2000 in Taraschansky [Tarashcha] District, Kiev [Kyiv], Ukraine. Examination of the remains on both dates were conducted at the Kiev [Kyiv] City Central Bureau of Forensic Examination.

During both examinations determinations regarding the biological profile of the corpse (sex, age, race, stature, and foot size) were ascertained. During both examinations multiple bone samples were collected for DNA comparisons by the US FBI – Federal Bureau of Investigation. Comparison of the biological profile of the corpse in question, to the known biological profile of Georgi [Georgi] Gongadze were found to be consistent. A detailed review of the skeletal elements found them consistent with that of a single individual. Examination of the remains also revealed evidence of old healed skeletal injury which was present on the right radius of the lower arm and the proximal and medial phalanges of the small finger (fifth digit) of the left hand.

Radiographs taken of these injuries were compared to known

antemortem radiographs of Georgi Gongadze. The antemortem radiographs of Georgi Gongadze were provided by his mother, Olaksandra [Oleksandra] Gongadze on April 26th , 2001, the day of the second US team examination. Comparison of the radiographs of the corpse in question to the antemortem radiographs of Georgi Gongadze revealed matching skeletal morphology, including evidence of like skeletal injury and presence of metallic shrapnel. A review of the DNA comparisons conducted by the FBI corroborate the findings of the forensic skeletal examination that the remains are of a single individual.

Comparison of the DNA profiles obtained from Oleksandra Gongadze, Miroslava [Myroslava] Gongadze, and her two daughters, Salome and Nana Gongadze are reported not to exclude the corpse as being offspring of Olexandra [Oleksandra] Gongadze. Furthermore, DNA comparisons also are reported not to exclude the corpse as being the remains of the father of Salome and Nana Gongadze. The combined DNA comparisons provide supplemental support to the radiographic identification of the corpse.

In conclusion based on the forensic skeletal examinations, radiographic comparisons, and DNA findings the badly decomposed remains examined are positively those of the missing journalist, Georgi Gongadze.

Signed
William C. Rodriguez III, Ph.D.
Chief Deputy Medical Examiner
Special Investigations
Armed Forces Institute of Pathology

(Source: Letter issued by the US Embassy in Kyiv on May 8, 2001)

A comment on sources

Investigating this murder, in which the person ordering the crime is allegedly the president, was fraught with dangers, especially for those providing the information. I cannot name many of those who gave me information; they know who they are and I am deeply grateful to them.

The following will not suffer from being named: the editor of pravda.com.ua, Olena Prytula; Gongadze's wife, Myroslava; his life-long friend, Konstantyn Alaniya; the lawyer representing Gongadze's mother, Andriy Fedur, and the director of Radio Continent, who for many years worked professionally with Gongadze, Serhiy Sholokh.

I especially want to thank Gongadze's mother, Lesya Gongadze, who was fearless and very cooperative in the interviews.

The most important evidence as to why Gongadze was targeted by the president came from the recordings made by his guard, Mykola Melnychenko. They cover about eleven months of President Kuchma's rule, from about the last week of October 1999 to the end of September 2000. However, a word of warning about using the available transcripts of the recordings. The transcriptions, whether they be done by Melnychenko, pravda.com, Radio Liberty, Moroz's socialist party, or 5element.net – have not been done professionally. Transcribing the Melnychenko recordings requires a high level of skill and attention because of their poor sound quality as well as the need to be proficient in Russian and Ukrainian as well as in the popular Surzhyk - a mixture of the two, widely-spoken in Ukraine, and a hall-mark of President Kuchma.

I used an excellent transcriber, who will not be named, for two excerpts, as his time didn't allow for more. The best published transcriber, despite his idiosyncratic views on the subject, was Oleksiy Stepura (see for example, "Te, chego ne sdelal Melnichenko (What Melnychenko didn't do," cripo.com.ua). Finally, the English translation is only as good as the transcript and the translator.

257

Bibliography

Most of the materials on the Gongadze-Kuchma saga, other than my interviews, are available from internet sites, of which pravda.com.ua, is by far the best. In English, the BBC does an excellent job of monitoring and producing translations of the most important official statements and reports from Ukraine's TV, radio and press. The best site in English is kpnews.com, the web site of Kyiv Post.

As for the Melnychenko recording; a collection of 45 hours can be obtained on CD-Rom from IPI (International Press Institute in Vienna). The IPI collection also can be downloaded from the Harvard site (wcfia.harvard.edu/Melnychenko). However, the Harvard site has renamed the files, with the consequence that the recording dates that appeared in the file names were lost. The Crime Ukraine web site, cripo.com.ua, has many transcriptions and analysis of the Melnychenko recordings. The new web site, www.5element.net, which appeared in 2002, promises to provide many more hours of recordings as well as transcripts. Its weakness is that the transcripts are strictly in Russian, though the recordings are in a mixture of Russian and Ukrainian.

The selected bibliography has been arranged according to the three persons who dominate the book – Georgi Gongadze, Leonid Kuchma, and Mykola Melnychenko.

On Georgi Gongadze

Tarashcha corpse
"Is the corpse found near Tarashcha … Gongadze's?", *Fakti*, Nov. 17, 2000.
"Statement by Prytula to the press about the disappearance of the Tarashcha corpse", *Fakti*, Nov. 17, 2000.
Vasyl, Mariya, "Interview with Vorotyntsev", *Fakti*, Nov. 17, 2000.
(also all the above in pravda.com.ua, Nov. 17, 2000)
DNA tests - American FBI
US Embassy in Ukraine, *Statement on positive identification of Heorhiy*

Bibliography

Gongadze, Kyiv, May 8, 2001.

Rodriguez III, William C., *Positive Identification of Georgiy Gongadze*, Kyiv, May 8, 2001.

Gongadze, Lesya, *Letter to General Prosecutor Potebenko*, May 31, 2001 (her criticisms of the FBI tests and demand for additional tests), pravda.com.ua, May 31, 2001.

German Genedia test

Holovaty, Serhiy, *Press release of Genedia test results*, March 20, 2001.

Holovaty, Serhiy, "Comments on Artem Shevchenko's interview with Pavlo Ivanov", *Dzerkalo Tyzhnya (Zerkalo Nedeli)*, June 16, 2001

Prytula, Olena, *Pytan vse bilshe (Confusion increases)*, pravda.com.ua, March 20, 2001.

Russian Health Ministry tests

"Kuchma: corpse - Gongadze's; and Tymoshenko - guilty", Pravda.com.ua, Feb. 17, 2001 (in the NTV program recorded on Feb. 17, 2002 for broadcast on Feb. 22, Pavel Ivanov said that his DNA test showed 99.9 percent that Tarashcha corpse was Gongadze's).

Shevchenko, Artem, "Interview with Pavlo Ivanov", *Dzerkalo Tyzhnya (Zerkalo Nedeli)*, June 9, 2001

Investigations into Gongadze's disappearance

AZhR, "Smert Georgiya Gongadze byla vygodna slishkom mnogim (The death of Georgi Gongadze was convenient for many)", *Taynyi sevetnik*, no. 19, June 8, 2001

Chobit, Dmytro, Chas pidloii vlady (Time of the vile government. Kyiv-Brody, Prosvita, 2001.

Fedur, Andriy, "Sprava Georgiya Gongadze (The Georgi Gongadze Affair)", unpublished memorandum, May 13, 2001

Kroll Associates, Kroll report on Gongadze, Kyiv, Working Ukraine, Sept. 18, 2002; also published in Russian and Ukrainian.

Moroz, Oleksandr, Khronyka odnoho zlochynu (Chronicle of a crime). Kyiv, Politrada SPU, 2001.

Mostova, Yuliya, "Review of the Kroll report", *Zerkalo Nedeli*, Sept. 29, 2001.

Nezhyvyi, Oleksiy, "Eto tumannoe delo Gongadze (That foggy Gongadze affair), *Krymskoe vremya (The Crimean Times)*, Dec. 12, 2000.

Reporters without borders, "Ukraine - mutilation of the truth, inquiry into the murder of journalist Georgiy Gongadze", rsf.fr, Jan. 22, 2001

Beheaded

Shmelev, Konstantin, "Kak iskaly Georgiya Gongadze (How they searched for Gongadze, eight part investigation into the disappearance of Gongadze)", fontanka.ru, Nov. 11and13, 2000.
Stepura, Oleksiy, "Sledstviye vedut varyagi (investigation led by barbarians)", cripo.com.ua, undated, 2001.
Unknown, "Vremya varyagov (Time of the barbarians)", cripo.com.ua, undated, 2001.
Yeltsov, Oleg, "Piterskaya versiya ubiistva Gongadze (The St. Petersburg version of the killing of Gongadze)", cripo.com.ua, undated, 2001.
Parliament - stenographic reports from www.rada.kiev.ua
Nov. 16, 2000, Dzhyha's report on Tarashcha corpse.
Dec. 12, 12, 2000, discussions, resolutions and votes about the Boryspil incident.
Dec. 14, 2000, discussions, resolutions and votes about Gongadze.
Jan. 10, 2001, Prosecutor General Mykhaylo Potebenko's report on the investigation into the Gongadze and Melnychenko cases.
May 25, 2001, Interior Minister Yuriy Smirnov's and Prosecutor General Mykhaylo Potebenko's reports on those suspected of killing Gongadze (see also Korchynsky, Oleksandr, "Gongadze killers ... wedding, Segodnya, May 25, 2001).
Dec. 24, 2001, Report by Oleksandr Zhyr, head of the temporary commission on the Gongadze affair.
TV documentaries listed by reporters
Mangold, Tom, "Killing the story", BBC2, April 21, 2002
Clover, Charles, "PR", ICTV, March 17, 2002
Kiselov, Sergei "Discussion on PR", ICTV, March 19, 2002
(see article on who paid for PR: Maryna Melnyk, "All the truth about film 'PR'", pravda.com.ua, March 27, 2002)

On Kuchma

Biography, politics and economy
Kuchma's letter to Financial Times, Feb. 27, 2001.
Lukanov, Yuriy, Tretiy presydent, politychnyi portret Leonida Kuchmy (The third president, the political portrait of Leonid Kuchma). Kyiv, Taki Spravy, 1996.
Lyutyi, Petro, "Corruption in Kuchma's administration and Interior Ministry", pravda.com.ua, Feb. 18, 2002.

Omelchenko, Hryhoriy, and Anatoliy Yermak, Explanatory note to the par-
liamentary resolution on impeaching President Leonid Kuchma, Sept. 14,
2000, and see part of the evidence against Kuchma in Svoboda, Sept. 12,
2000.
Siedenberg, Axel, and Lutz Hoffmann (editors), Ukraiina na pozdorizhzhi
(Ukraine at the Crossroads). Kyiv, Feniks, 1998; also available in English and
German from Springer-Verlag, Berlin-New York.
Interviews with Kuchma newspapers, radio and TV
CBS 60-minutes, April 29, 2001.
CNN, Feb. 23, 2001.
FT, Feb. 10, 2001.
ICTV, Feb. 25, 2001.
Kolomiychenko, Alena, Radio Liberty Russian Service, Dec. 30, 2000
(excerpts of the interview appeared in English in *Kyiv Post*, Jan. 18, 2001)
UT1, 7days, Feb. 7, 2001.
UT2, Epicenter, Oct. 17, 1999.
President's statements to the nation
Dec. 6, 2000, on Melnychenko recordings and Gongadze.
Feb. 13, 2001, on demonstrators being "Ukrainian Nazis".
Sept. 28, 2002, on Sept. 16, 2002 demonstrations.
Violations of UN arms embargoes
UN panel of experts, Reports to Security Council:
on Sierra Leone, Dec. 2000; and on Liberia, Oct. 17, 2001.

On Mykola Melnychenko

Interviews with Melnychenko
Boyarko, Oleksa, First interview with Melnychenko, Radio Svoboda in
Ukrainian, Dec. 30, 2001.
Boyarko, Oleksa, Second interview with Melnychenko, Radio Svoboda in
Ukrainian, Jan. 9, 2001.
Holovaty, Serhiy, Viktor Shyshkin, Oleksandr Zhyr, Interview by parlia-
ment's Gongadze committee, Dec. 7, 2000 (shown on video to parliament
on Dec. 12, 2000).
Kroft, Steve, CBS 60-minutes, April 29, 2001.
Krushelnycky, Askold, "Ukraine: Ex-Bodyguard says there is no greater crim-
inal than Kuchma", rferl.org, Feb. 27, 2001.
Tyler, Patrick, E., "From under a couch, an effort to stop corruption in

Ukraine", *NY Times*, Feb. 26, 2001.
Warner, Tom, Interview transcript, www.ft.com/Ukraine, Sept. 15, 2002.
Statements
"Why I recorded the president", given to MP Oleksandr Moroz and (shown on video to parliament on Dec. 14, 2000).
Sworn statements to Prosecutor General S.M. Piskun.
On Gongadze, NYC, Aug. 27, 2002.
On the Yelyashkevych incident, NYC, Aug. 27, 2002.
Tests on Melnychenko recordings
BEK-TEK, tests on the July 3, 2000 excerpts on Gongadze, pravda.com.ua, Feb. 16, 2002.
IPI (International Press Institute) test results in letter from Fritz, Johann P., IPI director, to Oleksandr Lavrynovych, head of parliament's Gongadze committee, Feb. 22, 2001.

References

Andrushchak, H., Marchenko, Yu., Telemko, O. (editors), Ofitsiyna ukraina sohodni, informatsiya stanom na hruden, 2000 roku (Official Ukraine today, information as for December 2000). Kyiv, KIS, 2000.
Yurchenko, Yuriy, Oleksandr Telemko (editors), Khto ye khto v ukraini (Who is who in Ukraine). Kyiv, KIS, 1999.

Web sites with Melnychenko recordings

5element.net (organized by Petro Lyutyi and totally dedicated to Melnychenko recordings).
cripo.com.ua (Oleh Yeltsov's Crime in Ukraine web site) has many analyses of Melnychenko recordings. Its best one was by Oleksiy Stepura, "Te, chego ne sdelal Melnichenko (What Melnychenko didn't do), no date, 2001).
Pravda.com.ua, has a large collection of recordings and transcripts
radiosvoboda.org.
Radio Liberty's collection of 21 fragments from Melnychenko recordings, April 2, 2001.
wcfia.harvard.edu/Melnychenko (has IPI collection of Melnychenko recordings, and guide to internet sites with English translations).

Index

H